SPECIAL DOGS DESERVE SPECIAL ATTENTION.
THE COMMON SENSE BOOK OF PUPPY AND
DOG CARE
WILL HELP YOU GIVE IT TO THEM.

Whether you keep a dog for sport, protection, companionship, or fun, this book will help answer all the questions you face. Here is everything you need to know. How to . . .

- find the gentlest, most even-tempered breeds
- select the best veterinarian
- provide all the necessary shots and licenses
- travel long distances with a dog—without hassles
- give him all the exercise he needs
- deal with problems like obesity, arthritis, fleas, etc.
- ensure your dog gets all the essential nutrients
- breed winners for dog competitions
- handle all accidents, injuries, and other emergencies
- make your dog a full-fledged member of your family

THE DOG LOVER'S GUIDE
TO COMPLETE DOG CARE

THE COMMON SENSE BOOK OF PUPPY AND DOG CARE

Harry Miller

Director Emeritus, Gaines Dog Research Center

Foreword by Hadley C. Stephenson, B.S., D.V.M.

THIRD EDITION – REVISED

BANTAM BOOKS
NEW YORK · TORONTO · LONDON · SYDNEY · AUCKLAND

THE COMMON SENSE BOOK OF
PUPPY AND DOG CARE
A Bantam Book / September 1956
2nd printing ...... *June 1957*   3rd printing . . . *September 1957*
4th printing . . . . *October 1960*
Bantam Reference Library revised edition / February 1963
24 printings through October 1981
Bantam 2nd revised edition / April 1987
3 printings through July 1988

Library of Congress Catalog Card Number: 56-11111

ISBN 0-553-27789-8

Published simultaneously in the United States and Canada

*Bantam Books are published by Bantam Books, a division of
Bantam Doubleday Dell Publishing Group, Inc. Its trademark,
consisting of the words "Bantam Books" and the portrayal of
a rooster, is Registered in U.S. Patent and Trademark Office
and in other countries. Marca Registrada. Bantam Books,
666 Fifth Avenue, New York, New York 10103.*

PRINTED IN THE UNITED STATES OF AMERICA

O   12 11 10 9 8 7 6 5

Foreword

Why write a book? Every author has a purpose, be it to state a theory, support a cause, make available information which is difficult to find, or present new information for the first time. In this book, *The Common Sense Book of Puppy and Dog Care*, Harry Miller has drawn upon his extensive knowledge of dogs and his close association with many research projects devoted to their welfare: his cause—to help dogs live longer and better lives through lifetime care; the result—a book that can rightfully be called a classic in the field of dog care.

The puppy needs good care during his early formative months if he is to lead an active life when he is full grown and enjoy his final years. Consequently, this book discusses the growing puppy month by month and, in addition, devotes full chapters to the grown dog and the old dog. In the latter sections the latest findings of research in nutrition and veterinary medicine, general care and training are presented in a popular and practical manner.

Finally, *The Common Sense Book of Puppy and Dog Care* contains an index which makes all of its valuable information and sound advice readily available. If this advice is followed, more dogs will live to a ripe old age, more disease will be prevented, more dogs and more people will be happy.

HADLEY C. STEPHENSON, B.S., D.V.M.

Preface

Not less than 55 million American homes keep one or more dogs for sport, for protection, for companionship and fun around the house. The army of dog-owners would doubtless be larger still were it not for the fact that many people believe the task of dog care to be more difficult than it really is. The responsibility of owning a dog can make people, especially first-time owners, a bit nervous.

In this book we have tried to approach the whole subject from a "common sense" standpoint. Let me illustrate:

Dogs come into homes at various stages of their lives, each stage presenting special problems that require particular attention. We have tried to group these problems—and the answers to them—within the ages when they normally would occur. This has been done many times with baby books, but we believe this is the first time anything of the kind has been attempted in a dog book.

We are strong believers in professional veterinary care for both the prevention and the cure of illness. However, all dog-owners do not live within easy reach of a veterinarian. Our recommendations, therefore, must take into consideration the practical necessities faced.

We may have gone too far in recommending care for the young puppy like that given to a baby. But like a newborn infant, the first few weeks a puppy spends in your home are crucial. You must set the pattern for his life so he will thrive and grow and learn. We can only plead that too much care is better than too little.

In the following pages we have tried to anticipate—and answer—most of the problems that a dog-owner may have to face in the lifetime care of his dog. Being human and fallible, we may have missed some. But our interest in you does not stop when you own a copy of this book. Anytime you need an answer to any question on a dog topic, please feel free to write to the Gaines Dog Care Center, 660 White Plains Road, Tarrytown, NY 10591. We will certainly do our best to help you—without charge.

Contents

1

The Selection of a Dog

Selecting a dog can be more confusing than it used to be because there are now so many available from which to choose. Today there are over 500 breeds of dogs throughout the world, approximately 350 of which are recognized by the kennel clubs of various countries. In the United States alone, there are more than 130 kinds of purebreeds recognized by the American Kennel Club, to say nothing of the countless crossbreeds and mixed-breeds. The American dog population, according to the American Veterinary Medical Association, is more than 55 million. A recent survey shows that about 45 percent of all households in the United States shelter one or more dogs. So if you love dogs, you're not alone.

Origin of the Breeds

What do we mean by a breed? Insofar as dogs are concerned, a breed is a group of dogs, more or less uniform in size and structure, produced and maintained by selective breeding. Man selects the dogs which have the qualities he admires or considers best for his purpose, and by breeding them over a period of time, gets pups which look alike and which, when grown and mated, will produce pups like themselves. That is why this type of breeding is known as selective breeding—man selects the dog and bitch he thinks, mated together, will produce the kind of puppies he wants. All of the breeds, from the tall Irish Wolfhound to the small Chihuahua, have been perfected by selective breeding.

Man did not start this idea. He borrowed it from nature,

1

which used just such a method in the wild for producing animals able to live under widely different natural conditions. When nature does the selecting, we call the method natural selection. Man took up the work of perfecting the breeds where nature left off, for way back in the dim past, evolution had begun to produce different types of dogs.

Ten to fifteen million years ago in the Miocene epoch, there lived a wolflike animal called *Tomarctus* that is believed to be the true ancestor of the genus *Canis:* domestic dogs, wolves, jackals, foxes, coyotes, and so forth. He was a small, predatory animal, similar in appearance to modern dog, with flexible legs and compact feet for high-speed running to efficiently chase game animals that were abundant at the time.

Long before the time of Christ, several main lines came down from *Tomarctus:* the herding dogs, the northern dogs and spitz-type toys, the hounds, the terriers, the sporting dogs, and the guard dogs. From these, our modern breeds have developed.

Much as we would like to classify them for the sake of easy understanding, we cannot be too exact about it because we can only guess what happened ages ago. Over the years, nature, it would seem, divided and subdivided dogs to fit them for certain climates, terrains, and occupations. Nevertheless, in tracing the paths of evolution, we find much overlapping, and so our groupings of type and breed can never be absolutely correct.

The herding dogs were the shepherds on Old World hillsides. Practically every country had its native sheepdogs: the Shepherd Dogs of Germany, for instance, the Collies of Scotland, the Komondorok and Pulik of Hungary, the Briards of France. These were the natural-type animals produced by nature rather than by man's selective breeding. Most of them were rectangular in body, had weather-resisting coats, and great endurance.

The northern dogs were the cold-country types of the Arctic Circle: the Samoyed, Alaskan Malamute, Norwegian Elkhound, Siberian Husky, Chow Chow, and others; all had a wedge-shaped head, ears which stood straight up, a heavy coat, and an upcurled tail that screened the nose from sub-zero air while they slept. Here, too, developed the tiny dogs, the toys, some like the Pomeranian closely related to polar types, others more or less removed from them as, for instance, the Maltese, the Pekingese, and the Pug.

The hounds were either swift sight hunters like Greyhounds, Afghans, Salukis, and Deerhounds, or scent hunters like Beagles and Bloodhounds. The sight hounds were tall and reachy-necked, streamlined for speed; they watched their prey as they chased it. The scent hounds were trackers, running nose-to-earth, with longer ear flaps that waved over the ground to stir up scent.

The terriers were so-called from the Latin *Terra*, or earth. These were the ground diggers, with strong forelegs and with powerful jaws for ratting and trapping vermin. They were made so hard-mouthed they could literally snap their quarry to death. Then there were the sporting dogs, that large group which includes spaniels, pointers, setters, and retrievers. Hunting with head high to catch airborne scent, these were the soft-mouthed finders and retrievers that brought in their birds without a tooth mark.

The guard dogs are descended from ancient Assyrian war dogs, and from the fighters of the Roman amphitheaters—the magnificent creatures that opposed human gladiators as well as lions, tigers, bulls, and bears. Down from them came Mastiffs, Bulldogs, Boxers, Great Danes, and others. Here were the stouthearts of the dog family, with size, weight, and courage to spare.

These at long last developed into the hundreds of breeds we know today. For thousands of years, of course, they were not thought of as breeds but as different types of workers. Only within the last one hundred years or so have we known enough to breed dogs according to definite patterns, hence to call them breeds.

For judging in the show ring, we have tried to group dogs along somewhat the same lines as those early natural groupings. Breeds recognized by the American Kennel Club are classified into seven groups: sporting dogs, hounds, working dogs, terriers, toys, non-sporting dogs, and herding dogs. We cannot strictly group the various breeds—we can only decide the divisions to which they seem best to belong.

Purebreed, Crossbreed, or Mixed-Breed

A *purebreed* is a dog of only one breed, that is, both its parents are of the same kind of dog. The puppies of a purebred Pointer male and a purebred Pointer female, for instance, are purebred Pointers. If different kinds of dogs are mated (for example, a Pointer with a German Shepherd, or a Poodle with a Cocker Spaniel), the resulting pups are called *crossbreeds*. A *mixed-breed* is a dog whose ancestors are of mixed-breed origins or unknown. In fact, the mixed-breed usually is such a conglomeration that no one distinct breed type can be recognized. Is there any difference between the three kinds as far as companionship is concerned?

Basically, all normal dogs are much alike—bighearted, faithful, kind. However, the fact that the crossbreed or mixed-breed is frequently "given away," whereas the purebreed often costs quite a sum, suggests certain differences. Cost does not always mean value, but it is a guide. What one gets for nothing is often worth nothing, or else it comes with strings attached. There must be a reason, then, why we can get a crossbreed or mixed-breed for little or nothing, and why we must pay for a purebred dog.

Crossbreeds and mixed-breeds are often given away because someone wants to get rid of them. Usually bred by accident or neglect, they are an unnamed product, with no market value. The purebreed, on the other hand, has always been bred from selected parents and raised under the best conditions for health and good development. Each purebreed has its own standard of perfection, or written description, by which it is judged. The standard is a detailed list of characteristics which together describe the "model," or word picture of a perfect Poodle, Boxer, Cocker Spaniel, and so forth. Therefore, when you buy a purebreed, you know more nearly what you are getting. You may be sure that the purebred puppy has a good chance of looking like his parents; that his size, weight, coat type, and general traits when he is grown will be fairly close to those of his father and mother.

When you get a dog other than purebred, you are getting uncertain quality and quantity; it's practically impossible to determine what he will look like or how big he will be when matured. But his heart is in the right place, and he will give just as much devotion and affection to you. Far better a crossbreed or mixed-breed than no dog at all! Many a happy home has been blessed with fascinating-looking, hearty, and loving creatures of dubious ancestry.

What Purpose Will a Dog Serve?

Before you buy a dog, it's a good idea to determine what purpose he will serve. Are you looking for a sedate and loving companion, a rugged outdoor sidekick, a gentle child's pet, or a small dog to pamper? Are you interested in breeding, or in exhibiting the dog in conformation shows or obedience or field trials? Do you want a watchdog? Usually when the term "watchdog" is mentioned, one thinks of a large breed, or an attack dog. Size has little bearing on alertness or vigilance, and many medium-size breeds make capable watchdogs. For the average person, a dog's role should be that of deterrent rather than savage aggressor. There are too many dangers involved in owning a ferocious dog, and too frequently innocent persons are attacked or bitten, perhaps seriously. Always know why you want a dog, and how it will fit into your lifestyle.

Which Is the Best Breed?

There are so many breeds. How are we to know which is the best? Which breed is smartest, which the most affectionate, which the cleanest in the house, the least likely to run away? To all such questions, we must give the same answer: there is no best breed. All are brothers and sisters under the skin, all very much alike, all very much what their owners make them.

The average person can be forgiven for thinking that one breed is smartest, one cleanest, one most affectionate, because for a long time owners and breeders have given their favorites just such labels. In their enthusiasm they have put mistaken ideas into the minds of buyers. Many expect to find special personalities in the dogs they select, and then perhaps are disappointed. Let us not blame these enthusiastic owners; let us try to understand them. In their loyalty to a favorite dog, they give him all the good qualities in the book! In time, you probably will do that very same thing!

Just remember this: no puppy comes with a special ready-made personality. It is strictly up to you, the owner, to develop, by proper socialization and by teaching, such qualities as you want your pet to have.

A dog of any breed will run away as fast and as far as another if he is not *taught* to stay at home. A dog of one breed will be as clean as another in the house if he is *taught* to be clean. Every dog can learn how to heel, sit, stay, lie down, and come on command, and how to be a civilized and well-mannered companion at home and in public places when he is *taught* basic obedience training.

There are differences, of course, in intelligence; that is, some dogs are smarter and more trainable than others. This, however, is more a matter of the parents; it has little to do with whether a dog is a purebreed, crossbreed, or mixed-breed. There are smart dogs and dumb dogs, geniuses and morons. Even so, a dog does not have to be a mental giant to be lots of fun; the "featherbrain" can still give much love, comfort, and companionship. In short, your dog, whatever his breed, will grow up to be the kind of pet you make him, if he had sound parents.

What Should You Pay for a Puppy?

It is difficult to say *exactly* what you should pay for a puppy. The price depends on the puppy's age, his lineage, his conformation to the breed's standard of perfection, his breeding or show potential, and the expenses involved in whelping and raising his litter. However, you can reasonably assume that toy dogs will cost more than medium- and large-size breeds (because there are fewer in the litter), rare breeds will be more expensive than common breeds, and older puppies sell for more than younger ones.

Depending on the breed, you should be able to purchase a good-quality purebred puppy in the $100-to-$300 range. For that price you are buying a lovable pet, *not* a show dog or a potential brood bitch or stud dog. Breeding- and show-quality animals cost more. If you were interested in a show-quality Poodle, for instance, you might have to pay a minimum of $600 to $750 for a sixteen-week-old puppy, and more than $1,000 for a nine-month-old puppy (even more if the dog has earned points toward his championship).

Before you begin looking for a purebred puppy, learn

what the average prices of pet- and show-quality animals are in your chosen breed. Then deal with dedicated, reputable breeders. Remember, they plan matings, and try to improve a breed with each generation by producing puppies that are better than their parents.

And if price is a consideration, don't be discouraged. Consider adopting a crossbreed or mixed-breed. *Millions* of dogs of all ages and sizes in animal shelters all over the United States are literally dying for homes. They cost very little and make faithful and loving pets. Immunization and neutering are often included in the low adoption fee.

Which Is the Best Puppy?

During your visits to reputable breeders, see as many puppies as possible. Good physical condition and temperament are most important because you are going to live with your dog for a long time. This suggests the importance of the parents of the puppy you plan to buy. Try to see the mother and the father for yourself; watch them, their manner of meeting you, their friendliness, their vigor, and their condition. Ask all about them: were they easy to train, clean, sensible around the house? "Like father, like son" is still a fairly good rule to go by.

Ask to see an entire litter at once, if that is possible, even though you may be understandably confused. They are all rollicking little balls of fur. Which is the smartest, which will you love the most? It is difficult to tell. The one that makes friends with you quickest is not necessarily the firmest friend in the end. One may be a bold little rabble-rouser, another as reserved as a bashful child. Curiosity has long been considered a fairly good yardstick of intelligence, yet it is no sure guide in judging the very young.

The main thing, then, is to pick a puppy of good sound parentage and whose health and vigor are unmistakable. The healthy puppy is sprightly but not nervous or overactive. His eyes are clear and bright, his nose has no mucous discharge, his coat is glossy, and the skin healthy-looking. His ears can hear; that is, he responds when you talk to him, when you make a noise. The listless, cringing pup should not be discarded as mentally backward. Such a one may not feel well because, perhaps, he needs worming or some medication. If your heart sets on a pup of this sort, *do not take him now*. Instead, ask the breeder to get him in tip-top condition, then visit him later.

There is nothing quite so discouraging as having to doctor a puppy the moment you bring him home. It should not be necessary, and it will not be if you insist on perfect health and nothing less in the dog you buy. Perfect health means two things: that the puppy is in good condition at the moment, and that he has not been exposed to any disease or type of infection which might develop in a few days.

Everything else depends upon taste alone. Some folks prefer a dog with a long tail, others one with a short tail. Some want stand-up ears, others dropping ears. Some like long coats, some short, while larger sizes appeal to many, and the medium and toy sizes to others. Color is also a matter of taste, and there are plenty of shades from which to choose. Suppose you make a list of what you want in a dog, and then consult "The Story of the Breeds" chapter, which describes the various dogs. See whether you can find one which matches up with your preferences.

After all, the pet that is going to make you happy is the one you like. This is to be *your* dog, one you will live with for the next ten to fifteen years. Get the pet whose looks please you; do not allow anyone to dissuade you. And remember that size, sex, and coat type will determine in some measure the kind of care you must provide.

Large or Small Dog?

What size dog should you get? Most breeds are capable of adapting to various environments, but realistically, large breeds need more living space and exercise than medium-size and small breeds. Important questions governing size include: Do you live in an apartment or a house with a yard? Do you have a private entrance or come into an apartment-house lobby? Do you use a public elevator? How close is your nearest neighbor? How will the dog get regular exercise? If you live in an apartment building, will the dog's exercise depend solely on you? And will certain giant- or large-size dogs intimidate your neighbors or other residents on the elevators?

Many a person who has to hand-exercise his dog on leash does a more thorough job than the one who lets his dog run free in the backyard. The free-running dog often just sits and suns himself, while the hand-exercised dog must keep pegging along as far as you make him go. You cannot keep a large dog in good mental or physical condition if you shut him in a house. A little fellow can exercise by running upstairs, downstairs, and all around the house, but for the large dog this is not enough. Large dogs also eat more food than smaller ones, so feeding costs will be higher.

How Big Is a Dog?

In studying the description of the breeds in Chapter 16, you will find information about weight. This will tell you something about the average size of the adult dog and will guide you in making your selection. But since some dogs are slender, some round, others rangy, and still others low to the ground, weight alone will not tell you very much. A tall dog with a slender body might weigh the same as a dog of smaller but chunkier build. How, then, do we determine a dog's size? We must also measure him for height.

The height of a dog is always reckoned as shoulder height, and has nothing to do with the measurement from the top of his head to the ground. In fact, when dogs are measured, their heads are disregarded entirely. Instead, they are measured from the withers (or top of the shoulder blades) to the ground. The withers are the point on the shoulder blade that is the highest portion of the body proper, that is, the spot where the neck and body meet.

To measure a dog: stand him broadside against a wall. Balance a stick across his back, as close to the joining of the neck and body as you can get. Then, on the wall, mark the spot where the end of the stick touches. The number of inches from this mark to the floor is the dog's "shoulder" height. The heights listed in Chapter 16 will tell you approximately how tall a full-grown dog will be. There is less size variation among puppies of the different breeds than there is among grown dogs, so when you pick your puppy, consider the size he will be as an adult. Only then will you know how much dog you have to live with when he is full-grown.

Male or Female?

Which sex makes the best pet, male or female, dog or bitch? Actually, there is no clear-cut answer. People who have always owned males are firm in the belief that a male makes a better pet, while those who have always owned females insist that a female is the only kind of dog to have around. It really is a matter of taste.

It must be remembered, though, that a female will need protection as well as confinement twice yearly for a period of three weeks while she is "in season." If a female is allowed to run free during her heat period, she will attract a lot of stray dogs and can be bred accidentally. Having her spayed will avoid accidental matings and unwanted litters, and it should be seriously considered if a female is not to be bred or exhibited at shows. (See pages 60–61.)

The female has been called more affectionate, more reserved, more of a homebody than the male, and while this may be true, we believe it has been overemphasized. The male, properly handled from puppyhood, can grow up to be as settled and sweet-natured as the female. When not trained to stay in his own yard, a male may run away at the first opportunity; but so will a female if she feels so inclined. We can think of no breed that is less likely to run away than any other. In fact, the answer to the runaway problem is basic obedience training, plus a secure fence.

Then there's the man up the street—he owns a female. He says, "Bring your dog over, let's breed them, it will be good for them both and we'll divide the pups." You take your male along. You all sit in the basement for hours as the two dogs fuss and fuss, accomplishing nothing, except that the female grows weary and your male all but exhausted. You see, when a male is raised by a breeder for stud work, he is expertly trained. Your inexperienced dog may bungle things, even injure himself because no one knew how to assist both dog and bitch throughout the mating. Then your male comes home, a wiser but not by any means a better dog. He is not the same, in fact; he's not quite as much yours as he was before.

Smooth or Long Coat?

All breeds need some kind of regular grooming. When you choose your dog, the length of coat is important because you will have to learn to care for it yourself or pay someone to do it. Smooth-coated, short-haired breeds need little or no trimming; brushing and an occasional bath (which you can do at home) will keep the coat in good shape.

Long-coated breeds like Collies, Pekingese, Afghans, Shih Tzus, and Lhasa Apsos need regular brushing to keep the hair in good order, but you can manage it yourself. Other long-haired dogs, including Poodles, Bichons Frises, Cocker Spaniels, Miniature Schnauzers, Wire Fox Terriers, West Highland White Terriers, Bedlington Terriers, and Kerry Blue Terriers, need regular clipping, scissoring, hand-stripping, plucking, or thinning periodically, and if you haven't the time or talent, you'll have to pay a professional groomer to do it. Patronizing a professional grooming expert does not relieve you of certain responsibilities, however. Breeds that require complicated grooming usually need plenty of care between regular appointments.

The Child's Pet

Dogs make wonderful companions for children, and they can help a child develop humane instincts and respect for other living creatures. But if you want a dog for a child's pet, first consider the child. The rough little boy had better have a tough dog, one that can take a lot of knocking around, and strong enough to keep on the go. For this youngster, a terrier, a spaniel, one of the scent hounds, or some of the herding breeds would be ideal. For the dainty little girl, a small dog might be best; she can cuddle it, make a baby of it. Be skeptical, however, about accepting this or any such suggestion as a certain guide. As we have said before, a dog grows to be what his keepers make him. Sometimes you can make a quiet-mannered pup into a boisterous tough if you give him the idea that you want him that way; just as you can sometimes take a headstrong one, full of vigor and vim, and make him gentle as a lamb. So much depends on the way he is handled and social-ized as a young and growing puppy. The strongest trait of the good-natured domesticated dog is the desire to please his mas-ter. When he understands what his master wants, that is what he will usually be.

If you want the dog to guard the child, then a medium-to large-size breed might be best. Even so, the dog brought up with a child, whether large, medium, or small, will in almost every case take on himself the job of protection. While he may not go so far as to bite or attack, he'll raise enough ruckus with his barking to send the intruder packing without delay.

When you go to buy a dog, beware of the seller who guarantees *this breed* is perfectly safe with children. That is a highly questionable statement. There is hardly one breed that is any more safe with children than another. A dog, any dog, is safe with children only after he has proved himself to be so. He must learn to love the child, and he *will* learn to if he is brought up with the youngster from puppyhood. When he has attached himself to the child with real affection, he will suffer any discomfort for the child's sake. Given sound par-ents, any puppy raised with children learns to be loving and trustworthy. Once he is used to little people, he accepts them, and follows them to the ends of the earth.

Ears and Tails

Some people object to the cropping of ears and the dock-ing of tails. If you should favor a breed to which either or both of these procedures are done, remember that you do not have to do it. When the tail is to be docked, however, it is done at a very early age—in fact, long before most puppies go to their new owners. As for ears, cropping is done early in certain breeds; in others, Bostons for instance, not for several months.

It is quite usual for a buyer to take a puppy in the nest; that is, he chooses it while it is still nursing and pays a deposit on it for future delivery. In such a case, you can say, if you so desire, that you do not want your puppy's tail docked or ears cropped. There is no law against docking tails, but there are laws in several states which prohibit the cropping of ears.

The Black Mouth Theory

A common mistaken notion is that the roof of a dog's mouth must be black or at least dark-colored if he is a true purebreed. This is nonsense, so do not use it as a yardstick when selecting a puppy. Of all the purebred dogs at present, the Chow Chow and Chinese Shar-Pei are the only breeds whose tongues and inner mouth membranes are always bluish-black in color. If any other dog has a dark mouth, it is mere chance. It means nothing.

The "Police Dog"

While studying the chapter on breeds, do not be disappointed when you fail to find one called the police dog. There is no such breed. The expression "police dog" simply means a dog used by police forces and law-enforcement agencies throughout the world.

Police dogs are particularly adept at patrolling, chasing and cornering criminals, tracking, and narcotics and bomb detection. They are also used in factories and department stores as night guards against thieves, on farms to protect stock and poultry, in warehouses to protect equipment, and on war fronts to find the wounded and to carry messages.

Although German Shepherds are used most often, many other breeds—Rottweilers, Doberman Pinschers, Boxers, Airedales, and various others—have also been trained for police work.

Breeding Is Not Necessary

One common myth about dogs should be dealt with here: *the female does not have to be bred*. She does not have to give birth to a litter of puppies in order to remain healthy.

Sentimentalists have decreed that no female can be perfectly happy or healthy unless she has suckled a litter. Nonsense! You are her world; with you she will be completely happy, even if she never sees another dog. She doesn't know she is a dog, she thinks she is part of your family, as indeed she is. The carrying and whelping of a litter means a certain amount of danger. Do not subject your pet to it just because you have been told it is good for her or because you think it will be educational for your children to witness the "miracle" of the birth of a litter of puppies.

The same goes for the male dog. It is *not* necessary to mate him. Sex for a male dog does not satisfy any sensual pleasures, nor does it involve love as we humans know it. It is only a reaction to being near a female in season. Mating a pet male is a big mistake, since even the cleanest dog may soon forget his manners and start lifting his leg and urinating in the house. If there is one thing above all that causes males to roam, it is an occasional mating. Whereas before, a male was a quiet, contented pet satisfied with the joys of human companionship, he becomes filled with big ideas about his place in the scheme of things. Every female dog he sees is fair game and every time he scents one in season, off he goes.

The Dog's Background

Perhaps, when you read the chapter on the breeds, you will be disappointed because not one is just called a pet. I don't want a hunting dog, you say to yourself; I don't want a herder of sheep, or a dog that fights bulls and badgers. I merely want a pet, a friendly dog to play with, to walk with. Do not worry. No matter what kind of dog you select, you will get a pet if you bring him up to be a pet. His past is so far behind him he will forget all about it.

The dogs of ancient times worked hard for their living. Man worked hard also, and dogs were the only animals that worked with him, the only animals that turned from their own kind to be the friends of man. Down through the ages, dogs have stood by man's side as hunters, guards, and protectors, helping him to find food and clothing, to track the snows and the jungles, to make life possible oftentimes where it might not have been possible without their aid.

The brief histories in "The Story of the Breeds" will show you that the dog you take into your home has a long and honorable history of service as selfless and as untiring as he will give to you. The very qualities of devotion that were his in ancient times are his today. Count on him for faithfulness and love of man, his master. Take the dog, then, and teach him to be the well-behaved friend you want him to be.

2
The 2-3-Month-Old Puppy

Introduction to the Home

Let's suppose that you have just acquired your first puppy. You bring him home; you take him indoors and set him down. He is only eight to twelve weeks old, remember, and it's quite understandable if he is completely bewildered by all these new sights and faces. Perhaps you brought him home in your car. He had been bounced and jounced, or at least had butterflies in his stomach from the unaccustomed motion of riding in an automobile. All gone is that delightful playfulness he showed when you picked him out at the kennel or shop. Don't be surprised if he looks like a wilted bouquet.

Puppies are not all alike, however. Even at this tender age they are individuals. While one puppy will seem utterly crushed by the strangeness of new surroundings, another will trot about boldly as if anxious to investigate this charming place and all these lovely people. Whatever the pup's reaction to this new scene, there are three important DON'TS: 1. Don't reach down quickly and make sudden grabs at him. 2. Don't permit children to tease or handle him roughly. 3. Don't let children shriek over him in their delight. Sudden movements, rough handling, and unaccustomed loud noises frighten puppies. And uncontrollable, running children may accidentally step or fall on the puppy and injure him. Your role is to gain his confidence. When you get that, it will serve you all of your dog's life: in obedience, in training, in whatever you want him to do or be. Talk to the new pup. He won't understand a word at this point, but he will understand a friendly tone of voice and there is nothing more successful in creating confidence.

All of a sudden you are astonished at yourself for daring to bring home such a very young puppy. You feel so inadequate to cope with the problem. Hesitantly he comes toward you and looks up as if you were all in the whole world he could depend on. That does it! You pick him up in your arms and hold him close. He's yours and you are going to do the best you can.

You will, too. You are just as able to take on this job of puppy raising as anyone else. It's a wonderfully rewarding job and not at all hard to do. You can learn it, step by step, as the puppy grows. That you love him already and have anticipated his coming is proved by the fact that you have prepared for him.

The Puppy's Bed

Before the puppy is brought home, consider the place where he is to stay while he's little. Young puppies need warmth and an even temperature. You can block off a small section in the kitchen or an unused bedroom, or you can use a bathroom or pantry. There are two good reasons for giving a young pup a special place. At this age, puppies have very little bladder and bowel control and, when given the run of the house, can't avoid soiling anywhere and everywhere. Second, dogs are "den" dwellers by nature. They feel most comfortable and secure in their own snug little nests. A bed in a small area is the puppy's own territory or "den," the only part of the house not intruded on by the rest of the family. The feeling of security in having a place of his own will help him fit into his new life and its routine.

Arrange a box or bed of his own, not overly large but big enough so he can stretch out or turn round and round in his inherent fashion to get comfortable, at one end of the blocked-off area and a few layers of spread newspapers at the other. Your puppy may have been partially paper-trained when weaned. Whether he was or not, he soon gets the notion of what the paper is for because it is natural for him to leave his bed when he is ready to eliminate. Always have a newspaper within easy reach.

His bedding, first of all, should be washable. Fleas, for instance, cannot be controlled unless the bed and bedding can be kept clean. You might use a small discarded cotton blanket, fold it down to pillow size to fit the puppy. Or you can use a piece of folded flannel, or a blanket. It should be fairly thin: a thick cushion might be too deep for the pup's short legs to negotiate. Whatever the bedding material will be, have two or three on hand so that you can wash one and air it in the sun periodicially.

The bed or box itself may be as plain or as luxurious as you wish—the puppy will not care. A variety of designs and sizes are available, from toy dog to giant size. Remember that most puppies are chewers and anything expensive might be torn or chewed to shreds in no time. Until the teething process is complete, a good temporary solution is to use a cardboard carton with the front cut away so the pup can get in and out. Place it in a quiet, draft-free area. The bed or box should be underlaid with carpet or a blanket to keep its floor warm. Drafts and cold are a puppy's worst enemies.

A wire-mesh cage or crate with a door that can be closed is not necessary but can be useful, especially for house training. The crate should be large enough for your dog to stand up in without touching the top, and comfortable enough for him to turn around and lie down in without being cramped. The crate can be used as a bed, and also as a place to confine your dog when you will be away for a few hours.

You can purchase a crate at most pet stores, or the man of the house can make an excellent puppy enclosure out of a packing case. Nail strips to the bottom to keep it an inch or two off the floor. For the front, make a door with a four-sided frame, its center covered with wire. Don't use very fine-mesh wire. It is too easily chewed and, more important, its fine mesh can trap the puppy's toenails. Use quarter-inch-square mesh; nail or staple it on the outside of the frame, and cover the edges with strips of molding. Fasten a good catch on the door, one the pup can't pop open by bouncing against it.

When a puppy is kept in an otherwise unused room, do not shut the room door tightly at night; leave it open a crack so you can hear what goes on. Constant crying during the night can be stopped by the simple command "Quiet!" so the puppy may know he's not entirely alone.

You may prefer to keep the puppy's box or crate in your own bedroom for a few nights until he learns to sleep by himself. Always place the crate away from any possible draft. If the room becomes cold, throw a blanket or shawl across the top. Use your own judgment as to how much air to give the pup. Don't let him take cold, but don't smother him, either.

If you have a puppy of a sporting breed or another large breed, you may have planned to have him live in an outdoor kennel. In that case be sure to have a well-sealed, draft-proof dog house, one that has a snug box within, filled with suitable bedding material—washable blankets, rugs, cushions, or a layer of straw—so the puppy can make a warm nest. The kennel should be placed in a dry, sheltered area, raised off the ground and positioned so that the door faces away from the prevailing winds in the winter and from the midday sun in the summer. It must also be placed within an enclosure, such as a wire-fenced yard, or your puppy may wander, or be prey to straying dogs, mischievous children, or thieves.

So, after the comforting hug you've given your new puppy, you're going to place him in his new bed. He's had enough excitement for a while. Too many introductions, too much attention at first appearance, will only be confusing. Probably he will just sit in his bed and think things over, glad at last to be rid of the motion of the car. Since he has undoubtedly not been fed for several hours, he may whimper from hunger. If he remains quiet or sleeps, leave him alone. If he whimpers, give him a snack, some warm milk, or other accustomed food.

Crying at Night

You may be upset by the crying sessions of the first few nights. You feel very helpless and somehow to blame. This is a perfectly natural occurrence—nearly all puppies cry when they sleep alone in a new home for the first time. They miss the warmth and companionship of their mother and litter mates.

Try to make up for this lack by providing something warm for the pup to snuggle up to. Try letting the puppy cuddle up to a hot-water bottle wrapped in a terry towel. Fill it about two-thirds full of slightly hotter than lukewarm water.

An electric heating pad can also be used, but these are safe *only* when the connecting wire can be buried under the bedding so securely that it cannot be chewed. The ticking of an alarm clock placed near the puppy's bed may help to ease his lonely feeling.

Few Visitors

Next morning the puppy will be up bright and early, literally screeching for something to eat. Open the crate door and let him scamper around the floor as you clean out his box and give him a change of blanket and newspapers. Keep the door of his room closed if there is any chance of his investigating the stairway and falling down.

Now your problems will begin—and they will not come from the puppy. Everybody up and down the block is going to be interested in your pup; everybody is going to love him and itch to get their hands on him. And this can invite trouble. Perhaps they have a dog, too, and out of the kindness of their hearts they may bring him to sniff noses with your puppy. Or possibly their puppy is home sick and cannot call in person; but he can send his germs on the hands, the feet, and clothing of his owners. This is one way contagion is spread, especially among young dogs. Your puppy may have been safeguarded by inoculation against the serious puppy diseases. If not, explain the situation to your visitors or make up some excuse. Then select a veterinarian, take your puppy there and have him inoculated so you won't have to fear contagion. (See pages 32–33.)

Aside from the possibility of disease, young puppies are easily excited, upset, and overtired by too many visitors. Until your pup has become used to his new home, try to avoid attention from strangers; also do what you can to guard him from loud noise and confusion.

FEEDING CHART: FROM WEANING TO 3 MONTHS

BREED SIZE	WEIGHT IN POUNDS	CALORIES PER DAY*	NO. OF FEEDINGS PER DAY	AMOUNT PER DAY**			
				DRY (1 cup = 8 fl. oz. measuring cup)	SOFT-MOIST (6 oz. pkg. = 2 burgers)	CYCLE 1: complete and balanced food designed to meet the nutritional requirements of puppies.	
						DRY (8 oz. cup)	CANNED
Very Small (avg. 6-12 lbs. at maturity)	1-3	124-334	4 or self-feeding	1/2-1 1/2 cups	1/2-1 package	1/2-1 1/2 cups	1/2-1 can
Small (avg. 12-25 lbs. at maturity)	3-6	334-574	4 or self-feeding	1 1/2-2 cups	1-1 1/2 packages	1 1/2-2 cups	1-1 1/2 cans
Medium (avg. 25-50 lbs. at maturity)	6-12	574-943	4 or self-feeding	2-3 1/2 cups	1 1/2-2 packages	2-3 1/2 cups	1 1/2-2 cans
Large (avg. 50-90 lbs. at maturity)	12-20	943-1384	4 or self-feeding	3 1/2-5 cups	2-3 packages	3 1/2-5 cups	2-3 cans
Very Large (avg. 90-175 lbs. at maturity)	15-30	1113-1872	4 or self-feeding	4-6 1/2 cups	2 1/2-4 packages	4-6 1/2 cups	2 1/2-4 cans

*Requirements may vary depending upon breed, age, exercise, and environment.

**Divide the amount per day by the desired number of feedings per day.

How to Feed

Beginning on page 101 you will find a complete discussion on feeding. Read it as soon as you can. But right now you are faced with one hungry pup, and the suggestions below are made with the common sense approach to dog feeding there outlined.

The person from whom you got the puppy probably has spoken to you about feeding, or given you a feeding chart. In either case, continue the same diet for a week or so while the pup is getting used to the daily routine as a new member of the family. But remember that the breeder's feeding chart may have been designed only for the weanling pup. Many new owners follow the "baby" diet long after a husky, growing pup is ready for more substantial food.

Although some puppies are weaned to baby cereal and milk, the recommended method is to wean directly to a commercial soft-moist, dry, or canned puppy food, starting at three weeks of age, with the weaning process completed when the pups are five or six weeks old. (See pages 201–203.) In the latter case, you have no problem in changing the diet. If the pup has been eating baby cereal and milk, he should be started on a regular dog food at about six weeks of age. However, since any sudden change is apt to cause an upset, introduce new foods gradually. Add the commercial food a little at a time until the cereal food is replaced. The puppy's food should be served at room temperature, never too hot or direct from the refrigerator.

If, by chance, your puppy arrives before you have prepared yourself with the regular food you are going to give him, it is safe to feed human baby cereal, or toast mixed with slightly warm milk, or meat broth or raw beef chopped into small bits. The growing puppy requires even more food than a grown dog of the same breed, but his stomach cannot hold that much in one feeding. So the puppy must be fed several times a day. At this age, four feedings are needed: morning, noon, early evening, and shortly before bedtime. The feedings can fit the convenience of the household but they should always be about four hours apart. Changing feeding times will upset the routine that a pup has grown accustomed to.

Occasionally a puppy will turn up his nose at one feeding. If your puppy refuses a fourth feeding, skip it, but be sure to increase the amount of food in the other feedings.

The correct amount to feed will differ according to the size of the dog. We have many different purebreeds and mixed-breeds to consider, including a great many different sizes. Individuals differ too, even members of the same litter; some are voracious eaters, others pickers.

Step on the bathroom scale with your puppy in your arms. By subtracting your own weight you can estimate the pup's weight. Then, use the feeding chart as a guide, remembering that amounts are approximate.

As already stated, however, the individual puppy is the best measuring stick for the amount of food to be given in each feeding. As a rule, give as much as he will readily eat, and use your own observation. You can soon tell if you are overfeeding by just looking at your pet.

The average healthy young dog eats as if he were starving. Don't believe him for a minute; he gobbles by nature. Up to now he has been eating side by side with his brothers and sisters, so he eats fast. As time goes on, he will acquire better manners. Occasionally, however, a puppy misses the competition of his litter mates and may not eat as readily without them. He may dawdle at first and need some coaxing, but in time will get used to eating alone.

Your pup may clean up his dish in a few minutes. Good! The puppy who eats like an eager beaver, and gains and grows, is what you want. If he eats half his food and appears satisfied, take the dish away and give him a little less at the next feeding. Allow enough time for him to complete his meal—fifteen to twenty minutes or so. Allowing a puppy to dawdle over eating will only encourage "picky" eating habits. Fix a fresh dishful for each feeding. Mixed food left standing is likely to become spoiled, especially in warm weather.

If the pup skips one feeding, do not worry or tempt him with tidbits. Remove the food and feed him again at the next scheduled time. But if he stops eating entirely, and appears listless, then make a quick visit to your veterinarian.

You will soon learn the right amount of food to give your puppy to keep him satisfied and well-filled-out without becoming obese. Watch the little fellow's stomach as he eats; if it is so enlarged that he sways and waddles when he gets through, then he may have had too much. Cut down on the next feeding.

After he has finished eating, take him outdoors or put him on his "paper" for a few minutes to relieve himself. Puppies always have a bladder or bowel movement soon after eating. Then put him in his crate or his den to rest. Do not handle him much, and don't romp with him directly after eating. Increase the amount of food gradually as the puppy grows.

Because the young puppy's food is very moist, water is not quite as necessary now as it will be later. Sometimes puppies may actually overdrink water just before or after meals and upset their stomachs. Offer a drink regularly, then remove the dish. When the room is very warm, or during hot weather, offer fresh water more often or keep it available. Unlike cats, dogs are very fond of water; they delight to dabble in it and strew it around; water must be available for puppies that are on dry self-feeding. (See below.)

Feeding Dishes

The feeding dish will depend on the length of the puppy's nose and the shape of his face. Flat-faced, short-nosed pups—Bulldogs, Pekingeses, Boston Terriers, and Pugs, for instance—eat more easily from a shallow dish. Longer-nosed dogs—Collies, Fox Terriers, German Shepherds, Dalmatians, and so forth—can reach into a deeper dish, while Poodles, Cocker Spaniels and other long-eared breeds may need a slant-sided dish to help keep ear flaps and fringes from dipping into their dinner.

When a puppy is just learning to eat, however, he may be started on a fairly flat dish, then after a week or two given the type of bowl best for his muzzle shape and ears. Dog feeding dishes are made of stainless steel, plastic, aluminum, and ceramics. Select one that is easy to clean, chewproof, and sturdy enough not to tip over or slide around the floor while the dog eats. Stainless-steel dishes are the best, but ovenware crockery and plastic are also serviceable.

Self-Feeding

If your puppy prefers his meal-type food dry—without the addition of any liquid—you might like to try something called self-feeding, which is becoming very popular. The dog feeds himself from a container in which the dry food is always kept available. He can eat what he wants, when he wants it. When left alone in his "den," he has something to do; nibbling at his dry food will very likely take the place of nibbling at a chair leg or the corner of a rug. Also, if you work every day and are kept away from home past the puppy's regular feeding time, you know that he has food and can satisfy his hunger. An important advantage is that the blood-nutrient level is maintained more evenly.

However, when starting self-feeding, do not begin at a regular mealtime—that is, when the dog is very hungry—or he may gorge himself beyond his needs. Feed him his regular meal, then put out the filled container.

Although some puppies may overeat and become fat on a self-feeding regime, most will eat the correct amount to keep their proper weight and continue growing. Dry food usually increases the need for water, so the pup on self-feeding should have unlimited access to water.

You may not want to put the puppy entirely on self-feeding, in which case you may feed one or even two mixed feedings each day as well. However, keep the self-feeding container filled and available at all times.

Keeping the Puppy Clean

After meals, the puppy will need cleaning off, since his muzzle may be smeared or caked with food, and his ears, if they are long, may have dragged through his dinner. Wipe off his mouth, his muzzle, and ear fringes with a slightly dampened cloth; otherwise the hair, which is only puppy-fluff right now, will mat and annoy him until he scratches. He can be wiped off with a dampened cloth or brushed clean and perhaps combed very gently to separate the hairs. Occasionally little clumps of hair mat together and irritate the skin. These should be separated with your fingers before large tangles have a chance to form. There is no harm in trimming off small mats, but use blunt-tipped scissors to avoid accidents. Puppies are unbelievably quick in turning, so do not risk injury to the eyes.

Trimming Toenails

Toenails grow rapidly, and in the case of the young puppy they are not worn down to proper length because he usually walks on only soft or smooth flooring. The ends of the nails are often sharp as needles. They'll prick holes in stockings or clothing, but worse than that, as they grow they take on a curved shape which makes them difficult to disentangle once they are caught. When the nails do catch into things, the puppy may injure himself in trying to pull away. Long nails also make his footing less secure. Therefore, you should periodically nip off just the transparent tips of the nails with dog nail clippers. Remove only the point, without trying to shorten the nail, but merely blunting it. Do not cut into the "quick," which is quite sensitive and may bleed. (See page 132.)

Dewclaws

On the inside of the front legs (and sometimes on the hind legs), just above the feet, you may find a set of extra claws. These are called dewclaws, and their attached nails should be trimmed like the others. At this age, the dewclaws are loosely attached by cartilage only. They are useless toes, unsightly, and often dangerous when they get caught in fabrics. Most breeders have their veterinarians remove dewclaws several days after the birth of a litter. There are a few breeds of dogs, the Great Pyrenees, for instance, whose dewclaws are left on. For the most part, dewclaws are a nuisance and might as well be removed. The earlier they are removed, the better, since they become attached to the leg bone with growth. During early puppyhood a veterinarian can remove them under local anesthesia. With older dogs, dewclaw removal is a more serious procedure.

Soft Spot

Besides the joints, tendons, and leg muscles, which may be injured by a fall, the puppy has a very tender surface on top of his head known as the "soft spot." While the chance of incomplete or slow hardening of the skull differs in breeds or individuals, the top of a puppy's head is always a highly vulnerable spot.

See to it that your pup is never dropped on his head. Take care that he doesn't strike himself against chairs, beds, and in fact any hard object during those earliest play periods when he is just beginning to use his legs. Perhaps the best answer to this problem is to give him a place to play where there is little or no furniture. The most important precaution of all is to instruct the children not to pick up the puppy until they have been taught how to hold him safely. (See pages 36–37.)

Play

The puppy that plays quietly is usually playing safely, whereas the one that tears around boisterously may be exhausting himself nervously and physically. This does not mean that a normal puppy is not lively, for he certainly is. But just as he gets enough sleep by means of short naps, so does he get his best exercise in short sessions.

Don't egg him on to play when he tires or wants to rest. When he is ready to quit, leave him alone. It is a great mistake to excite a resting puppy or to permit children to urge him on. He will play when he feels like it, and when he is tired he should stop.

Play is the young animal's instinctive method of exercise. He will find ways of playing by himself, too. The age-old game of chasing his tail is usually puppy play; but if he actually bites at his tail, look for matted hair, debris, or even fleas that might be annoying him. Since a normal, healthy puppy is chock-full of vim and vigor, he may exert himself beyond his strength. After a play period of twenty minutes or so, pick him up and put him in his box. Stopped in the midst of a boisterous game of chase-and-pull, he may rebel, but never mind! Shut him up and leave him alone. Before you know it, he'll be sound asleep.

The puppy that plays quietly in his own place or box cannot come to much harm no matter how long he keeps at it. His footing is secure because he is on his papers or his blanket. When taken out for play, however, he meets certain risks, not the least of which is slippery flooring. Many folks floor the puppy room with vinyl tile or linoleum, or they let him scamper around the kitchen or bathroom, since these places suffer less from periodic mistakes. Nevertheless, the frisky pup is none too sure on his feet. He can easily slip and fall, injure a knee joint, or pull a tendon. Therefore, the puppy that plays on vinyl floor coverings or waxed hardwood floors needs the protection of some kind of carpeting. Especially suitable is a discarded cotton rag rug that can be washed as often as needed.

Toys

Your puppy needs toys to play with. Be sure they are the right kinds of toys. The little rascal's ability to rip and tear things apart with his teeth is surprising indeed. He is not being naughty but merely natural. Using his teeth is innate to a dog and a puppy learns this at a very early age.

All kinds of toys can be found in pet shops: rawhide bones, twists, chips, and chews; hard rubber toys; latex and vinyl figures, digestible chewies, and more. Whatever you buy, select it with the following in mind: *can it be torn apart and can it be swallowed?*

Don't buy toys that could crumble easily, or toys made of synthetic rubber. The latter, even if not swallowed, can irritate the stomach and intestines and do a great deal of harm. Toys with bells and squeaking devices that might be chewed off and swallowed should also be avoided. Thin, soft rubber balls will be destroyed in five minutes, the pieces swallowed, perhaps, and the puppy made sick. Steer clear of toys stuffed with sawdust or grain, as these can be potentially dangerous, too.

The safest toys are those made of hard, natural rubber, natural rawhide, "treated" natural bone, and leather. Remember to select toys of appropriate size. Don't give large toys to small breeds, or tiny items to large breeds, especially things that can be chewed apart, caught in the throat, or swallowed whole. A pair of discarded stockings, knotted together, makes a good toy, as does a bunched-up clean cloth or a strip of heavy burlap stitched into a roll for the pup to haul about.

Bones are sometimes given to puppies as playthings. Small bones, like those from chops or chicken, will splinter and the sharp pieces may tear the throat and seriously injure or kill the puppy. The larger, harder knuckle and shin bones cannot be splintered and are safe.

Sleep

A puppy needs a lot of sleep. When he finishes eating, he will usually feel sleepy, so put him on his paper or take him out to relieve himself and then put him in his crate for a nap. This helps his digestion and avoids excitability.

Your puppy should not be allowed to romp directly after eating. Too much activity, handling, or excitement may make him nauseated. Keep him quiet and undisturbed for a short time, and before you know it he'll be napping. Instead of going to sleep, he may prefer to stretch out and quietly mouth his toys. This is all right, too.

Paper Training and Housebreaking

The chances are that your puppy was started on paper training when he was weaned; even so, he is by no means perfectly broken as yet. He is too much of an infant to remember anything very long. So let's start again from the beginning.

Paper training—standard practice for puppies too young to go outdoors (especially those that are not fully immunized), or those not yet physically or mentally developed— means teaching the puppy to relieve himself on spread newspapers. Although paper training is convenient, to save the trouble and possible frustration of having to retrain the pup to go outdoors when he is older, it's better to start taking him outside from the beginning. However, papers should be kept at one end of the puppy's sleeping place or den for emergencies. Paper training is particularly suitable for small dogs and for apartment living.

Cover a three-by-four-foot area of the floor in the puppy's den with several layers of newspaper. If the floor is slippery, tape down the corners of the papers to keep them from sliding. Following a nap, the puppy is usually ready to urinate. If you can be on hand just as he wakes, so much the better; if not, wake him gently after a reasonable period of sleep. Place him on the paper immediately. Do this the first thing every morning, after each meal or drink of water, after play periods or naps, and before bedtime. You will be surprised how soon he connects the feeling of paper beneath his feet with the duty expected of him. Always praise him so he will know that he has pleased you.

Burning all soiled papers is the most sanitary method of disposal, but while the puppy is learning, save one soiled piece to remind him what the papers are for. Puppies, in fact all dogs, prefer to use a spot they have visited before, so take advantage of this during the early stages of paper training. However, remove all droppings promptly so the puppy doesn't play with them.

For the first few days, cover a large area with papers so the puppy is more likely to locate them, then gradually reduce the size of the papered space until it covers only a small corner of the den.

Watch him closely. When you see him sniffing the floor, hurrying round and round, he probably needs to relieve himself. Pick him up quickly and put him in the proper spot. Then be liberal with your praise. He may leave a trail—when he starts, he can't stop—and though one spot may be easier to clean up, remember the object is to train your puppy, and the proper place must be associated with the deed.

If you prefer to train your puppy to go outdoors from the very first, you can do so, provided he is fully immunized against certain canine diseases. Puppies taken outdoors can pick up disease from places where infected dogs have urinated or defecated. The puppy is protected, however, when properly inoculated. (See pages 136–137.)

For dogs that will eventually urinate and defecate outdoors, this is the wiser course. It means that you must be ready to take the puppy out the first thing in the morning—usually early morning, too—in the beginning. Since a puppy needs to eliminate right after meals, that means another four trips, and still another walk just before bedtime. That makes six trips at least, especially while the puppy is young. It may seem like more trouble than paper training, but you will not have to retrain when switching from papers to the outdoors.

The puppy's crate becomes an important part of outdoor

training too. When your puppy is confined to it at night, he won't soil his bed if he can possibly help it, but he will let you know very early in the morning his need to go out. Pull on some clothes in a hurry, then take the pup from the crate and carry him outdoors. Don't set him down until you get him outside, for he may squat immediately. Let him wander around until he finds a spot that he likes. If he doesn't do it right away, be patient. When he does, praise him extravagantly. Each time he does his duty, give him a great show of approval. Try to avoid "mistakes" by watching the puppy when he's indoors. If you catch him starting to squat, hustle him outdoors. If you really work at it, your pup will soon be housebroken. Mistakes are bound to happen with young pups, however, since they can't totally control themselves when they get the urge.

Under certain conditions, both paper and outdoor training may be wise. Strangely, many dogs never forget their paper-training lessons, and this is often a good thing. When a dog is ill or cannot go out-of-doors, or when he is old and uncertain on slippery pavements, the paper toilet can be arranged indoors. The dog will remember what it is for.

A young puppy urinates frequently and in small amounts. At this age, the bowels move several times a day; the movements are often not quite formed, but rather soft and of medium brown color. A change of food, particularly different milks, and even water, may loosen the bowels for a day or two, after which they return to normal. Overexcitement, more food than usual, or the strangeness of a new environment may also cause a temporary loose bowel condition. This need cause no alarm, unless the stools are definitely watery, black, or greatly increased in number. A highly offensive odor suggests some type of infection, and the veterinarian should be consulted promptly.

Umbilical Hernia

You may find a soft, movable bulge beneath the skin of the puppy's stomach. When the puppy lies on his back, the lump disappears; when he stands up, it descends again. This is probably an umbilical hernia which occurred at the point of attachment with the placenta when the puppy was whelped. It is not painful, nor is it irritated, but it may be unsightly or subject to injury. It may or may not correct itself in time. In any case, do not attempt any sort of home treatment. Your veterinarian will advise if it can be surgically repaired.

The First Medical Examination

Your first trip with your puppy should be a visit to the veterinarian for a thorough examination. Early inspection of every young puppy is just good common sense. Most breeders and pet shops are experienced and reliable enough to offer for sale only puppies which are in good health. Some, unfortunately, are not as careful as they might be. Many a pup is purchased on impulse before the buyer is sure about the reputation of the kennel or pet shop. Then too, things can happen suddenly which change a sound and healthy youngster into an ailing or injured one requiring immediate professional care.

Should you find out that the dog has a serious medical problem or hereditary fault, get a statement from the veterinarian and return the puppy immediately to the kennel or pet shop. It may seem heartless, but it will be less painful in the long run to return the puppy than to raise him, become attached to him, and see him suffer or have to be put to sleep at an early age because of a serious defect.

Immunization

Depending on his age, your puppy may have received some or all of his required inoculations. If you obtained a health and immunization record from the breeder or pet shop, show it to your veterinarian so he can determine if additional inoculations are required.

All puppies and adult dogs must be inoculated against certain highly contagious canine diseases, including distemper, hepatitis, parvovirus, leptospirosis, and parainfluenza. These are explained more fully in the "Practical Health Care" chapter.

Usually the dam (the puppy's mother) is immune to these diseases, either because she has had them and recovered or because she has been inoculated against them. Her colostrum—another name for the milk which her newborn puppies get in the first few hours of nursing—gives them protection until they are weaned. Beyond this period, a puppy's protective antibodies dwindle, and he becomes very susceptible to disease unless he is immunized.

Selecting a Veterinarian

If you don't already have a veterinarian, ask the puppy's breeder or your dog-owning neighbors for recommendations. The local veterinary association can also give you the names of veterinarians in your area. You will find conscientious and competent veterinarians conveniently located almost everywhere.

It's wise to choose and get acquainted with the veterinarian of your choice before trouble occurs. Today's veterinarians are busy professionals; they do not often go to one's home. Their more complicated equipment for examination and treatment is office-bound, so you must go to them.

Learn if the veterinary hospital is located within a short drive of your home; find out what the office hours are, and whether it is possible to obtain emergency care after hours or on weekends and holidays. Once inside the hospital, see if the facilities are clean, bright, and pleasant-smelling. Does the veterinarian handle your dog carefully? Is he or she willing to discuss problems, treatments, and fees? Are the staff courteous and cheerful and, most important, kind to animals?

The important point is to seek professional assistance before an ailment is advanced and the treatment unnecessarily difficult or expensive. Don't forget that, like everything else these days, the cost of animal care has increased considerably. Some large cities have pet clinics for those unable to pay normal fees. Your local human organization can direct you to these.

3
The 3-5-Month-Old Puppy

The Developing Puppy

Your puppy is growing rapidly now, not only in size but in other ways as well. He is much more certain on his feet than he was a short time ago: his leg muscles are stronger, his coordination better. Most striking, perhaps, is the development of his intelligence. He seems more aware of his surroundings, more eager to reach out and make friends with the people around him. He wants to play, play, play, and he expects everyone to join in with him. He especially enjoys children. They, too, are always on the go, and that pleases him. Children are small, and since the pup's line of vision is close to the ground, they appeal to him even more than grown-ups for his ever-ready frolicking.

Message to Parents

Because so many puppies are purchased as children's pets, it's time for some advice to parents. Some of them will hesitate to add a dog to the household for fear it will injure the child.

You have no cause for fear. Most puppies are friendly creatures. Born with complete confidence in people, they will not be anything but friendly unless their trust is destroyed by ignorance or neglect. If a good-natured puppy goes to a home where it receives lots of affection and attention, and learns what is and what is not acceptable behavior, it will not be a problem with children. Of course, in playing with a toddler, certain pups may topple the child over—that is not so much the dog's fault as the fault of the parents who, without thinking about it, gave too large or too rambunctious a dog to a young child. Actually, the dog risks the greater harm in most cases. Quietly, he takes an unbelievable amount of pummeling, and he'd give his very life for the child if he could.

In addition to the physical protection a dog gives a child, he provides constant companionship. Rainy days present fewer problems for the only child in the house when a dog is around. Letting the youngster think the dog is his and his alone develops his sense of responsibility and humane instincts. In caring for a dog, a child learns how to treat another living creature with justice and humanity. Such wholesome friendship can teach him the proper attitude toward any member of society who suffers physical or other misfortune. Failure to grasp this lesson causes some of the greatest evils of society. A child must learn that the world is not his, to do with as he likes; only when he treats others with kindness and understanding can he really grow as a human being. Without a doubt dog ownership plays a big part in the social education of the young.

A dog will not teach the child kindness unassisted—you will have to help. By his patience, a dog may even give the child an exaggerated idea of his own powers and privileges, for the dog is unbelievably long-suffering. The slightest growl is a real exception. Usually the dog simply gets up and walks away.

Sometimes children, and even grown-ups, tease a puppy because he is so "cute" when he gets angry and tries to bite with his baby teeth. This is a serious mistake. Besides the cruelty of tormenting a pup, it is very likely to make him mean-tempered and snappish when he grows older.

What about a dog's service to adults? It is as great as that given the child. Let us disregard for the moment the war dogs, the herding dogs, farm and factory guard dogs, and leaders of the blind. Thousands of these have served, and continue to serve, man. But let us also salute the millions of dogs in private homes where, as pets and companions, by their love and devotion they make life happier and less lonely.

The Child and the Dog

At what age can a child have a pup of his own as a companion? This question cannot be answered exactly because it depends on the amount of help given by the parents. Respect for others is one of the things a child must learn as he grows. He cannot always be expected to treat a puppy humanely without help. He will learn, however, if he sees his parents handle the puppy carefully, and if they insist that he be gentle and considerate every step of the way.

No child is old enough to play with a pup by himself until he has learned to treat the dog properly. He must be taught not to chase the puppy. An uncontrollable, running child may accidentally step or fall on the dog and injure him. He must be taught not to stick his fingers in the puppy's eyes and ears, not to pull the hair or tail, not to lift him by the legs, not to pull or twist the legs or tail to cause pain, not to drop the pup on his head, nor to frighten him with screams and cries.

He must also be taught not to antagonize the dog while he is eating, not to take food or toys away from him, or to startle or touch the pup while he is sleeping. A child must learn never to "corner" a dog (or any animal for that matter). It is natural for animals to protect themselves when cornered, and a pup that has the most gentle nature may snap or bite to protect himself under certain conditions. All such things have been done to dogs by children who knew no better because their parents did not realize the need for teaching them.

And so the age at which a child may be given a puppy of his own will depend upon the child and the amount of time given by the parents for teaching as well as for watching over the play periods of both little ones.

How to Pick Up the Puppy

Always use both hands to pick up the puppy. Place one hand between the forelegs to support the chest and the other hand under the belly to support the hind parts. As you lift, take care not to spread the youngster's elbows. Held with both hands in this manner, the puppy cannot use his feet to wriggle free, nor is he strained as when lifted at one end only. *Never* try to lift a puppy by his front legs or grab him by the scruff of the neck—these actions will hurt him and frighten him. Never use his tail as a handle, since the tail is easily injured.

Put the puppy down as carefully as you lift him. Suppose you are holding him on your lap. Keep one hand ready to stop him in case he should suddenly try to leap off or squirm to the floor. When you put him down, hold him with both hands and carefully put him on the floor so that all four feet touch at the same instant.

Very young children should not pick up the puppy at all. They go through a phase of dropping things on the floor and you cannot do anything about it *except* by your own watchfulness. To prevent serious injury, see that your child does not lift the pup; if he should, get to his side as quickly as possible. Naturally, puppies of the smaller breeds suffer greatest damage since they are most easily lifted. Older children can be taught the proper method of picking up and putting down an animal, but even they should be told to sit on the floor when they handle a tiny pup.

Naming

The puppy is now ready to start his education. His first lessons will be simple enough to fit his youthful understanding. If he is a purebred dog, his name may have been chosen by the breeder and already registered with the American Kennel Club (see pages 189–191.) Registered names often incorporate the kennel name of the breeder. A dog's registered name cannot be changed once it is recorded by the AKC, but it can be shortened into an attractive call name. If your purebred puppy has not been named officially, you may select a name (limited to 25 letters) when you fill out the AKC Registration Application. His "informal" name, of course, can be whatever you choose, for this is merely a call name to be used at home. The informal name, however, should be short and crisp-sounding.

Every time you approach the puppy, speak his name clearly, distinctly, and in a moderate tone of voice. Shouting is not necessary; he hears much better than you do. Loud noises may frighten him and confuse him. In a short time he will connect his name with himself. Maybe he'll reply with a tiny yip, perhaps he will run toward you. This is excellent. Reinforce it by kneeling or stooping down as he approaches and petting him under his chin. A fully grown person, standing, can be rather intimidating to a little dog on the floor, so get down to his level and your voice will have far more appeal.

Collar and Leash

You will need more than one collar before your puppy grows up. He'll grow through several sizes as he matures, so don't spend a lot of money at first. Select a lightweight, narrow collar, then replace it as soon as it becomes too small. Round leather collars won't pull out or break the hair on long-coated breeds, while flat leather collars are good for short-haired dogs. The collar should fit correctly, that is, loose enough to be comfortable but not so loose that it can slip over the pup's head if he balks at the leash. To find out the correct size, measure around your puppy's neck, then add two inches. A dog measuring 12 inches around the neck, for instance, would wear a size-14 collar. When on the dog, see if you can slip two fingers between collar and neck—that spells comfort—and then with both hands see if you can pull it off without unfastening it. If you can, then it is not safe, for the puppy may put a paw through and hobble himself.

Attach the collar for a short time each day, especially during playtimes. Your pup may be one of those devil-may-care youngsters that doesn't mind a bit, or he may resent it by pawing and rubbing himself along the rug. Don't worry. He will get used to it, but right now try it on him for short periods only, perhaps just before mealtime.

Next comes leash training. When your puppy has learned to accept the collar, tie to it a piece of string or snap on a lightweight leash. Let him trail it over the floor, wherever he wishes to go. He'll be a bit bewildered, especially if it catches on a chair leg and gives him a yank. Stand by and see that the puppy doesn't tangle himself up and become frightened or injured.

After a few sessions of trailing, hold the leash loosely in your hand and follow the puppy around the room. The next step is to lead the puppy where you want to go. This is the first time he has been made to do something he may not want to do. If he balks, drop the leash, play with him a moment, then pick it up and try again. As you guide him along, talk to him continually, praising him, telling him what a very good dog he is. Soon he will disregard the tug at his neck. Once things go well inside, take the puppy outdoors. Always use a well-made leash for outdoor walking, because even a tiny toy can break a string, get away, and run into the street.

The earliest and simplest lessons have been dealt with at length to stress the need for patience and understanding. Avoid frightening the puppy now and you will also be paving the way for all later training.

"Bed!" "Place!"

When a dog does something especially smart or surprising, we tend to fall back on the instinct theory. "Oh, he does that instinctively," we exclaim. Perhaps he does; then again, perhaps his mother taught him.

Much of the supposedly instinctive animal behavior is taught the young by their mothers. Puppies form their first bond of attachment with their mother when she feeds them, licks them clean, and looks after them. As they grow in the nest, they learn much from their dam, especially if they are free to trail her and she is able to show them the sights and the dangers. When we get a young puppy, we are literally taking him out of elementary school; so let's get him right back in again, and teach him what a little dog on his own ought to know.

The simplest of all the puppy's obedience lessons is *"Go to bed!"* or merely *"Bed!"* or *"Place!"* or whatever expression you may want to use. Its advantages are too many to name; you will learn that as you proceed.

Remove the puppy's toys from his bed, and use one of them to start a little game. Take his toy away, give it back, then take it away again. Naturally, he'll want it. Hold it up so he can see it, and as you walk toward his bed or box, say, *"Go to bed!"* He will scamper after you, and as he sees you drop the toy in the box, he will jump to get it. You are telling him to do what he is already doing, but the point is that you are impressing upon his mind the sound of the order *"Go to bed!"* at the very moment he is hopping in. Repeating the order will

soon associate the words with the act. When he understands
what is wanted, you can skip the toy. Merely issue the command and give a signal with your hand in the direction of the
box.

Don't overtire the pupil by continuing the lesson longer
than five minutes at a time. Four or five lessons daily are
enough. Be regular in your teaching, be patient, and above
all, be encouraging. *"Go to bed!"* is an order, not a punishment, so be cheerful, sociable about it. All the lessons will not
go well. Sometimes the pup will be confused; he'll look up at
you, worried, as if to say, "What am I to do?" Stop everything. Pet him, talk to him. Wait a while and then start all
over again. Once he gets the idea, his eyes will shine as he
scampers to obey. Then, be liberal with your praise.

A young puppy's memory is short, so "little and often" is
a good teaching rule. Several short training periods per day
are best, without one day skipped if it can be avoided. Even
after the lesson has been learned, use it often or the puppy
will forget. Gradually increase the distance until the youngster can be sent to bed from another room.

The Carrying Case

Conditioning the puppy to a carrying case, like crate
training, is best done while young. Adult dogs often show re-
sentment and fear when they are shut up in any kind of enclosure. Of course, if yours is one of the larger breeds, you will
not be carrying him in a small case for very long. He will ride
free or in his crate in the car, and he will be crated when he
has to travel by plane. Nevertheless, at some time during puppyhood, most puppies have to be taken somewhere in a carrying case, so it is sensible to teach them that a satchellike
enclosure is nothing to fear.

Place the puppy's own blanket or pillow in the case so he
will feel at home, and keep the top or door open. Put the case
down on the floor. Perhaps he will hop in; if not, put him
inside, lower the top or shut the door and latch it. Don't attempt to move the case, but just sit down beside him so he will
know you are there. If he cries, reassure him by talking softly.
Open the top or door and let him hop out if he likes, or if he
cares to take a nap in the case, so much the better. Leave the

case around for a while so it becomes familiar to the puppy. Next time you put him inside, carry the case around a little to accustom him to the motion. Take the puppy outdoors and carry him down the street a short distance, just so he will learn to accept the case as a matter of course.

Feeding

The puppy's basic diet continues without change (refer to the "Basic Nutrition and Feeding" chapter). As the puppy grows, however, he needs more food so you must increase the amount in each separate feeding. The amount to be fed at any age can usually best be determined by watching your puppy. He will show weight changes from day to day. If he is getting on the plump side, reduce the quantity. If he appears thin and seems anxious for more to eat, increase the amount. The quantity also depends on the puppy's breed and activity. The feeding chart for different-sized pups can serve as a guide.

When your puppy reaches four months of age you can reduce the number of feedings to three a day—morning, noon, and evening. But, of course, to compensate for the dropped feeding and also because the puppy is still in a growth stage, you will increase the quantity.

If you prefer to vary your pup's menu, the morning and afternoon feedings can be commercial dry dog meal moistened with slightly warm water or milk, and the evening feeding either dry meal (moistened with meat broth), semimoist, or canned dog food.

In buying commercial dog food be sure to get the best kind you can buy, since whatever else you add, this is the foundation of your dog's diet.

Under certain circumstances, you may want to feed dry dog meal alone. This can be done on a self-feeding regimen, which is described on pages 24–25.

Fresh drinking water should always be available to the pup. If it is not convenient to give him free access to fresh water, do not forget to offer a drink several times during the day, but not directly before feeding or after rigorous play periods or exercise.

During the teething stage, usually commencing at the age of four months, a large shank bone is a good thing for the

FEEDING CHART: 3 TO 6 MONTHS

BREED SIZE	WEIGHT IN POUNDS	CALORIES PER DAY*	NO. OF FEEDINGS PER DAY	AMOUNT PER DAY**			
				CYCLE 1: complete and balanced food designed to meet the nutritional requirements of puppies.			
				DRY (1 cup = 8 fl. oz. measuring cup)	SOFT-MOIST (6 oz. pkg. = 2 burgers)	DRY (8 oz. cup)	CANNED
Very Small (avg. 6–12 lbs. at maturity)	3–10	334–816	3 or self-feeding	1½–3 cups	1–2 packages	1½–3 cups	1–2 cans
Small (avg. 12–25 lbs. at maturity)	5–15	494–1113	3 or self-feeding	2–4 cups	1–2½ packages	2–4 cups	1–2½ cans
Medium (avg. 25–50 lbs. at maturity)	12–25	943–1645	3 or self-feeding	3½–6 cups	2–3½ packages	3½–5½ cups	2–3½ cans
Large (avg. 50–90 lbs. at maturity)	20–40	1384–2352	3 or self-feeding	5–8½ cups	3–5 packages	5–8 cups	3–5 cans
Very Large (avg. 90–175 lbs. at maturity)	30–70	1872–3542	3 or self-feeding	6½–12½ cups	4–7½ packages	6½–12½ cups	4–7½ cans

*Requirements may vary depending upon breed, age, exercise, and environment.
**Divide the amount per day by the desired number of feedings per day.

puppy to chew on; it helps to loosen the baby teeth and to relieve the irritation of sore gums; helps his jaw to develop normally; and gives him a lot of innocent pleasure. Never give the puppy fowl or chop bones that are sharp; these may splinter and stick in the throat if swallowed.

Mischievousness

Every healthy puppy is going to be mischievous. You might as well make up your mind to it and not worry. Worry more when your puppy is so good he never tears up anything; this one needs a bracer, for he's below par!

When we say that puppy mischievousness is not a fault but a virtue, we can hear objections popping up on all sides. But a dog's teeth are his fingers, you see, and he must use them if he has the normal vitality and curiosity of a healthy young animal. Books and magazines within reach will be gnawed; that hanging corner of the tablecloth will be yanked unmercifully. The world is his, and everything he can grab is a toy to play with.

There is just one way to prevent all this. Keep things out of his reach. You cannot teach him yet to leave certain objects alone. So be sure to provide safe and interesting toys to push and pull and tear and wreak his small vengeance on; and then remove all else from his inquiring teeth.

A special warning about base plugs: electric outlets with their wires attached are fair game for any puppy. He'll try to chew them, and possibly cause a fire or shock himself. If your puppy does get a shock from chewing through an electric cord and becomes unconscious, don't touch him while he is in contact with electrical current. *Always unplug the cord from the wall first.* If you can't, wrap a towel around your hand, or use a pencil, a broom handle, or some other nonconductor of electricity to push the wire out of the pup's mouth. Wrap him with a blanket to keep him warm. If the dog is not breathing, start artificial respiration (see page 158), then get to your veterinarian as soon as possible. Another word of advice: do not drop rubber bands, paper clips, and other small items on the floor, because they could go into a curious puppy's mouth and be swallowed.

Can He Go Outdoors?

Can a 3–6-month-old puppy be taken outdoors? Of course. But use common sense. If it rains or snows, the puppy belongs inside the house. If it is extremely cold or very hot, keep him indoors. Wind, draft, and too much direct sunlight can prove harmful. It's best to avoid them. This is most important with small and medium-size breeds. The larger breeds at this age will be better accustomed to being outdoors.

Bear in mind that most puppy coats are not thick and weather-resistant enough to keep him warm or to screen his body from the sun's rays. He is more sensitive to cold, too, since he has more body surface for his weight than a grown dog.

In fairly warm weather, a certain amount of exercise on natural grass is good; but it is not safe for any length of time. Especially when left to himself, the puppy will dig up dirt and stones and may swallow them. He'll delight in sprawling out on the grass, but if he lies there very long he may get chilled from dampness even though the ground seems warm. If the owner plays with the puppy for ten or fifteen minutes, two or three times daily in good weather, that is fine, and that will be enough. Keep the youngster moving and he will benefit from the outing. The safest kind of outing for a young pup is in a playpen.

The Playpen

To get sufficient exercise your puppy must have more space to play in now. He may be very mischievous, too, or not totally housebroken, so he cannot be given the freedom of the house. Put a tension-bar gate (made for small children and dogs) in the doorway of the room you want him to stay in. At this age, weather permitting, dogs of the large or heavier-coated breeds can spend some of their time in an outdoor enclosure. They can be confined in a puppy exercise pen or baby playpen. You can buy a puppy exercise pen from most pet-supply dealers, or you can make one.

Four wired frames can be screwed together and bolted to a wooden platform with casters or wheels. If the height of the pen is an inch or two less than the width of the house doors, it can be carried from one room to another, or outdoors. When covering the frames, *nail the wire on the outside*. It's safer because the puppy won't scratch himself.

Since you may wish to confine the puppy in the pen for a few hours, it is wise to add a bed in which he can curl up for a nap. For most puppies, a wooden box will do nicely. Cut an opening in the side to serve as an entrance. Hinge the top for a cover that can be raised for cleaning or left open if the weather is very warm. Place a blanket or other bedding inside and you have created a snug little harbor free from draft and chill. Occasionally a pup will refuse bedding of any kind and claw it out of his box, basket, or kennel. Don't worry about it. If he prefers a bare bed, there is nothing you can do about it.

Place the pen in the sun when it is cool, and in the shade when it is hot. Face one long side and one short side with canvas as a windshield. The outdoor yard for larger breeds should have some shade as well as sun, and a place protected from drafts or wind, such as a doghouse. If you leave the house, even for a short time, bring your dog inside. Never leave him alone in an outdoor enclosure when no one is at home, even when your yard is fenced.

Keeping the Dog in the Basement

How about keeping the puppy in the basement? It depends entirely upon the basement! A dark, damp, poorly ventilated basement is no fit place for a dog of any age—it is just as unpleasant and unhealthy a place for him as it would be for you. The average basement, however, is not what it used to be, particularly in today's modern home. If it is light, dry, and clean, it can serve for at least part of the time. It can be his bedroom for sleeping at night, for instance, if care is taken to guard against dampness. Construct a wooden platform, raised off the floor for ventilation, shield the sides against drafts, and furnish a comfortable box or basket for the pup to stretch out in. (Watch those wicker baskets, though, at this

age; teething pups often chew them and swallow the pieces—
to their, and your, sorrow.)

Due to lack of sunlight (even in the best basement), however, your dog should not be confined in the basement during
the day. To make a long story short, the basement that is fit for
you is equally fit for your dog as a part-time shelter.

Sleeping with People

Should the puppy be allowed to sleep in your or your
child's bed? By all means, if you want it that way. As long as
the pup is sweet and clean and *housebroken*, no harm will be
done to adults or children, except in the rare case of human
allergy to dog dander. Taking the puppy with him is one of
the best means of persuading a child to go quietly to bed. It is
also a great comforter for lonely people, young, old, or
middle-aged.

So far as the puppy himself is concerned, he sleeps warm
and draft-free, with no danger of chilling when the house
heat goes down. If you are afraid of coddling your puppy,
remember that some need coddling—if such a term may be
used to mean sleeping warmly. A puppy's energy is limited; it
can be used for keeping warm or for growing. So let him grow.

There are drawbacks to letting the puppy sleep with people. Once you start it, you may have to keep it up. The puppy
will be quite definite to tell you that. Furthermore, sleeping
covered will "soften" him to a certain degree. He should not
sleep in a warm bed one night and alone in a cold room the
next.

The short-coated, thin-skinned little puppy accustomed
to sleeping covered should be given a blanket to curl up in for
daytime naps. Make a flannel cover for the blanket or pillow,
and leave the ends open so he can crawl inside. The older
puppy knows enough to do this. When it is warm, he'll sleep
outside; when it is chilly, he'll crawl in, snug as a bug in a rug.
If you have occasion to board out a dog that has always slept
in bed, tell the kennel so they will provide the additional
night warmth required. If they cannot, then board the dog
elsewhere.

The Teething Process

When the puppy is about four months old, his baby teeth will begin to loosen and fall out as his permanent teeth start coming in. In the course of his life, a dog has two sets of teeth, temporary and permanent. The temporary set, sometimes called "milk teeth," consist of six quite tiny incisors, upper and lower, directly in the front part of the jaws. On each side, upper and lower, is a fanglike or shearing tooth (these are called the "canines"), and behind them the molars.

A puppy starts to cut his baby teeth at three weeks of age, and by six or seven weeks he has his full set of 32 temporary teeth. For the time being, the milk teeth are strong enough for chewing rather soft foods; but since his jaw strength has not yet developed, they cannot crack or crush really hard substances. Nor are they strong enough to support the puppy's weight without injury. A common method of play is to let the puppy grab a rag and hang on as you lift him high. Owners often do this as a matter of pride, to prove what a good grip the youngster has. Needless to say, lifting a pup by his teeth is bad practice, and ought never to be permitted.

During the fourth month, you may notice that the gums are swollen and irritated. The little teeth will gradually loosen and fall out. The puppy rarely if ever cries from toothache, yet his mouth is sore; he champs his teeth together, may vomit occasionally, lose his appetite, and act as if he has lost his last friend. However, the teething process does not always disturb puppies. Some go through it without batting an eye. But practically all puppies want to chew on things at this stage. You can help the puppy by giving him safe toys or a hard knucklebone to chew on in an attempt to pull his own teeth. (See pages 41–43.)

When a baby tooth refuses to give way to the permanent tooth coming up beneath it, it will be pushed aside rather than out. Then the veterinarian will have to extract the baby tooth. Give the puppy time; don't be too eager to get those baby teeth out. Ordinarily, they will shed themselves and you won't even notice the process. However, if you notice two teeth, one large and one small, trying to occupy the same place in the jaw, do something about it to avoid problems in tooth alignment and the adult bite. By six months of age, the 42 permanent teeth are usually in place.

Worming

Contrary to what people may say, not all puppies have worms. *Do not dose your puppy, therefore, with strong and dangerous medicines merely because you think he needs them.* Be very sure before you go ahead, and then proceed with caution and exactness.

Most reputable dog breeders worm their puppies before delivering them to new owners, so your puppy may not need worming again for several months, if at all. However, since worms are fairly common in young dogs, it is wise to be on the alert for them.

There are many signs of worms, for they upset a puppy in various ways. His abdomen may appear bloated or overly fat, especially after eating, more than the amount of food consumed seems to warrant. He may spit up or vomit often in small amounts. He may be lethargic and disinterested in play. His appetite may be irregular: one day he may eat hungrily, and another day refuse food entirely. His bowels, too, may be loose or watery. Roundworms, which resemble one-to-three-inch pieces of string, are often expelled in the stool. They may also be vomited. These are the most common kind of worms that infect young dogs, and puppies can be born with roundworms, infected in the womb from their mother.

If worms are suspected or actually seen in the stool, it is wiser for the new dog owner to let his veterinarian prescribe the dosage instead of trying to do it himself. Take the pup, along with a specimen of his stool, to the veterinarian, who will determine the type of worm present by microscopic examination, and prescribe medication. The fee for the examination will be modest. If you don't know the type of worm present, never give your dog an over-the-counter worming preparation. The dosage recommended on the package cannot take into consideration the condition of every individual puppy, meaning that your dog may be less rugged than normal. He may be weakened by the worms or some other ailment and his resistance lowered for the time being. If such is the case, even the normal dose for his size and weight might be dangerous. That is why a veterinarian's prescription is preferable to patent remedies.

With present-day over-the-counter medicines, it is not difficult to rid a puppy of roundworms. Directions for dosing will be found on worm medicines sold in pharmacies and pet stores. If you use one of these, consult your veterinarian about the safety of the brand, then be sure you follow instructions precisely for dispensing the medicine to puppies.

The amount of worm medicine varies with the puppy's age and weight. This is where the danger lies, when the inexperienced dog-owner attempts home worming. Worm remedies are irritating to tender intestinal membranes. They are hard on the digestion, too. It is important to give some worm medications only after a period of fasting. The dose is usually given the first thing in the morning, on an empty stomach; that is, before any food or milk is allowed. And then no food is given for at least two hours or a specified time. You will find detailed directions on the package. *Be sure you follow them to the letter*.

Stool Eating (Coprophagy)

Once in a while a puppy will eat his own or another dog's stool. This disgusts and disturbs the owner but it need not become a habit. The dog may merely be hungry—puppies are frequently ravenous and ready to pick up whatever is available. It may be a good idea, therefore, to keep some dry dog meal or biscuits in your dog's play area for him to nibble on when he suddenly feels like eating.

Boredom, inactivity, and too much confinement are other causes of stool eating and point to the need for more attention, more exercise, and a good assortment of toys so the dog will have something to drag about. Puppies often play with stools. Since uncollected feces may be responsible for the practice, clean up all bowel movements promptly.

Stool eating can also result from a deficiency of the digestive enzymes amylase, lipase, and protease, causing a dog to eat feces to replace them.

This repulsive habit must be corrected immediately, especially since a dog can become infected with roundworm, hookworm, or whipworm eggs from eating the feces of other dogs. A sharp "No!" in a disgusted tone of voice will stop a puppy when you catch him in the act. Then, of course, remove the stool. A well-balanced diet is essential. Adding the enzyme papain (contained in meat tenderizers) sometimes discourages the tendency to eat feces. Try sprinkling a teaspoon of Adolph's Meat Tenderizer or Accent on your dog's food. Your veterinarian can help, too, by giving you an ingredient to add to the dog's food that will make his stools unpalatable.

Things to Watch Out For

There are certain infectious diseases which will prove far less serious if treated without delay. Symptoms include listlessness, loss of appetite, coughing, running eyes and nose, and high fever. If you notice any of these signs, consult your veterinarian immediately.

As you brush the puppy's coat every day, or every other day, watch for fleas and ticks (see pages 123–125), for they infest dogs of all ages. Look sharply along the back, at the root of the tail, under the vent and the forelegs, on the creases and flaps of the ears, and between the toes. If you see the slightest trace of these pests, especially the black, granular leavings of fleas, get to work with the fine comb, and use an insecticidal shampoo or spray on the dog.

Learn to use the regular brushing sessions as a means of checking your dog's health. Report any sudden loss of hair, inflamed areas, signs of tenderness, or lumps under the skin to your veterinarian.

4

The 5-7-Month-Old Puppy

The period between five and seven months is the age of gangling youth, a trying time for any dog. Ordinarily, it is his most unattractive age. He has lost his puppy plumpness and may appear to be all legs and neck. He is leaving behind some of his sweet, trusting puppy ways, but he has not yet acquired any mature dignity and good sense. The puppy is rambunctious; he barks more and generally asserts himself. His coat is undergoing changes, too. Gone is the soft, fine baby hair and in its place are the beginnings of his adult coat.

Dog Licenses

Your dog is still very much a puppy and, if normally healthy and intelligent, something of a little wild Indian. But according to the records of your municipality's city or town hall, he rates as an adult dog at six months and, as such, must be licensed. A dog license is a sort of tax, a charge for the privilege of keeping a dog, and the fees supply the local canine-control agencies with much-needed funds.

If you are new to dog-keeping and unfamiliar with your area's licensing ordinance, check with the city or town clerk to determine exactly what the laws are, since regulations vary from one area to another. Fees are generally higher, for example, for unspayed females and unneutered males. The license must be renewed yearly. If you need more information, call your local humane society and they will advise you.

In return for the license fee you will receive a printed form containing the dog's license number. Be sure to record your dog's call name, breed, sex, and markings on the form, a copy of which is retained at headquarters. You will be given a metal license tag along with the receipt, which should be securely attached to the dog's collar. The license and tag not only provide him with the best form of identification, but also may avoid his being picked up as a stray and possibly destroyed. If your dog gets lost and some good samaritan finds him, his license number will tally with his description; he can be identified and returned to you.

This is the best reason why your puppy should wear his collar at all times. He may slip out the door, chase after someone or something, and get lost. If he is not wearing his license tag, he may be picked up by the local dogcatcher and popped into the pound, after which you may or may not see him again. If he wears his license tag, he will be held for several days, during which time you can claim him.

Another means of identification is a metal collar plate or tag engraved with your name and address. Neither the license tag nor the identification plate or tag, however, can always be depended on to furnish proof of ownership. If your dog strays and gets into a fight with another dog, his collar could be chewed off, or if your dog is stolen, the thieves could remove his collar and tags and destroy them.

The only foolproof method of identification is a tattoo. You can have your dog tattooed on his inner right hind leg. The process is accomplished quickly and painlessly with an electric needle by a veterinarian, or through local groups such as kennel clubs or humane societies that offer tattoo clinics. The marking is permanent and cannot be removed. His number should then be registered with an agency such as the National Dog Registry or Tattoo-A-Pet. These and other registries are usually open twenty-four hours a day, 365 days a year. Once an animal is tattooed and the number registered, they will notify the owner as soon as the pet is located anywhere in the United States by an individual, the police, an animal shelter, or other source. For more information, contact the National Dog Registry, Box 116, Woodstock, New York 12498; or Tattoo-A-Pet, 1625 Emmons Avenue, Brooklyn, New York 11235.

Feeding

Most 5–7-month-old puppies will not need the same number of daily feedings as they did when they were younger. Now is the time to skip the bedtime feeding and give only two meals a day: morning and late afternoon or early evening. The amount of food he consumes, however, must be increased to compensate for the dropped meal and also because his rapid growth puts an extra demand on the puppy at this stage.

The amount of food required depends on the individual puppy, the extent of his activity, exercise, size, and weight. You will find more information in the chapter on "Basic Nutrition and Feeding."

An important point is that at least three-fourths of your puppy's diet should consist of a balanced, prepared dog food that will give him all the necessary food elements. You will probably be able to judge the amount of food needed to keep your puppy satisfied and in good weight, neither too fat nor too thin, by observing him. The feeding chart, based on the puppy's weight and caloric need, can serve as a guide.

There is a method called self-feeding in which dry dog meal is kept out for the dog to eat at will. Although self-feeding more often appeals to the kennel owner, it can also be adapted to house pets, especially when the owners are away during the day. The self-feeding method is described on pages 24–25.

Bones—should they or should they not be given to your dog? Let us consider the negatives: bones provide little nourishment, can cause constipation, and can irritate or even tear the digestive tract when swallowed. Continuous gnawing of bones wears down the teeth. On the positive side, bones provide chewing exercise and most dogs enjoy them tremendously. At one time bones were considered quite beneficial for dogs, but today they are looked upon as more risky than nutritious. Most pet owners give synthetic or rawhide bones instead to satisfy their dogs' chewing urge. If you want to give real bones to your dog, though, limit the number to about one a week. Never give him a bone near his regular feeding time. And only give a well-cooked large bone, such as a beef shank or knuckle bone, that will not splinter. Poultry, chop, and other small bones are too sharp; they can splinter or be swallowed and do great harm.

Don't forget that your dog needs water as well as food. In fact, a dog can live without food a great deal longer than he can without water to drink. Keep fresh water in a bowl where he can drink at will unless you make it a practice to offer a drink several times a day. The water should be renewed frequently, especially in hot weather when it can quickly become warm or fouled by insects.

Drooling

People often worry when they see saliva stringing down from the corners of a dog's mouth. This is very common and frequently occurs while he is waiting for his food, especially in breeds with pendulous lips. The sight or the smell of fresh food is enough to start the mouth watering until it spills over. Drooling is common, too, when a dog feels sick at the stomach, such as when he rides in the car. Teething can also cause drooling, as can a foreign object caught between two teeth. If the drooling continues, however, have your veterinarian examine the dog's mouth and throat.

Outdoor Exercise

Outdoor exercise, especially walking, is extremely beneficial to puppies. It keeps them in shape both physically and mentally. An exhilarating jaunt at least once a day is more healthful to both dog and owner than any other form of exercise. Walking is a good way to acquaint a puppy with the world outside his home. He experiences new sights, noise, and scents. He has an opportunity to meet other people and animals while under your supervision, and all these contribute to his socialization as well as satisfy his natural curiosity. When regular walks are initiated during puppyhood, an adult dog will eagerly await his daily outing.

Controlling your dog is mandatory during walking, but his play periods should be pure enjoyment. Puppies love to chase balls, to retrieve sticks, and to play other outdoor games. These are excellent forms of exercise, provided you determine that sticks will not splinter and that balls will not lodge in the puppy's throat. "Safety" is the guideline for outdoor exercise. Nothing that jeopardizes your dog's life can be considered beneficial exercise. This means that you don't let him walk off leash on busy streets and that his play periods should take place in an enclosed yard.

Heeling

Since leash control is required by law in most communities, begin correct leash-walking at a fairly early age. The first leash lessons were discussed in the preceding chapter. By this time your puppy should be used to being led with a leash fastened to his collar.

Heeling is another name for walking correctly under leash control; it means walking with the dog's right shoulder in line with your left knee. When this lesson has been learned, you will hold the leash in your left hand; your right hand will be free for other duties. However, throughout the training period, the leash is shortened by coiling and is held in your right hand. At the same time, your left hand, palm downward, grasps a part of the leash closer to the dog's collar to execute firm correction or control. Just how near the collar you place your left hand depends on the size of the dog.

Keep the dog on your left side. Walk at a fairly brisk pace. Find a quiet path or sidewalk so the pupil's attention will not be distracted by other animals or people passing. Your goal is to make your dog walk willingly and easily. He may charge ahead like a little bull, or balk and pull back. If he does, jerk the leash with your left hand, call his name, and command *"Heel!"* to bring him in line. You'll have to repeat the command frequently the first few times you try heeling. Every time the dog moves ahead, falls behind, or crosses in front of you, jerk the leash, call his name, and repeat the command *"Heel!"* After a few minor corrections, your dog will adjust his steps to your movement.

There is a difference between giving commands and making corrections. All commands of motion should be issued in a calm and pleasant tone, in conjunction with the dog's name. The sharp word and the jerk of the leash are corrections to be used when the dog lags behind, for instance, or charges ahead, or when he stops to sniff the ground. And when your dog understands and obeys, be liberal with your praise. Several lessons daily, about ten minutes each, will be about right. Puppies tire easily, so "little and often" is the rule.

Sweaters and Coats

When your dog goes out walking he may need protection against wintertime cold. The general rule is: when you put on a topcoat yourself, put a sweater or coat on your dog if he is accustomed to living in a heated house. Of course, when he is let out for a few minutes to scamper around the yard or when he goes for a walk on a mild day he need not be bundled up. But when he is out for any length of time, or walked in cold or wind, he should wear a covering.

Should every dog wear a sweater or coat? The larger, long-haired breeds do not need clothing of any sort, especially when fully grown. By that time their dense undercoat, overlaid with a coarser outer coat, protects the body from the cold. The thin puppy coat, however, is not weather-resistant. Therefore, if your pet is still carrying his puppy coat during his first winter, keep him moving outdoors and dry him thoroughly if his hair gets wet. As for the thin-skinned, fine-haired small breeds kept as house pets, these will need sweaters or coats on cold days.

Pet shops generally stock many different kinds of sweaters and coats for dogs. When choosing one, make sure that it covers the dog's chest, since this is the area that needs the most protection. Fancy styles that are made of flimsy materials may be pretty to look at but are not much defense against the cold. Raincoats serve a different purpose, of course, and protect the neck and back as well as the chest. These save the owner a lot of work, too, since a dog that is walked uncovered in the rain must be dried thoroughly when he comes in.

Get your puppy used to clothing of some sort while he is young, for you never know when it may be useful. In illness, a housebroken dog often *insists* upon going outdoors to relieve himself and, at such times, will need extra protection. Be careful when putting on a sweater for the first few times. Don't frighten the dog by pulling it over his head and ears. Instead, hold the sweater in one hand, then place your other hand through the neck opening and spread it enough to slip over the head gently.

Conditioning to Noise

The longer your puppy is protected from noise and confusion, the greater his shock will be when he encounters them. You walk along the street—pop goes the exhaust as a car goes whizzing by. The puppy shies. He is not only frightened; his eardrums actually bother him. Stoop down, reassure him, and if the noise continues, put your hands over his ears to deaden the sound. He will undoubtedly have already learned that the world is not the most quiet place. We cannot stop the noises but we can introduce the puppy to them gradually.

Make some sort of racket at home; for instance, just before you feed the dog, rattle his pan unnecessarily. Because he so enjoys his food, he will be less disturbed by the noise that goes with something pleasant. When he has learned to heel fairly well on leash, walk him down a street where traffic is heavy. Have a treat or two in your pocket, and if fire engines roar past, offer him the tidbit then and there. All this noise, he begins to think, is not so bad after all!

Overexposure to Sun

Direct sunlight out-of-doors is beneficial for puppies, but in summer or very hot climates, too much is harmful. The first sign of overheating will be increased panting. A dog cannot rid his body of extra heat as rapidly and efficiently as can a human being. A dog perspires mostly through his tongue rather than through the pores of his skin. As he pants, his tongue drips and, if he continues to pant, he loses a lot of body fluids. Give him water to drink and move him to a semidark, cooler place until the panting ceases. Ten to fifteen minutes of direct sunlight is sufficient for a young dog, unless he has shelter into which he can retreat when he gets too hot.

Hot-Weather Tips

It is easier to keep a puppy warm than to keep him cool. When a dog becomes overheated and perspires, he needs plenty of drinking water to replace lost fluids. A pan of water placed for him in the morning is not enough. Provide fresh, cool water several times daily. Be sure that both the water and the bowl it is served in are clean.

During hot weather, exercise your dog in the morning or evening and keep him out of the midday sun. See that his outdoor exercise pen has a section of shade.

Don't worry if your dog goes a little off his food during a hot spell; he may be quite sensible about eating less at such a time. Give him the same kind of food but not quite so much of it. Do not take him for long rides, especially if you have to leave him alone in the car for any length of time. A car parked in direct sunlight gets hot inside very quickly; in a matter of minutes, the interior temperature can soar to 110° F.

Do not clip off his coat since it will help to screen the skin against sunburn and insect bites. Daily brushing will remove much of the dead undercoat which adds to overheating and discomfort. Heavy coats can be thinned out but never given a "crewcut." Never use poisonous weed killers or plant sprays where your puppy plays. They can kill your dog or make him very sick. Fresh paint and varnish must also be kept out of reach.

Correcting Bad Habits

This can be a time of great destructiveness if you permit it to be. A normal puppy is playful and curious; his jaw strength is rapidly increasing; his gums and teeth are becoming less sensitive and he is eager to try them out on everything. Add to this the fact that a puppy does not know right from wrong, and you have on your hands an animal capable of doing considerable damage.

Every dog can develop bad habits. The important thing is not to punish him for these but, instead, to teach the dog what he may and may not do.

Dogs learn commands and corrective words the same way children learn to count or to recite the alphabet: by repeating and repeating until they are fixed in the memory. Some dogs learn more quickly than others, but every dog can eventually learn basic commands and the meaning of the word "No!"

Approval and disapproval are demonstrated by tone of voice. The higher-pitched, encouraging "Good Dog!" or "Okay!" and other words of praise mean approval. A dog's name is always spoken with affection and enthusiasm, too, never unkindly or in conjunction with discipline. The lower-pitched, definite "No!" signifies correction. "No!" is the only negative word you should say to your dog. All corrective actions must be firm, but kind; firm because the puppy feels greater security when controlled; kind because you don't want to destroy his confidence. Dogs thrive on praise and stop, surprised, when scolded.

Suppose you find your dog blissfully gnawing away on the table leg. Fetch one of his toys quickly, maybe a rawhide bone. Pull him away from the table with a quick jerk of his collar as you scold "No!" Your tone of voice will let him know exactly how displeased you are. Offer him his bone. Praise him as he takes it. Then watch him. If he returns to the table, order "No!" again, and confine him to his crate and leave him alone. Sooner or later, he will understand that he may chew certain things but not others.

Much of the difficulty in teaching this lesson is caused by temptations that you unconsciously leave in the dog's path. Sometimes you make it difficult for the dog by not using common sense. Take the case of the table leg again. When you are at home, you scold him for chewing it. But if you go out and don't confine the puppy while you are gone, you're giving him *carte blanche* to chew the leg to his heart's content. No one is around to follow through with correction, consequently that lesson is lost.

Once you insist that the puppy leave something alone, see that he obeys, or remove the tempting object from his reach. If you give him an old shoe to play with, don't blame him when he noses into the closet and drags out a new pair. This is your fault, not his.

Praise your puppy lavishly when he does something right, and correct him immediately when he misbehaves. To make the correction effective, he should be caught in the act. Actions and consequences are interrelated to a dog, and he does not understand discipline for a misdeed that occurred in the past. Remember: when you catch your dog misbehaving, voice your displeasure immediately with a firm "No!" Never hit your dog or slap him with a folded newspaper. You will only frighten him and make him resent you.

Spaying and Neutering

If your dog is a female, you will want to decide whether or not she should be spayed. Spaying, or ovariohysterectomy, is the removal of the ovaries, uterus, and cervix. It is an operation often performed to prevent a female from being bred and having puppies. Spaying does away with the female's three-week "season" which attracts male dogs to her. During her season, which occurs approximately every six months, you would have to keep her confined indoors or board her in a kennel to keep her from being accidentally bred.

The best time to spay a female is before her first heat period, or when she is between six and eight months old. The operation can be performed at any age, but the earlier it is done, the simpler the procedure is. At this age, healing takes about one week, and in from two to three weeks, the patient is back to normal. At first, however, physical exertion, particularly running up the stairs and jumping, should be avoided.

If your dog is a male, and you do not want him to sire puppies, he can be neutered or castrated. Neutering, or orchiectomy, is a procedure involving the tying of the spermatic cords and the removal of the testicles. The best time to perform this operation is when a male is between six and eight months old, before he becomes sexually mature and before bad habits are established.

Spaying and neutering tend to make dogs less aggressive, more contented and affectionate. Males are less likely to roam and get into fights. On the average, spayed and neutered dogs live longer and healthier lives. Almost half of the unspayed females develop breast and ovarian tumors as they age. Spaying (especially before the first heat) greatly reduces the risks of breast cancer and uterine and ovarian disease. As unneutered males mature, they frequently suffer from enlarged prostate glands, testicular tumors, or cancer of the prostate. Neutering lowers these risks.

What are the disadvantages of spaying and neutering? Altered animals are ineligible to compete in the show ring. Naturally, a female can never give birth, and a male can never sire puppies. For those who desire a dog merely as a pet, companion, watchdog, or guard, however, these things are not disadvantages. On the other hand, if you should plan to enter your dog in shows, or to breed your female or use your male at stud at some later time, then certainly she should not be spayed and he should not be neutered.

5
The 7-10-Month-Old Puppy

Changes are now taking place very quickly. You can almost see your puppy grow. He is still a bit awkward, and still enthusiastic about everything, especially play. He probably has lost most of his babyish looks. At seven months he is shooting up on his legs; as he nears ten months he will begin to fill out, unless he happens to be one of those ultra-low breeds whose framework develops somewhat differently from the average. His appetite is voracious. He needs more food because of his growth and increased activity, and must still be fed twice a day since he can digest larger quantities at a time.

Psychologically, at this stage a puppy generally becomes rather self-confident. He begins to get his own ideas about his rights and independence. You'll have to be firm more often in order to maintain your authority. This is critical with a large breed, which may need obedience training. Raising a puppy is very much like raising a child. They both need plenty of love and discipline, especially at this age.

As puppies approach sexual maturity, their masculine and feminine tendencies become more apparent. Males become more aggressive; they dislike confinement and feel the urge to roam freely. (During mating season, it is normal for free-roaming adult males to travel in packs, following the trails of females in heat.) Females begin to show a stronger homing instinct. This is as critical a training period as early puppyhood. Be firm, and be especially affectionate and tender, to compensate for all the scolding you'll have to do. Your puppy's perception of power and ownership of his property and territory is also developing.

Your puppy watches you keenly, trying to understand everything you say. As a matter of fact, he probably does, for the more you talk to him, the more he understands. Talk to him simply and clearly—and often. Dogs love conversation. He'll even try to communicate with you, too, telling you that he is hungry, that he would like to go out, or that he wants to play.

How to Feed

Until your puppy reaches eleven or twelve months of age, feed him twice a day, morning and evening, with possibly a snack at noon. The feeding chart included in this chapter can be used as a guide to the amount of food your puppy needs, in line with his size and age.

The amounts recommended in the chart can, of course, be changed to fit the individual pup. An active, well-exercised dog will burn up more food than one of more quiet habits. An amount that is right for one puppy can make another overweight. You can determine the correct amount to feed by watching your puppy's weight. If he is well-filled-out and seems satisfied with less food, feed less. If he seems forever hungry and is growing rapidly, feed more.

Small-breed dogs are reaching maturity at this age and their requirements for food intake will decrease. With maturity they will eat less of their own accord. Large-breed dogs do not mature until well over a year of age, however, and their food requirements remain high. Ample quantities of food are essential to satisfy a large puppy's nutritional needs. In fact, many pups of the large and giant breeds seem almost to have bottomless pits for stomachs at this age.

Tidbits and Supplements

Although your dog will be eating mostly commercial dog food, there are usually good table leftovers in every household that can be included in his food. Economy can be combined with taste variety, and you may be sure that your dog is get-

FEEDING CHART: 6 TO 12 MONTHS

BREED SIZE	WEIGHT IN POUNDS	CALORIES PER DAY*	NO. OF FEEDINGS PER DAY	AMOUNT PER DAY**		CYCLE 1: complete and balanced food designed to meet the nutritional requirements of puppies.	
				DRY (1 cup = 8 fl. oz. measuring cup)	SOFT-MOIST (6 oz. pkg. = 2 burgers)	DRY (8 oz. cup)	CANNED
Very Small (avg. 6-12 lbs. at maturity)	6-12	574-943	2 or self-feeding	2-3½ cups	1½-2 packages	2-3½ cups	1½-2 cans
Small (avg. 12-25 lbs. at maturity)	12-25	943-1645	2 or self-feeding	3½-6 cups	2-3½ packages	3½-5½ cups	2-3½ cans
Medium (avg. 25-50 lbs. at maturity)	20-50	1384-2750	2 or self-feeding	5-9½ cups	3-6 packages	5-9½ cups	3-5½ cans
Large (avg. 50-90 lbs. at maturity)	40-70	2352-3542	2 or self-feeding	8½-12½ cups	5-7½ packages	8-12½ cups	5-7½ cans
Very Large (avg. 90-175 lbs. at maturity)	70-100	3542-4640	2 or self-feeding	12½-16½ cups	7½-10 packages	12½-16 cups	7½-9½ cans

*Requirements may vary depending upon breed, age, exercise, and environment. Pregnant, nursing, and hardworking adult dogs may require 2-3 times more food than is required for maintenance.

**Divide the amount per day by the desired number of feedings per day.

ting proper nourishment when scraps are *only additions* to a balanced commercial dog food. Leftover meat, trimmings, and vegetables can be mixed in the food with leftover gravies and soups. But remember that such additions should be limited to not more than 15 percent of the total dietary intake to prevent nutritional or digestive upsets. Fats, especially, are highly palatable and supply additional essential fatty acids. A teaspoon of vegetable oil or bacon drippings can be mixed in the pup's food occasionally.

Some dogs get bedtime tidbits all their lives; it is very much a household ceremony as various members of the family go to the refrigerator for the same purpose. Make this just a snack: a dog biscuit fed from the hand. The multiflavor dog biscuits now on the market are ideal for snack feeding or as training "rewards." They are nourishing and offer plenty of taste variety. Feeding too many tidbits, however, and constantly adding table scraps can result in poor eating habits.

Although the majority of dogs of this age are hungry and wolf their food, some may be slow, even picky at times. Do not try to find something your dog likes when he refuses the food offered. If he is healthy and active, remove his dish and give nothing else until the next mealtime. If you let him grow choosy instead of eating what you give him, he may become finicky. Some dogs show good sense by skipping a meal now and then for no apparent reason. A feeding or two refused occasionally need cause no alarm. By always refusing one of two feedings, a dog may be ready to have the number reduced to one.

If you prefer, there is a method known as self-feeding, which means that the dog eats from a container in which dry or soft-moist food is always available. He can consume as much or as little as he wants whenever desired. This is explained on pages 24–25.

Unless your veterinarian recommends the addition of vitamin-mineral supplements, they are not necessary when your dog eats a complete and balanced commercially prepared food as the major part of his diet. As many problems exist today from excess vitamin-mineral consumption as from deficiencies.

It is essential with any feeding regimen that the dog have ample drinking water available continuously. Keep it fresh. Dogs dislike stale water as much as we do and often will not drink unless their water is kept fresh.

The Female's First Heat Period

If your dog is a female and has not been spayed, your most important concern at this age will be safety during her first heat or seasonal period. The average female first comes in season at about eight months of age, although some begin at six or seven months, and others not until ten or twelve months. The heat period occurs at approximately six-month intervals. Most females have two heat periods each year. A few come in season only once, while others go to the opposite extreme and have as many as three heat periods a year. The female whose periods are more often than once every six months should be examined by a veterinarian.

Each heat period lasts about twenty-one days. Early signs include extra friskiness and affection, more than usual urination, and a swelling of the vulva. An occasional mucus discharge for a few days is followed by a bloody discharge which usually continues for two weeks. During the third week the vulva swelling subsides and the discharge lessens as the parts return to normal.

During her heat period the female will be attractive to male dogs and can be bred by them; in fact, it is the *only time she can be bred*. Heroic measures are needed for her protection. She cannot be allowed outdoors alone for one minute. Either board her in a kennel or confine her securely for the entire three weeks. The instant she sets foot out-of-doors, males from far and wide will congregate in your yard, to your annoyance and her danger.

Every time a female in season squats to urinate, she leaves an odor for male dogs. Her urine contains a special chemical that is produced only during her heat. This is why males you've never seen before will hang around your yard. If your female is habitually kept in an outdoor kennel run, shut her *securely* in her yard for the entire three weeks. The fencing must be escape-proof. It must also keep out visiting males, who will try all sorts of daring stunts, such as climbing over or digging under it, to reach her. There is a monetary consideration, too. Some municipalities levy a substantial fine against an owner who allows a female in season to run free. Don't blame male dogs if they congregate on your doorstep. It is your fault for allowing your female the opportunity to attract them.

For lack of a fence or protected yard, the female will have to be hand-exercised—on leash, of course. Do not let her out of your sight until her season is finished.

If your female is bred accidentally, get her to a veterinarian immediately. He may be able to prevent conception by hormone injection. This treatment must be given within twenty-four hours after the breeding, and is estimated to be about 80 percent successful. Remember that one misalliance will not ruin your female for future breeding or giving birth to purebred puppies. Each litter is complete in itself and has no bearing on any later litter.

Care of the House Pet in Season

The care of the house pet in season presents certain problems. Some females, especially small ones, flow so little that their discharge is hardly noticeable; others flow enough to stain furniture, floors, and coverings.

Your furniture, of course, can be protected with covers, which is not too difficult a task when the female is kept in a single room. When she has the run of the house, however, she can be dressed in commercially available sanitary panties. There also is a type of canine chastity belt to avert mating. But the vigor of male dogs makes such contraptions not altogether safe. They cannot be completely relied upon. Neither can ointments or pills taken internally, advertised as protective for females in season, though they are helpful in masking her scent.

The sensible procedure is to imitate the practice of the professional kennel owner, who shuts the female in season securely in a separate run or room. In the home, windows and other enclosures should be locked or otherwise safeguarded against accidental opening. Screened or storm doors leading to the yard or street should be carefully latched lest the female push them open and slip out.

Remember, wherever your female sits down and whatever the amount of her discharge, the scent will advertise her condition until a rousing good rain wipes it out. And when the female has returned to normal, that is, after three full weeks, give her a thorough shampoo-and-water bath to remove all traces of scent.

Caring for a female in season is not too difficult a task, but if you decide you would like to have your dog spayed (see the preceding chapter), you can still have it done. The operation is not performed during a seasonal period. Wait until about midway between seasons.

Fences and Fencing

Whether your dog is a male or female, he or she is going to be healthier and safer if provided with a fenced yard in which to play and exercise. But, you say, your dog loves his home and will not wander away. Nevertheless, all dogs at some time in their lives may roam if they get the chance. And this urge may be strongest at the approach to maturity. Your dog may find his way home again, but his disheveled state will tell a tale of travels with other escapees. It is no reflection on the comforts of home when your dog takes off for parts unknown. Dogs are social creatures, and like to travel in packs. In fact, the pack instinct is something which man, with all the frills of domestication, has not succeeded in eliminating.

There will come a time when the male dog desires a mate; the scent of a female in season will blind him to all other joys and prompt him to follow her to the ends of the earth. The female may also get the wanderlust, especially when near or actually in season.

To confine a dog properly, a fence must be high enough that he cannot jump over—the exact height depends, of course, on his size. Since you want to keep your dog in and other dogs out, choose a heavy wire fence such as woven chain link, rather than a light mesh that can be spread apart. The wire should be sunk at least six inches in the ground, and the posts driven well below the frost line. Dogs can dig under a fence; the only way to discourage them is to sink the wire into the earth or to pour a concrete wall a few inches thick into the ground. A diagonal mesh that pinches their feet will deter dogs from climbing, as will an overhang of about a foot, braced inward, all around the top. The most effective fence for the female in season is double-wired; that is, a fence within a fence, about a foot apart.

The gate must be strong and rigid so it cannot be pried open at the bottom. Use a secure latch, one that cannot be accidentally opened by deliverymen or by curious children. And remember that many dogs can use their paws like hands to turn a knob or lift a latch.

Trolley-line Leash or Running Chain

Without a fence a puppy may occasionally have to take his airing on a trolley-line leash or running chain in the backyard. String a stout wire taut across the yard and fasten it securely to two posts, after first attaching a swiveled ring so that it will easily slide along the length of wire. One end of the dog's leash or chain is then latched into the ring, the other end to the dog's collar. A swivel at both ends of the leash or chain will allow turning as the dog runs up and down. It is essential that the taut wire be higher than the dog, to lift the weight of the leash or chain off his shoulders.

The trolley-line exerciser has only limited use but, intelligently employed, serves as a short-term aid. The danger is that the leash or chain may tangle, hobbling the dog and, in extreme cases, even choking him. The space all along the wire must be kept free of objects on which the leash might catch.

The dog on the trolley line cannot stray. But he is at the mercy of other dogs or children who are free to enter his yard and plague him. He cannot fight back or protect himself, so he should not be chained unless someone can keep an eye on him. He should also be walked and receive other exercise, since the small space in which he is free to run, always up and down, never across and around, can make him restless and resentful of such a restriction.

The Outdoor Shelter

Should dogs live outdoors? Puppies under six months of age and dogs that are sick or old should not live outdoors. Sturdy and long-coated breeds can live outside year-round if they are properly conditioned. Small breeds and those with smooth coats should remain outside only in mild weather. Even so, a shelter can be of great benefit to them during the day.

The dog left in the yard, even temporarily, will require a shelter—a snug house, for example, where he can rest in comfort and security when it rains or snows. In a small house, the animal's own body heat will help to warm him in winter. The shelter should be roomy enough for the dog to be able to stand up, lie down, and turn around with ease. The bottom should be raised off the ground, the entrance protected by a flap of heavy canvas or burlap to serve as a windshield, and the whole, of course, must be waterproof. Such a shelter can be kept in the open in mild weather, and hauled into the garage or barn if the weather becomes unusually severe.

For summer, a platform sunshade will be enjoyed. Build a wooden platform long enough for the dog to stretch out on: put the platform on four legs at least high enough for him to crawl under. When he wants to sun himself, he will lie on top; when he wants to cool off, he'll settle in below.

The dog living outside in all weather will need a really sturdy kennel or house. Remember, though, that only the heavy-coated or more rugged breeds can stand full-time outdoor living in winter. It's not a good idea to keep your dog inside during the day and outside at night or vice versa. Frequent temperature changes can make a dog sick.

If the dog will live year-round in a kennel, the building should stay at an even temperature all year long. If the kennel is unheated, the dog's sleeping quarters must be draft-free.

If the dog will live in a doghouse, the structure should fit his size: large enough for him to be able to stand up and turn around comfortably, yet small enough for his body to heat. The house should have a double floor, with insulation between the layers. The roof and side walls should also be insulated. The roof should be pitched to shed rain and snow and to give additional headroom. It should also overhang the walls to keep them dry. One-half of the roof may be hinged, to be laid back from time to time for cleaning and for better ventilation in the summer. Place the house in a dry, sheltered, and hard-standing area. Face its entrance east or south, at least away from prevailing winds and the midday sun in summer. For extremely cold weather attach a portable vestibule or right-angled storm door to keep the wind out—this can be merely two sides of a box.

The year-round doghouse needs floor space fully twice as long as the adult dog, with a bed placed at the back, well away from the door, and protected by a partition. The bedding, which may be held in place by a slotted slide, may consist of washable rugs and blankets on a layer of cedar shavings, cured hay, or straw. If there are no shade trees, make a lattice across the front and over part of the entrance. Convert it in warm weather with a length or two of deck canvas.

Shade trees are more satisfactory than any awning. They give off moisture, helping to equalize the temperature in summer; they act as windbreaks in winter by keeping the snow from drifting into the yard. However, trees should not be too close to the siding—leave several feet beyond their widest spread to allow for the circulation of air. If the trees are already grown, this can be provided for when the dog shelter is built; if the house comes first, then allowance must be made for the growth of the trees. Avoid fruit trees for the dog's yard if they eventually will be sprayed with material which can poison the dog when dropped on the grass or licked off the feet.

Whether the yard is designed for part-time or full-time use, outfit it with a container for water—if possible, of fountain type, to keep the water cool and clean.

Do remember, when the temperature drops below freezing, to bring all breeds indoors.

The Sit Exercise

Once your dog is *Heeling* on leash, you should teach him to *Sit*. The two lessons are closely associated because they are used together when the puppy is walking on leash.

The puppy is trotting along at your left side. The leash is held in your right hand, your left hand just now being reserved for another action. Coil up the leash into a fairly short length. Stop and command him to *"Sit!"* Your dog doesn't understand this command, so you will have to demonstrate what you have in mind. As you give the command, pull the leash upward with your right hand while you press downward on his hindquarters with your left to put him in a sitting position. Press gently, slowly, and do not remove your hand too quickly. You want the dog to sit but not to lie down, so you may have to continue the upward pull on the leash. As you issue the order, *keep your feet still*. If you move your feet the puppy will move.

The first few times, your puppy may be surprised at the pressure and perhaps even try to break away. If he resists, order *"Heel!"* immediately, and start walking to calm him down. (*Heeling* is explained on pages 55–56.) Then try the *"Sit!"* again. Keep at it, and he will soon be performing perfectly.

If he lies down instead of sitting as he should, chances are that your hold on the leash was incorrect. A slow, firm up-pull on the leash as you issue the order *"Sit!"* should produce the right pressure. When your grip on the leash is not strong enough, and the dog lies down, do not try to correct by jerking. The mistake was yours, not the dog's. Reach down, and with your right hand between the forelegs, raise him to a sitting position, then pet him to show approval.

If he gets up the instant you take your hand away, that, too, is your fault. Keep your hand pressed to his hindquarters long enough for him to understand what you want, even if it takes several seconds. Gradually, less pulling and pushing will be needed and, finally, none at all. Should your dog sit diagonally instead of squarely, nudge his hindquarters to the right or left so that he faces directly forward.

Turns

The pupil must now learn that you will not always walk straight ahead, that you may turn to the right or left, and that he must turn with you without tangling you up or making you fall over him.

You are walking forward now, the dog on your left side, the leash end coiled in your right hand, and your left hand fingering the leash loosely but ready to stiffen your hold at the proper moment. Command *"Heel!"* if only to alert the pupil's attention as you turn sharply, squarely to the left, at the same instant tightening up on the leash with your left hand to prevent the dog from walking across your path. You turn on the left foot and bring your right foot around into the new direction. If the dog bumps against you instead of turning, jerk the leash and say *"Heel!"* rather sharply. He will probably bump your right leg as it swings on the turn, and this combined with the leash jerk will teach him what to do.

The right turn is done the same way, although the dog in this case has further to go. You turn on your right foot, swing your left around, and as you order *"Heel!"*, bring the dog around you on a taut leash.

Excessive Barking

From now on, for many months to come, life is going to be one lesson after another for your dog, but he will thrive on it. Learning new things keeps him out of mischief by giving him something to do, something to anticipate. Training matures him mentally; and he almost wiggles out of his skin with pride when you praise him for work well done.

Your puppy has learned to love you very much; you are his whole world, and if he has anything to say about it, you are not going to leave him alone, no sir. To make a long story short, he barks when you go out—the neighbors have complained. This will never do.

The first step is to teach him not to bark unnecessarily. To do this correctly, you must first decide when the barking is permissible and when it is not. To discourage all barking is to limit his value as a watchdog. So you correct only when the dog barks continually and for no apparent reason.

Go *to* the barker. Never call him to come to you for correction. With one hand hold his muzzle tightly shut even if it hurts. Use the other hand to finger-point as you command *"Quiet!"* Correct your dog every time he barks excessively. Occasionally a few such sessions will be enough, but if the bad habit is of long standing, or the dog unusually stubborn, then something more spectacular than the muzzle grip has to be used. You can surprise the yappy one into silence by means of a harsh sound—drop a frying pan or a tin. A shake-can can also be rattled at the dog as you command *"Quiet!"* To make one, place five to ten pennies in a clean soda can and tape the top. The noise produced by shaking the can should distract your dog and make him stop barking. This lesson can also be taught successfully by squirting him with water from a water pistol or plant mist-er.

Once you teach the *"Quiet!"* lesson, the dog will remain

quiet while you are with him, but the minute you are out of sight, he'll probably start barking again. Pet owners who live in apartments or settled communities must make sure their dogs behave when left alone. So put on your hat and coat and let the dog think you are going out. Order him to *"Bed!"* or *"Place!"* with an old sweater of yours to lie on, then say plainly and slowly, *"Quiet!"* and pretend to leave the house or apartment. Once the door is shut, stay close by.

Don't let the dog fool you, however, by stealing to the door and sniffing out the fact that you are waiting on the other side. That is why you ordered him to *"Place!"*—to keep him away from the door. As soon as your dog starts to bark or cry or howl, open the door immediately, rush back inside, and reprimand him with a firm jerk of his collar and the command *"Quiet!"* You may have to repeat this performance many times, and you may find yourself spending what seems like hours just outside your door waiting for the barks to begin. But keep at it until you are sure your dog has learned the lesson. Leaving him for short periods at first will also let him understand that you *are* going to return. If he feels assured of your return, he will learn to be contented alone. Young puppies that have learned this in the cradle, so to speak, rarely have to be trained to stay alone quietly.

Jumping Up on People

Jumping up on people on the street or in the home can be annoying, embarrassing, and frightening to strangers. It is a bad habit that, if caught early, can be easily broken. It is unfair to allow your dog to jump up when you're wearing work clothes, then to resent it when you are dressed to go out. The dog can't tell the difference. As the animal leaps toward you in greeting, bring your knee up and bump the dog in the chest or, if it is a visitor who is being jumped on, instruct him to do the same. If this does not work, try reaching out with one foot and stepping on his hind toes, and he will soon understand that his greeting must be given on all fours.

Do not discourage the greeting entirely, however, lest you repress the dog for his expression of joy. Instead, as you correct him for an unnecessarily boisterous greeting, substitute another form: The moment he is on all fours, pet him or shake hands with him, if he has learned that enjoyable trick (see page 174).

Car Chasing

Car chasing is a problem in most communities. This bad habit should be broken before the dog comes to harm or causes an accident. Cars on the road are not the only danger; many pets have been seriously injured in their own driveways while the family car was being backed out. A dog should be taught, therefore, to give wide berth to any moving vehicle.

Training can be begun in the home driveway if it is long enough, or on the street at a time when there is little or no traffic. Let one member of the family take the dog into the yard, or on the sidewalk, on a fairly long leash. As the car is driven slowly down the road, have someone sitting opposite the driver ready to shoot a spray from a water pistol or plant mist-er into the dog's face as he approaches the car and you order sharply and immediately "*No!*" This has a frightening effect upon most dogs and will discourage them. The use of your own car is best because, being familiar with it, the dog runs up to it expecting a ride. Controlled by the leash, he gets near enough to be squirted, but not near enough to risk injury. Sometimes this is all that is needed to teach him to stay away from moving wheels.

If, however, the dog becomes a confirmed auto chaser, stronger measures may be needed. Have a friend drive a car up and down a quiet street. He will know what you are doing and will therefore be on guard to prevent injuring the dog. Snap on a long leash and walk the dog along the side of the road, letting the leash out to full length as he lunges. As he nears the wheels, jerk him off his feet so sharply that he tumbles over, and command "*No!*" This may have to be repeated many times, and though it seems rather severe punishment, some dogs need it for their own safety.

Objectionable Habits in Males

The male's testicles should be descended and visible by this time. If they have not descended, or if only one can be seen, consult your veterinarian.

The urge of approaching maturity sometimes causes a male dog to begin the objectionable habit of riding your arm or ankle when overexcited in play. And it's quite normal for male puppies to mount other pets, children, and even pieces of furniture and become sexually aroused. The best way to deal with this is to grasp the dog by the collar, give him a quick shake, and say *"No!"* sharply. If he tries the trick on someone or something else, push him away as you give the command.

Because children and dogs like to roughhouse together, dogs unfortunately misbehave in this manner more often with children than with grown-ups. Parents should instruct their children accordingly. When they actually see it happening, they should simply say, "Don't let Rover do that!" There is no need for parents to be embarrassed at such a time, however. Animals are animals, and they often show their sexual feelings, especially before they reach puberty. On the brighter side, once the dog is fully grown, he'll usually outgrow the habit. If he doesn't, ask your veterinarian about having him neutered. If you do not intend to use a male for breeding, it is inconsiderate to keep him sexually frustrated.

Objectionable Habits in Females

The female dog, prompted by a desire to mate, occasionally tries to mount a male or another female. When this happens during a seasonal period it is a natural occurrence. It is obvious, though, that the female should be isolated at such times.

Should this behavior continue when she is not in season, your female should be examined by the veterinarian, since ovarian cysts or tiny growths in the vagina may be the cause. Furthermore, the odor given off by cysts and infections may attract the attention of male dogs, who will probably attempt to breed her.

Infections of this kind may cause a female to undergo

seasonal periods more often than normally. She is not actually "in season," although she appears to be for a period of a few days at a time when she discharges a very small amount of mucus. If the female comes in season, or seems to, at other than her regular six-month intervals, she should be examined by a veterinarian. Two periods per year are enough; more than two would suggest spaying (see pages 60–61) to avoid any chance of malignancy.

Dogs and Cats

Dogs and cats need not be enemies, although they are often made so by thoughtless owners who shout "Sic 'im" to the dog every time he sees a cat. Don't ever be guilty of doing this!

When introduced carefully, and especially when puppy and kitten grow up together, they become firm friends. True, some dogs chase after cats at the slightest opportunity. The cat flees, the dog legs it after him. That is precisely why he does it, because movement excites the age-old desire to pursue. The cat in the home, however, will affect a dog differently; it is an animal to be sniffed, investigated, and finally accepted with affection.

When bringing a cat into a home where there is a dog, it's a good idea to keep them in separate rooms for a few days. In that way the dog can smell that a cat has joined the household, and the cat smells the presence of a dog. Then when they are brought together they are more prepared for the introduction.

A kitten and a puppy of fairly equal age apparently do not recognize each other as cat and dog but merely as playmates. When a kitten is brought into a grown dog's family circle, or a puppy is added to an adult cat's household, the resident pet and the newcomer immediately become competitors for attention and affection. If you get a cat when your dog is already grown, choose a kitten, cuddle him securely in your arms, and let the dog see and smell him. Pay lavish attention to the dog, as jealousy can be a problem. If the new arrival gets all the attention, the dog will feel threatened and may refuse to eat or become destructive. Separate the two after the first meeting. For the next week, allow the pair to get closer with each encounter, until they become friends.

6

The Adult Dog

Maturity

The small or medium-size dog will probably have reached his full height by the time he is ten months of age, although his shape will continue to change for a few months longer. Larger breeds mature more slowly and continue growing up to eighteen months. Except for the slower-developing large dogs, growth beyond the ten-month stage is mostly rib spread, or rounding out, and settling into the body conformation of the breed. In most cases, then, except for the large and giant-size breeds, the ten-month-old dog can be considered an adult.

While the basic food requirements are the same as those of the earlier, or 7–10-month stage, the amount of food consumed daily will be slightly but not a great deal more. It is recommended that two feedings per day or self-feeding be continued for the remainder of the dog's life. Some dogs, however, are content with only one meal a day, offered in the morning or evening. It's not wise to abruptly switch from feeding two meals per day to a single feeding. For perhaps two weeks, offer a biscuit at the missed mealtime. When cutting down on the number of meals, though, be sure to supply the correct amount of food at the remaining mealtime. Serve it at room temperature or warmed, but never too cold or too hot.

How to Feed

The feeding of an adult dog can be as complicated or as simple as you choose to make it. Simplicity seems to make the most sense.

By this time you have probably chosen a complete and balanced prepared dog food that will assure all the essential nutrients. Perhaps it is the dry type, moistened with water or broth; the semimoist type packaged in airtight cellophane pouches or as individually wrapped patties; or the "wet" type served right out of a can. Perhaps you combine the dry and canned types, feeding them mixed or separately. High-quality dog foods contain all the required nutritional elements—proteins, carbohydrates, fats, vitamins, and minerals—in accordance with the recommendations established by the National Research Council.

When a dog becomes an adult, his caloric requirements gradually decrease when the primary growth period is completed. In general, the amount of food necessary will vary due to differences in size, breed, environment, temperament, activity, and stress. In the stress category, for instance, would fall police and sentry dogs, hunting and field trial dogs, show dogs, boarding dogs, and patients recuperating from surgery.

The hardworking or hyperactive dog as well as the growing puppy naturally needs more food than the adult dog that spends most of his time lying around the house. Females need more food during pregnancy and lactation. The amount of food is reckoned not entirely on the dog's body weight but also on the amount of body surface area. Strange as it may seem, the larger dog often needs less food in proportion to his weight than the slightly smaller dog.

A feeding chart is provided here to be used as a guide. Due to diverse activities as well as individual differences, the eating habits of dogs vary widely. Feed your dog at the same times each day to establish a steady appetite and regular routine. After a trial period, you can adjust the amount of food necessary to maintain, gain, or lose weight. For further information consult the "Basic Nutrition and Feeding" chapter.

If you continue with two feedings a day you may divide the recommended amounts or vary the menu by a breakfast of dry dog food and milk. For dinner, which is the main feeding, mix the meal with water or broth, together with canned food or whatever leftover meat or vegetables you happen to have at the time. Vegetables may be fed; they are not necessary, but they do have a laxative effect which will help the underexercised dog. Cooked carrots, onions, beet tops, spinach, and string beans are especially suitable.

FEEDING CHART: NORMALLY ACTIVE ADULT DOGS

BREED SIZE	WEIGHT IN POUNDS	CALORIES PER DAY*	NO. OF FEEDINGS PER DAY	DRY (1 cup = 8 fl. oz. measuring cup)	SOFT-MOIST (6 oz. pkg. = 2 burgers)	CYCLE 2: complete and balanced food designed to meet the nutritional needs of active adult dogs.	
						DRY (8 oz. cup)	CANNED
Very Small (avg. 6–12 lbs. at maturity)	6–12	286–472	1 or 2, or self-feeding	1–1½ cups	½–1 package	1–2 cups	½–1 can
Small (avg. 12–25 lbs. at maturity)	12–25	472–823	1 or 2, or self-feeding	1½–3 cups	1–2 packages	2–3 cups	1–2 cans
Medium (avg. 25–50 lbs. at maturity)	25–50	823–1375	1 or 2, or self-feeding	3–5 cups	2–3 packages	3–5 cups	2–3 cans
Large (avg. 50–90 lbs. at maturity)	50–90	1375–2151	1 or 2, or self-feeding	5–8 cups	3–4½ packages	5–8 cups	3–5 cans
Very Large (avg. 90–175 lbs. at maturity)	90–175	2151–3675	1 or 2, or self-feeding	8–13 cups	4½–7½ packages	8–13½ cups	5–8 cans

AMOUNT PER DAY**

*Requirements may vary depending upon breed, age, exercise, and environment. Pregnant, nursing, and hardworking adult dogs may require 2–3 times more food than is required for maintenance.

**Divide the amount per day by the desired number of feedings per day.

FEEDING CHART: LESS ACTIVE OR OVERWEIGHT ADULT DOGS

BREED SIZE	WEIGHT IN POUNDS	CALORIES PER DAY*	NO. OF FEEDINGS PER DAY	AMOUNT PER DAY** CYCLE 3: complete and balanced food designed to meet the nutritional requirements for inactive or overweight dogs.	
				DRY (1 cup = 8 fl. oz. meas. cup)	CANNED
Very Small (Toy Poodle, Yorkshire Terrier and others)	6–12		2	1–1½ cups	½–1 can
Small (Cocker Spaniel, Fox Terrier and others)	12–25		2	1½–3 cups	1–2 cans
Medium (Dalmatian, Eng. Springer Spaniel and others)	25–50		2	3–5 cups	2–3 cans
Large (German Shepherd, Labrador Retriever and others)	50–90		2	5–7 cups	3–4½ cans
Very Large (Great Dane, St. Bernard and others)	90–175		2	7–12 cups	4½–8 cans

*Requirements may vary depending upon breed, age, exercise, and environment. Pregnant, nursing, and hardworking adult dogs may require 2–3 times more food than is required for maintenance.

**Divide the amount per day by the desired number of feedings per day.

Practically all kinds of meat leftovers may be given the grown dog. Because it often contains dangerous parasites, pork or rabbit should always be thoroughly cooked. Fish should also be cooked and, of course, carefully boned.

Although bones can be given occasionally, they are not nutritious unless considerable meat clings to them. Provide only large, hard bones such as knuckle, shank, or shin; no poultry or chop bones, which may splinter and pierce the throat or stomach.

Since dogs are classified as carnivores, we may think they require nothing but meat. Dogs are meat eaters by nature, but few people realize that in their wild state dogs instinctively ate a complete and balanced diet. They consumed their entire prey: the flesh, stomach, intestines, and internal organs to satisfy their needs for protein, carbohydrates, vitamins, and minerals; the fat, muscles, and bones to meet their needs for energy and maintenance. Meat, as furnished today, is not a complete diet. Moreover, the dog's instinct has been altered by modern civilization, and if he were given a choice, he probably would not choose as good a diet as you can provide.

Certain dogs show a liking for fruits, raw vegetables, and other "unusual" foods. Such things are not harmful if given only occasionally. However, offering unusual foods or feeding excessive quantities of table scraps only contributes to poor eating habits.

Self-feeding, a method that involves keeping dry food available for the dog to eat at will, has become an accepted feeding practice in recent years, especially for kenneled dogs. It can be started with puppies and continued throughout their lifetime, or the adult dog can be switched to self-feeding. For more details, see pages 24–25.

Remember that your dog requires water to drink. It may be offered at various intervals or kept available in a drinking bowl. Keep the bowl clean and filled with fresh water, especially during hot weather.

Weight and Weighing

Whether or not the amount of food given is correct will be indicated to some extent by your dog's weight. Once fully grown, the properly tended animal maintains his weight fairly well. Do not, however, try to judge your dog's weight by looking at him. Ounces and pounds can accumulate unnoticed; furthermore, a thick or fluffy coat can hide a thin body.

Put your dog on the scale from time to time. The wriggling puppy can be rolled in a bath towel for weighing. If the older dog is small enough to be picked up, step on the scale with him in your arms. Then weigh yourself alone. The difference is the dog's weight.

When weight increases out of proportion to overall size, you can be fairly sure your dog is eating too much. When weight decreases, feed more, but at the same time have the dog examined for worms, particularly tapeworms. Worms weaken a dog, and this debilitation is reflected by paleness of the mouth and eyes. Look carefully at the gums; pull the lower eyelids slightly downward. The skin should be pink in color, not bluish or ashy and seemingly drained of blood.

Even though the dog seems to be in the best of health, veterinary examinations from time to time are worthwhile: every two or three months for the puppy, every six months to a year for an adult dog.

Behavior on the Street

When your dog walks with you on the street, he will meet people and other dogs. You want to keep him from taking too much interest in them, but friends and strangers alike may have other ideas. They'll call him "nice doggy" and they'll pat him, smile, and whistle.

Your dog has already learned not to jump up on people (see pages 74–75); even so, he may greet the stranger by pawing, licking or just acting silly. If he is the reserved type, he may frighten the stranger by bristling or growling. This is not meanness; your dog is only trying to say *"Won't you please leave me alone?"* You know that your dog is kindness itself, certainly not a biter. But what you may not have learned is that a dog can be provoked into anger, the same as you or I.

In a case like this you cannot very well correct the dog; he's doing what comes naturally.

What a pity people do not treat dogs with the same dignity they show each other. Strangers do not rush up to one another and act as if they had been friends all their lives! Yet they do this to a dog, and the dog has every right to resent it. Pat a strange dog on the head and what happens? He may snap because he cannot keep your hand in sight. Hold your hand down, perfectly still, giving him time to get your scent. When he makes up his mind, he may be friendly or he may ignore you. Do not force yourself on a strange dog. Wait for him to make friends with you.

When passing a dog on the street, your dog will react according to his previous association with other dogs. If he is used to their company, he'll probably give them a welcome wiggle and continue on. But if he has never met other dogs, he may be shy or fearful, or he may kick up quite a fuss, growling and turning on the leash, or he may be anxious to make friends.

The fearful or the overly friendly dog is not corrected at a time like this. He needs a carefully chosen doggy friend to play with occasionally. The growling one, however, is jerked sharply by the leash as you order *"No!"* Then make him *Sit* until the other dog has gone by. Next time, when you see another dog approaching, make your dog *Sit* immediately. If the dogs are friendly, you and the other owner may let them play together awhile.

The Stay

The *Stay* is an extension of the *Sit*, and a most useful exercise, too. Your dog will be ready to learn this command as soon as he has learned to *Sit*. But this new exercise will take longer to teach because it demands more of the pupil.

Walk your dog on your left side, holding the leash in your right hand, then slowly stop and command him to *"Sit!"* Once the dog is in the *Sit* position, give the command *"Stay!"* At the same time hold your left hand, palm side down, directly in front of the dog's nose. Pull up on the leash with your right hand simultaneously, holding it taut for a few seconds to keep him still. If he moves, tell him *"No!"* and put him back into position, and praise him lavishly when he stays there. While the dog is in the *Stay*, transfer the leash to your left hand and slowly begin walking around him, stepping in front of him. Doing this blocks the dog from moving. Repeat the entire procedure several times, commanding the dog to *Sit* and *Stay* after you stop *Heeling*, until the exercise becomes automatic.

The next step is to practice with a slackened leash. If the dog moves, tell him *"No!"* and put him back into position. Eventually walk around or behind the dog as you give the command and the hand gesture. Continue until you are confident that the dog will stay at a distance of a few feet from you. When he does this, eventually drop the leash and gradually move farther and farther away and then out of sight for a few minutes to watch from a place where he cannot see you. To release your dog from the *Stay* position, use a distinct word, such as *"Okay!"* or command him to *"Come!"*

Coming When Called

You may think it's not worth bothering with this lesson. Your dog almost always comes when called, so why waste time, right? Wrong! *"Come!"* is one of the most important commands a dog can learn. When he obeys, you achieve total control over him. If he is not taught, a dog will come because he wants to. Sooner or later, he will refuse. You'll call him one day but he'll keep on going and risk his life in a fight or under a truck.

Start establishing a positive pattern early on by calling your dog to *Come* for feeding, to *Come* for his daily brushing or other activities. When he obeys, praise him lavishly. Never, never call your dog to *Come* for a scolding or discipline. He *must* associate this command with enjoyable experiences.

To begin training, attach a long leash to your dog's collar, and put him in a *Sit-Stay* position at your left side. Hold the leash in your right hand and move away from him as far as you can go without pulling the leash taut. Face the pupil, call his name, and command *"Come!"* If he doesn't start toward you, give a light tug on the leash to get him going. Praise him lavishly as soon as he reaches you. Practice day after day, until the dog comes promptly no matter how far you let him out on leash.

Later, let him off leash in a fenced yard or some place where he can't run into traffic. If he keeps on going instead of obeying your command, turn around and walk away from him. Perhaps he wants to romp; perhaps he's teaching you, and will be so disappointed when you do not chase him, that he'll change his mind and come back. When he comes, do not forget the praise.

Dogs, Gardens, and Lawns

Coming when called is a very useful command to teach your dog to observe your own property line, and to keep him from bothering your own or your neighbor's garden and shrubbery. If your property is large, walk around the edge once or twice a day, first with your dog on a long leash, later without the leash. When he starts to go toward the street or into the next yard, say "*No!*" sternly, then call him to you and praise him when he comes. Do this repeatedly. If the dog does not obey your command when he's off leash, go back to using the leash again.

If this doesn't work, get an assistant. Have him stand outside your hedge, or somewhere in the forbidden territory, armed with a shake-can (put five to ten pennies in a clean empty soda can and tape the top) or a few empty tin cans. When your dog ignores your command and goes beyond the "boundary line," have the assistant shout "*Go back!*", clatter the cans, and even throw some toward the dog. You will, of course, welcome your dog warmly when he comes back to you for "protection." Such measures, however, are usually unnecessary if you take regular boundary walks. Call him to you, during the walks, for a pat or a tidbit every once in a while. Of course, you should remember that a passing dog or cat, or a female in season on the next block, may cause even the best-intentioned dog to stray from his own yard. Therefore, if you cannot provide an enclosed area, your dog should never go outdoors unsupervised.

Dogs get spring fever and nothing is better to roll in or dig up than the soft earth of a freshly sown lawn or a flower garden. If dogs are constantly warned "*No!*" and called back when they go for your flower garden or special shrubbery, they will soon give it a wide berth. A few dousings with a water pistol, a plant mist-er, or a garden hose will discourage not only your own dog, but any strays as well.

The commercial dog repellents or cayenne pepper scattered around plants and shrubbery also will help discourage a dog's attention. The repellents have an odor that a dog dislikes, the pepper will irritate his nose and make him sneeze. All such material has to be renewed frequently, especially after rain. And, of course, the least trouble is to put up a low wire fence around a garden to protect it from dogs.

Wandering

In many communities it is unlawful to let dogs roam free. Even where there is no law, it's best to have a fenced enclosure for your dog, or a "trolley line" outdoors except when you can be near him. (See page 69.) Although many people believe that a dog must be free to be happy, a dog gets much more enjoyment out of life by being with his family and knowing he is wanted. Dogs that receive lots of attention at home rarely become wanderers. If your dog is called once in a while, and spoken to kindly, he won't be so inclined to stray away. There should also be regular play periods, walks, grooming sessions, and, of course, quiet times when you are together indoors. Just feeding a dog won't keep him at home. If he doesn't get the attention and affection he needs at home, he'll search elsewhere for it.

Occasionally there is the dog that is a happy-go-lucky tramp by nature, but this is the exception rather than the rule. If your dog does wander away one time and you have to find him to bring him home, don't waste time scolding him. Take him home, confine him, and treat him coolly for a while. In other words, let him know you are displeased but that you want him with you. And see that he gets more attention at home.

Digging

There are many reasons why dogs dig holes in the ground. Certain breeds, such as the terriers, follow their natural instincts to hunt underground. They may actually be looking for a mole or field mouse or, in fantasy, digging out badgers or foxes. With a determined digger there is not much you can do except to give him a place where he can dig when he feels the urge. Some dogs also dig to bury a bone or some other morsel. And in the summer, dogs often dig to find the cool spot the earth provides for them to lie in. This is another reason for giving a dog a cool shady place outdoors.

Digging also occurs when a dog is bored. Here again, play periods, safe toys, and regular walks and exercise will help prevent the habit.

Exercise

How much exercise and what kind of exercise does an adult dog need? Few dogs get enough. In urban areas, and in busy suburbs, dogs must be exercised on leash, and this takes time. It is time well spent, however, for exercise is a great conditioner. The steady pace of controlled leash-walking is more beneficial than the occasional dashing hither and yon of the yard-confined dog. Furthermore, even in a sizable yard, a dog can be as lazy as he likes.

If possible, walk your dog on leash twice daily as far as he will go without seeming tired. Two or three trips around the block every day are more beneficial than three miles on Sundays only, for dogs become used to exercise just as we do. The walk should be as long as the dog's legs—in other words, one city block for the short-legged dog equals several for the long-legged one. If you are uncertain about the distance your dog can walk, start with a few blocks, then gradually increase the distance each day. In addition to leash-walking, your dog should be exercised and played with regularly in his yard, or he can be taken for a free run in woods and fields.

Do not feed immediately before or after exercise. When it is very hot, walk your dog only in the cool of the evening or early morning. Do not expect him to hold his own on icy pavements, for he slips easily. If you get caught in a shower, towel him dry when he comes in, and when returning home from a tramp in the woods, check his feet for thorns, mudballs, or blisters and his coat for burrs and ticks.

Swimming

Swimming is a most enjoyable exercise. Not all dogs, however, swim by nature, but some can be taught. Get the pet into shallow water by floating his ball. If you, too, are in the water, he will wade in to get it, and may swim when he reaches out beyond his depth. The dog's swimming stroke is much like his walking movement—that's why it's called a dog paddle. He does not have to learn either stroke or timing, but he does have to keep his body fairly upright and his chin above the waterline. If your dog does not start swimming, don't force him; let him play around the shallow water to get the feeling of it. You can guide him beyond his depth later, while holding your hand under his chest.

Next, take him out into deeper water, always turning him toward shore before he begins to swim. He will continue swimming with paddling strokes until he reaches the bank and clambers up.

When you encourage your dog to swim, be sure there is a graded exit, that is, a slight rise or bank up which he can scramble. A dog cannot pull himself up out of a straight-sided pool. Unwatched and unaided, he can easily drown in this manner. Even if he tries and fails by his own efforts, he may be so frightened or exhausted that he will refuse to enter the water again. Once a dog learns to enjoy the water, he will jump in by himself, especially when chasing a stick or ball.

When your dog has finished his swim, dry him thoroughly with towels or an electric hair dryer. Be particular about his ears; dry them completely. If he was swimming in salt water, rinse his coat with fresh water. Salt water (along with sand) dries the hair, often irritates the skin, and causes itching and scratching.

7

The Old Dog

Albert Payson Terhune once said: "The pity of it is that the dog lives for so short a time." Isn't it so!

Things look brighter today, however, because better nutrition and veterinary care have greatly increased the dog's life expectancy. The average lifespan ranges from twelve to fifteen years. And while seventeen years can be considered old, it is no longer news when a dog reaches that age. The dog believed to be the oldest known, Adjutant, a black Labrador, lived for twenty-seven years.

How Dogs Age

As you can see in the following comparison from the Gaines Research Center, dogs age faster than humans.

EQUIVALENT AGES OF DOG AND MAN

Dog's Age	Man's Age
6 months	10 years
8 months	13 years
12 months	15 years
2 years	24 years
4 years	32 years
6 years	40 years
8 years	48 years
10 years	56 years
12 years	64 years
14 years	72 years
16 years	80 years
18 years	88 years

The development of a six-month-old puppy may be compared with that of a ten-year-old child; the year-old dog with the youth of fifteen. After two years, the dog's aging slows, with each single year equaling about four years in man. Dogs generally begin to show their age at about eight years. Not all breeds grow old at the same time, however, and what constitutes an old dog is different for each breed and each dog. An Irish Wolfhound or St. Bernard, for example, may begin to slow down at six, while a smaller breed may not show signs of age until he is ten.

Helping Your Dog Live Longer

We are never ready to give up our loving companion, so how do we help him to live longer? The puppy with long-lived parents has a better chance of reaching a good old age if he is correctly fed, housed, and cared for. A secure fenced-in yard is very important to the life of today's dog. If you have a backyard, enclose it, so that you can open your door and let your dog go out by himself. The sort of fence that helps keep your dog in and stray dogs out will prolong your life, too, perhaps, since you won't be forever worrying about where your dog is. He'll be safe.

As dogs grow old, their bodies go through natural aging processes. There is a slowing-up in every way, usually so gradual we hardly notice the changes taking place. Much as we regret the effects of age, we have to accept them. It is best to know what to expect so that we can be ready to deal with it.

Less Exercise, More Rest

The most obvious change probably will be a decline in activity. The first thing to watch for is tiring after exercise. The aging dog cannot walk as fast or as far. Do not take long walks; instead, walk him little and often, especially to new places. Use a more leisurely pace, stopping several times for rest along the way. Don't make the dog run up and down the stairs, for his heart is not as strong as it used to be. Do not force him to play if he does not want to. Those games of catch and run and fetch, which he used to enjoy, may still interest him, so don't let him think he is being put on the shelf by stopping them entirely. Do cut down on the time and see that he doesn't get overtired.

An aging dog will want to sleep more. Let him, and be sure his bed is a little softer as well as warmer in the winter. Be sure that he is not sleeping in a drafty place. Be aware of his intolerance for high and low temperatures and protect him from extremes. He feels the cold and heat as he never did before. Remember this when you bathe him and have both the room and the bathwater warm. Don't bathe him unless it is absolutely necessary; sponge him instead with a damp cloth, or use a dry shampoo to keep him sweet and clean. His hair will turn gray and lose its sheen. Brush him often; he'll like it, and brushing will help to stimulate his skin glands, which have become sluggish.

Impaired Hearing

As a dog ages, his hearing becomes less acute. Deafness, which is quite usual, need not stop the animal's activity, but it may risk his safety. The first sign of hearing loss may be inattention or disregard of your commands. Your dog is not being disobedient, he cannot hear your call. A dog can "hear" with his feet, as it were, and as his hearing weakens you can tap the ground to attract his attention. Or if his sight is still good and he is looking your way, you can start using hand signals. Often when one sense fails, another tries to make up for it; therefore, it is not unusual to find a deaf dog looking instead of listening for commands. He will watch you more closely than ever before.

Failing Sight

Failing sight is more serious, although much can be done to protect the dog from injury. Though not entirely blind, an old dog sometimes becomes frightened because he cannot see objects clearly. The condition may go unnoticed around the house, where everything is familiar, but if you change the furniture around, you may notice that he stumbles or perhaps hesitates to move. "Blue eye" or cloudy eyeballs in an old dog may mean cataracts, which, of course, will need veterinary attention.

The totally blind dog can get along fairly well and still enjoy life if a little extra care is taken for his safety and comfort. As long as he can smell and feel and hear his loved ones, he doesn't seem to mind at all. Blind dogs get around by memory. Don't rearrange the furniture. Keep his things in the usual places. He will remember where they are and can find his water bowl, his bed, his favorite toys, and, if need be, his paper. Walk though your yard to see that no low obstructions could trap or injure the dog. Block the stairways with puppy or baby gates. Keep rooms and stairways bright and free of obstacles. If the dog is totally blind, guide him safely up and down the stairs. He will still enjoy riding in the car, for his chief pleasure in going places is to sniff the scents along the way.

When picked up and set down, your dog may not know where he is and may bump into objects until he gets his bearings. When you pick him up, therefore, set him down again in his own bed or on a chair whose familiar scent will tell him exactly where he is. He can then make his way from one room to another without getting lost.

Constipation

Constipation can be caused by too little exercise and by lack of bulk in the diet. As a dog ages, his muscles lose their tone and strength. The muscles in the large intestine become sluggish and the feces do not pass through as quickly as they did when he was young. The longer the feces remain in the intestine, the more moisture is removed, making them very dry.

If the stools become hard and difficult to expel, you can relieve mild constipation by adding Metamucil to the food. Keep the water bowl filled because abundant liquids are important. You can also try adding mineral oil—one teaspoon per ten pounds of body weight—to the food to soften the stool. Do not pour the mineral oil directly into the mouth, though, because it can pass into the lungs and cause pneumonia. And do not give mineral oil for more than two days, since continued use decreases the absorption of vitamins.

Feeding

An old dog sometimes does not get the full benefit from the diet he has been eating. He may become thin, and his coat harsh and dry. Have your veterinarian look him over, for great progress has been made in the field of nutrition for geriatric dogs. If changes are necessary, make them gradually. Old dogs are creatures of habit and do not adapt quickly to changes. These may cause either meal-skipping or overeating. A different food, a new feeding dish, or a different person preparing the food may upset the dog.

You might try feeding more often. Give two feedings instead of one per day; or three instead of two. Smaller amounts at each feeding are easier on the digestive system, and don't forget a few treats now and then, such as custard.

Keep fresh drinking water available at all times. If you notice an increase in the volume of water consumed, especially accompanied by increased thirst, report it to your veterinarian. Kidney deterioration is common in geriatric dogs. Medication and prescription diets may be necessary. In fact, if your old dog has heart disease or stomach or intestinal problems, special foods are available in canned or semimoist form for these and other disease conditions through your veterinarian.

Obesity

Another common problem of old pets is obesity. An old dog may gain weight because he exercises less. The added poundage can contribute to many health problems. Sooner or later the dog gets tired very quickly, becoming short-breathed and actually lazy as the fat accumulates around the heart and squeezes the blood vessels. This is where real trouble begins, because the heart may begin to fail.

This condition can often be avoided by watching the

FEEDING CHART: ADULT DOGS OVER 7 YEARS

BREED SIZE	WEIGHT IN POUNDS	CALORIES PER DAY*	NO. OF FEEDINGS PER DAY	AMOUNT PER DAY** CYCLE 4: complete and balanced food designed to meet the nutritional requirements of older dogs.	
				DRY (1 cup = 8 fl. oz. meas. cup)	CANNED
Very Small (Toy Poodle, Yorkshire Terrier and others)	6–12	257–425	2	1–1½ cups	½–1 can
Small (Cocker Spaniel, Fox Terrier and others)	12–25	425–743	2	1½–3 cups	1–2 cans
Medium (Dalmatian, Eng. Springer Spaniel and others)	25–50	743–1238	2	3–5 cups	2–3½ cans
Large (German Shepherd, Labrador Retriever and others)	50–90	1238–1936	2	5–7½ cups	3½–5 cans
Very Large (Great Dane, St. Bernard and others)	90–175	1936–3308	2	7½–12½ cups	5–8½ cans

*Requirements may vary depending upon breed, age, exercise, and environment.
**Divide the amount per day by the desired number of feedings per day.

dog's weight. A dog can take on fat unnoticed until it becomes harmful. Make it a practice then to weigh your dog at least once a month. An obese dog, however, perhaps weakened by age, should never be put on a drastic reducing diet. It's better to increase the number of daily meals but reduce the total amount of food served. Cut down on tidbits and "extras" if you have gotten into a habit of giving these. This should cause a gradual loss of weight without weakening the dog. Special diets formulated for obese dogs may be beneficial.

Don't be too strict and take away everything the old dog enjoys. There are lots of nonfattening foods he can have. He has not long to live, perhaps, so he is entitled to all the pleasure you can provide.

The Temperature

Watch carefully for any changes in appearance. Even though slight, these are more important now. When he was young, a quick, high fever resulted when the forces of the body were fighting an infection. The old dog cannot fight infection as effectively—he takes it lying down, as it were.

If anything seems wrong, take the temperature (see page 166). Even a one-degree rise, which may mean nothing in a younger dog, is a danger sign in the old fellow. Though infection spreads slowly, nevertheless it does spread. Successful treatment must begin before damaging headway is made.

Growth and Tumors

Growths, too, are a common part of the aging process. Frequently no larger than a fingernail at first, they may remain small and then suddenly begin to grow. At first they are quite loose, being attached only to the skin; then as they get larger, they grow down into the flesh. Growths may be found on almost any part of the head or body. The flaps of the ears, the eyelids, and the flesh between the toes are likely places. They should receive immediate treatment by your veterinarian.

Warts on old dogs are usually hard, round, and smooth.

They are rather common and are caused by a virus. If they become irritated or bleed, have them removed. Warts are often found in the mouth. They often disappear spontaneously without treatment. In any case, they do little harm unless there are so many in the mouth that they interfere with eating. In such cases, they can be removed surgically.

Whatever the age of the dog, no growth should be disregarded. Handled by the competent veterinarian in its earliest stages, the average growth can be permanently removed. If neglected for any length of time, it may become deeply embedded or malignant. Tumors of the breasts or testicles often develop in old age when dogs have not been spayed or castrated. These, unfortunately, have a high malignancy rate.

Watch the Toenails

Long toenails strain the feet and make walking difficult. The pastern or wrist joints often weaken with age, then the arch flattens and the foot lets down. The nails can no longer grip the ground and so they grow rapidly. An old dog's nails rarely wear down to comfortable length naturally, so it is necessary to shorten them with a nail trimmer or a coarse nail file to give the dog better footing on smooth surfaces.

Whatever the state of the nails, however, an old dog is likely to become uncertain on his feet. He may not even try to jump anymore or, if he does, he falls back. If he is used to snoozing on your bed, don't deny him the privilege; he'll miss it. Instead, place a low chair beside the bed to let him hop up in easy stages. The same goes for the windows he enjoys looking out of to watch the world go by. Arrange a low chair or an ottoman close to the window so he can sit there and watch for you to come home.

Arthritis

Arthritis (usually noticed as a stiffening of the rear legs) and other degenerative bone disease is seen in many old pets. There is no cure for arthritis, so treatment is directed at relieving pain and making the dog more comfortable. Some dogs will show mild intermittent stiffness or lameness, while others experience much more pain and discomfort. Your veterinarian can prescribe pain-relieving medication. Don't leave your dog outside very long when it's very cold, and keep him off damp surfaces, which aggravate the condition.

Jealousy

You imagine one day how still the house is going to be when the old fellow is gone. You decide to get a puppy before the old dog leaves. When the new member of the family arrives, the old dog's nose is going to be out of joint. The jealousy may cause problems, especially if the old dog has been the *only* family pet. He has been the center of attention for so long, beloved and well-tended, and now everybody oohs and ahs over the cute newcomer. Pet the old boy first before you handle the little one! When both dogs clamor for attention, pet both at the same time or neither.

Without fear the pup plagues the old dog to play, bites his ears, jumps at him with great glee. Perhaps already out of sorts at having to share attention around the home, the old dog may resent the young one's onslaughts and perhaps nip him to put him in his place. Jealousy is powerful in doggy relationships.

Be very careful when introducing a new puppy to the old dog. First, keep the puppy in his cage where the oldster can sniff around him and say hello without being rushed, and meantime pet the old fellow lavishly. Feed the two separately, and watch them when they run together for the first few days. Always pay particular attention to the old dog to keep him from feeling neglected and ignored. Do not permit the two to sleep together or be alone together until definite signs of friendliness are shown by the old dog. Before you know it, they'll be the best of friends.

Boarding the Old Dog

It may be necessary to board your dog occasionally. Perhaps you are traveling to a place where dogs are not welcome;

perhaps your female is in season and you cannot guard her properly at home. Placing in the hands of strangers a pet that has grown fixed in his ways, as dogs do when they grow old, is a drastic change. Select a boarding kennel of good reputation, and pay without quibble the rates asked. Such accommodations are not cheap; if they are, they may not be good.

Have your dog as healthy, clean, and parasite-free when you take him in as you expect him to be when you get him back again. Explain to the kennel operator any conditions or habits that might make your dog difficult to handle. Find out if the kennel stocks the brand of food your dog is currently eating. If not, determine if it is possible to supply your own food. Weight loss is a common problem of boarding dogs. A change in diet with you away may be dangerous for your old dog. You should also determine if the kennel staff will assume the responsibility of giving your dog necessary medications on schedule. Ask permission to bring the dog's blanket or rug to sleep on, and perhaps a small piece of clothing with your "scent" to comfort him. And, of course, provide a sturdy collar and leash with identification securely attached. Deliver the dog a few days early, then telephone to make sure he is getting along before you leave.

If you can possibly avoid it, do not board an old dog at all unless he is already used to it. He will grieve more than a young dog, since, as we have already said, he cannot as easily adjust to changes.

When the End Comes

Journey's end. It comes no matter how much we would like the journey to continue. The life of your pet seems to have been short, all the more because it has been so happy.

Let the veterinarian decide when the time has come to say good-bye—he can decide better than you, for he will be scientific rather than emotional. Veterinarians no longer say "Put him out of the way" because they do not know what else to do. Better trained now, they are lengthening life and easing pain more certainly and humanely than ever before.

Even so, there comes a time when the penalties of age pile up and nothing remains but to put the sufferer to sleep. Euthanasia as practiced today does exactly that. The dog literally goes to sleep before the lethal dose takes effect. When the needle is administered, there is no pain, no struggle, no knowledge of what is happening. It is all so calm and quiet that you can hold the dog right in your arms.

8

Basic Nutrition and Feeding

The Balanced Diet

Like all living things, dogs have certain nutritional requirements. To stay healthy, they must be properly fed. They should eat a balanced diet containing all the essential nutrients to maintain good health and well-being through each phase of their life cycles: growth, adult maintenance, reproduction (and lactation), and old age.

Dogs can exist on a variety of diets but many of these will not keep them in the best of health. Poor nutrition, in fact, may even shorten a dog's life by several years. And growing puppies and old dogs are even less able to stand a poor diet.

It is important to remember that most of the required nutrients or food substances are not stored within the dog's body for any length of time. The principal exceptions are fat, which is stored in nearly all parts of the body, and vitamins A and D, which are stored for a time in the liver. If all the nutrients are to be fully used, therefore, they must not only be made available at each meal; they must also be present in the food in the correctly balanced amounts. Too much of one food substance can upset the contributions of some of the others.

All dogs need the same essential nutrients, but the amounts vary and are determined by age, breed, life stage, environment, and activity level.

The Essential Nutrients

The essential nutrients—proteins, carbohydrates, fat, vitamins, and minerals—work in several ways, including providing heat and energy, regulating body processes, and supplying material for growth and repair of tissues.

Proteins, the "building blocks" of the tissues, are composed of amino acids. These serve as building material for body, organs, muscles, skin, coat, nails, and blood. Of the 23 primary amino acids, there are 10 that dogs cannot synthesize within their bodies at an appropriate rate of need. These are called "essential amino acids" because they must be derived from outside animal or plant sources. If a dog is to develop to its full potential, his diet must contain all the essential amino acids in proper balance. Very little protein is stored in the body for immediate use, so each day's intake is critical.

Carbohydrates consist principally of starch, sugars, and cellulose. They supply energy and fiber to the diet, and help to regulate protein and fat metabolism. Cellulose helps to regulate the resorption of water in the lower digestive tract and regulates the formation and elimination of the feces.

Fats supply essential fatty acids needed for adequate nutrition and normal health. They also supply energy and make food more palatable. Fats are also essential for a healthy skin and shiny coat.

Vitamins are essential for growth, health, and life. They facilitate certain metabolic processes. They also maintain a balance between constructive and destructive cell changes and help dogs to resist disease.

Vitamins are either fat- or water-soluble. The fat-soluble vitamins—A, D, E, and K—are measured in international units and require fat in the diet to be transported and absorbed in the body. The water-soluble vitamins—the B-complex group and C—are measured in milligrams or micrograms. They are stored sparingly in the dog's body and require regular replenishing.

Minerals are chemical elements that perform several functions in the dog's body: they help build teeth and bone, aid muscle and nerve function, and help maintain the balance of body fluids. Their actions within the body are interrelated; that is, one mineral's function depends on another.

Calcium and phosphorus (along with magnesium and vitamin D) are essential for the development of bone and teeth. Iron and copper are needed for good red blood cells. Potassium, sodium, magnesium, and choline help regulate body fluids. Iodine and zinc play vital roles in the hormonal and enzymatic systems.

The Ready-to-Eat Foods

The proteins, carbohydrates, fat, vitamins, and minerals your dog eats can be given in one of two ways: you can shop for separate foods, then prepare, mix, and cook them; or you can feed the ready-to-serve foods found on store shelves.

Most veterinarians, breeders, and dog-owners find that dogs do best eating a well-balanced commercial dog food. Today, an array of foods—dry, canned, and semimoist—nourish all kinds of dogs. The commercial foods on your supermarket shelves are the result of years of conscientious research. Mixing many foods into a well-balanced diet requires a knowledge which few of us have. The chances of the average dog-owner coming up with a diet as nourishing as those put out by manufacturers who employ nutrition specialists and maintain research kennels is indeed slim.

In making a quality dog food, the manufacturer usually builds in a "safety factor" over and above the known daily allowances. In this way, tolerances are made for the individual dog with unusual requirements and for the alteration of the complete and balanced diet by owners who like to add "extras" or table scraps. Such additions should never exceed 10 to 15 percent of the complete diet.

The great advantage of feeding commercial dog food is that it involves very little time or work; the dog enjoys his food because of the variety, and you can be sure that he's getting proper nourishment. It also eliminates the digestive upsets common in dogs that are switched from one kind of food to another, as when only home-cooked meals or table leftovers are fed. Another danger in feeding table scraps is that, over a time, some dogs become spoiled and prefer the "extras" to a proper diet.

Types of Dog Food

Dry foods, the most economical kind of dog food, usually are complete and balanced. The best brands are formulated for various life stages of dogs. There are several different forms of dry foods: homogenized, pelletized, and expanded meals in a variety of particle sizes; and baked kibbles and biscuits.

The homogenized types contain such ingredients as cereal grains, vegetable products, meat and fish meals, fat, milk products, and vitamin and mineral supplements. The kibbles and biscuits are baked products, made by mixing such ingredients as wheat and soybean flour, meat meal, milk products, yeast, and vitamins and minerals.

The homogenized and kibble types can be served dry (with water on the side), moistened with broth or water (some form a gravy when water is added), or with a little meat to enhance the taste. The biscuit types usually are not fed as the sole diet (although most brands are nutritionally complete and balanced), but rather used as snacks or training treats.

Dry foods contain about 90 percent food solids and 10 percent moisture, and have a caloric value of about 1,500 to 1,600 per pound (300 to 400 calories per cup).

Soft-moist or semimoist foods are combinations of beef or other meats and their by-products, soybeans, fats, carbohydrates, vitamins, and minerals. Complete and balanced, they are especially palatable to dogs. Soft-moist foods are packaged in airtight cellophane bags or individually wrapped patties that do not require refrigeration. They are convenient and clean to handle, the portions being premeasured for easy use.

Soft-moist foods contain from 70 to 75 percent food solids and 25 percent moisture. There are about 275 digestible calories in a three-ounce patty, and 550 digestible calories in a six-ounce pouch. Six ounces of soft-moist food are nutritionally equal to approximately fifteen ounces of a complete and balanced canned dog food.

Canned foods contain about 25 percent food solids and 75 percent moisture. Depending on the ingredients, they supply between 500 and 750 calories per pound. There are three types of canned dog foods:

1. Complete and balanced canned foods are blends of ingredients such as meat by-products and meat, cereal grains, vegetables, and vitamins and minerals. The newest addition to this food category is the Gaines Cycle products, specially formulated for the following important stages in the life of a dog: puppyhood, the normally active adult dog, the overweight or inactive adult dog, and the older dog.

2. Canned meats supplemented with vitamins and minerals are combinations of beef, pork, horsemeat, poultry or fish, and meat by-products, supplemented with vitamins and minerals to make them nutritionally complete.

3. All-meat canned foods consist of beef, chicken, turkey, liver, and other meats, packaged without cereal, vitamins or minerals added. These are not considered complete diets, and should only be used for mixing with complete dog foods to add palatability.

You shouldn't have to add vitamin-mineral supplements when feeding a complete and balanced food. Nutritional supplements or extra fat may be necessary in special cases, such as for hardworking hunting dogs, sled dogs, or racing dogs; when a female is in whelp; or when puppies are in their early rapid-growth period. Don't add these, however, without checking with your veterinarian.

Most dog-food packages recommend the amount to feed. It's always a good idea to follow the manufacturer's suggestions. Quantity requirements vary with the age, weight, and size of the dog, and also with temperament, activity, climate, and digestive efficiency. The amounts suggested on the package should serve as a guide, but can be reduced or increased if your dog seems to be getting too much or not enough. Always rely on your veterinarian's advice on feeding problems.

Serving the Food

Feed your dog at the same time or times each day. Consistency will keep his appetite steady and his bowel movements regular. Don't feed immediately before or after hard exercise or play or before a long car ride.

It is important that you serve your dog fresh food at each feeding. Don't keep food standing until it becomes stale and unappetizing. The food should be served at room temperature, never hot or chilled. Put the feeding dish down, keep distractions at a minimum, give him about 15 to 20 minutes to eat, then remove the uneaten portion. This will teach your dog to eat promptly and not to linger over his food.

If your dog eats dry food, you might want to try the self-feeding method described on pages 24–25.

Dry food should be stored in a container in a cool place protected from insects and rodents. Once canned food has been opened, it should be kept under refrigeration. Soft-moist food does not require refrigeration but should be kept sealed until used.

There might be days when your dog will sniff at his dinner and walk away, or leave it after a nibble or two. This is nothing to be alarmed about in a healthy adult dog. In his wild state, the dog led a feast-or-famine existence, and this may be the dog's natural way of giving his stomach a rest. Tempting him with tidbits and table scraps will only encourage finicky eating habits. Simply take his food away and prepare a fresh dish for the next regular mealtime. Should the dog continue to refuse food after a day or two, however, consult your veterinarian at once.

Abrupt changes in diet can cause digestive upsets. When changing to a new food, do it gradually by adding a little of the new diet to the former food. Slowly decrease the latter and increase the new food until the change is complete.

Water

Water is an essential nutrient and its importance is often minimized. No living cell can exist without water and every cell requires a continuous supply. A dog can go without food and lose up to 40 percent of his body weight and survive; but he will die if his body loses one-tenth of its water content.

A dog's body should maintain its total water content at a relatively constant level; consequently, it is imperative that a continuous supply of fresh drinking water be available to maintain fluid balance. Water on the side is especially important in self-feeding.

Feeding Fallacies

Although they have been proved false, there are several popular superstitions about feeding dogs that continue to be handed down in families or handed out by self-appointed authorities.

While you are raising your puppy, someone may tell you not to give him milk because "milk makes worms." This could not possibly be true unless the milk contained worm eggs, which is not likely. Puppies that are fed *only* milk after weaning may well become debilitated from the combination of inadequate diet and worms they already have, but milk alone does not manufacture worms. Excessive amounts of lactose, the sugar found in milk, however, may produce diarrhea. Many dogs, especially puppies, are unable to metabolize lactose properly.

Another old wives' tale is that raw meat will make a dog vicious. The basis for this belief is difficult to imagine. It is true that a dog fed *nothing* but raw meat would be getting an insufficient diet and, as such, might not be in the best of spirits. But the raw meat would not make him vicious or bloodthirsty. Meat that can be eaten rare by humans can be consumed raw by dogs.

Raw meat is often blamed as a cause of worms. A dog may get tapeworm from eating a rabbit he has caught, or possibly from uncooked pork, but there is no other connection.

Another popular notion is that feeding garlic or raw onions will "cure" worms in a dog. Worms are eliminated only by medicines that are made of stronger stuff than any amount of garlic or raw onions. Because worm medicines are potentially dangerous, you should turn a deaf ear to those who say your pup "just needs worming" whenever he seems to be ailing. Your puppy may need worming, but on the other hand, he may be suffering from any of a dozen serious illnesses. Don't weaken him further by dosing with worm medicine. See your veterinarian.

When anyone advises you to feed your dog raw eggs to make his coat shiny, tell them that the uncooked white of an egg destroys the absorption in his intestines of an important vitamin, biotin. The yolks of eggs can be fed raw, but whole eggs should be cooked.

Many people worry when their dogs "wolf" down food. A dog's digestion doesn't start in his mouth as it does in humans. Eating fast and swallowing food whole is natural, and probably a regression to the time when dogs ran in packs and had to compete with others to get their share.

A block of sulfur placed in a dog's water bowl is credited with everything from preventing worms to curing skin diseases. Alas, sulfur has no medicinal or nutritional value, and is just an ornament in the water dish.

A common belief is that dogs should not be given the smallest speck of leftover potatoes because "starch *can't* be digested by dogs." This fact was disproved years ago by scientific tests. Dogs can digest cooked starch just as people can. Carbohydrates, so essential in the dog's properly balanced diet, come partly from starches. This does not mean, however, that a diet of potatoes, macaroni, or bread is recommended.

9

Housebreaking

Housebreaking is not a pleasant chore, but it is not nearly as difficult as it sounds. And once done, it is done for life. The dog rarely forgets this lesson. He is by nature a very clean animal, but he cannot stay clean without our help. In taking him into the home we make him live our kind of life. He must depend on us to take him out at the right time. Housebreaking is not teaching the dog to be clean; it is, instead, giving him a chance to stay clean.

The age at which housebreaking can be started varies among sizes and kinds of dogs. Intelligence has a bearing also, although not as much as people think. The problem is this: the earlier you try housebreaking, the more careful and alert you must be. In other words, the younger pupil cannot hold bladder and bowel movements for long periods. He needs relief more often, so the teacher must always be ready to take him out.

If the housebreaking is started too early, progress will be so slow that you may think the pupil is stubborn or stupid. But when the teacher gives enough time to the lessons, when he allows for the pupil's age and needs, progress may be surprisingly swift and sure.

When to Begin

Breeders and individual owners often disagree: one tells you that he started house-training his dog at three months, while another insists that six months is the earliest age at which to expect a dog to be house-trained. Each can be right, each can be wrong. A great deal depends upon the teacher.

To housebreak a dog quickly, arrange to teach him full-time. Housebreaking doesn't take long; by conforming to a fixed daily schedule, a healthy dog can be trained within 7 to 14 days, depending on his age. But if you train your dog in the morning and not in the afternoon, or train him for a few days and then go off and leave him alone for a day, you will have a confused and very slow learner. Keep at it hour after hour, day after day, and your dog will soon become a model of cleanliness.

Be patient. The slightest sign of temper will cause fear and slow learning. No matter how exasperated you feel, don't let it show. Be quiet, relaxed, gentle but firm, and above all, cheerful. Your manner is going to have a great deal to do with the way your puppy acts. He has much to learn. It is harder for him than it is for you, since he has to understand your language. You are not half as good at understanding his!

With these things in mind you *decide* at what age you are going to start the housebreaking—at three, four, five, or six months. But make it easy for yourself as well as for the dog. Don't begin housebreaking until you can see it through.

How to Begin

If you have watched your puppy closely, you should know what his needs are. At three or four months of age he still urinates and defecates often. Cold, excitement, and confusion add to the usual number of paper or outdoor visits, while feeding almost always promotes the urge. In other words, you will have to take him outside at least every two hours, and always the first thing in the morning and the very last thing before going to bed.

This seems like an awful lot of trouble. You are tempted to put off the housebreaking until, with growth, the puppy's needs are less frequent! Bear in mind, however, that regular outdoor visits teach cleanliness and control as well. So the earlier you start housebreaking, the sooner regular habits will be formed.

It's important to watch the puppy's manner just before he relieves himself. When about to urinate, does he hurry along, usually sniffing the floor or ground? When about to defecate, does he go around in circles once he has selected a particular spot? These habits are helpful, since they tell you of his needs.

To start the lessons, confine the puppy in his crate or in a small blocked-off area in the kitchen at night after he has had his regular outing or visit to his paper. Leave the usual pillow or blanket and a square of newspaper. He's probably going to need the paper during the night for a while. However, the paper should cover just a small section of his sleeping quarters, giving him just enough room to sleep comfortably. As the puppy grows, his instinct for cleanliness increases. He becomes more and more unwilling to soil the floor close by. Do not leave him room to get far from his waste matter, since he is learning to dislike it. He wants to keep his bed clean even if he does not know quite how.

Go to the puppy the very first thing in the morning and take him out. Better carry him out to be safe—he is likely to relieve himself the minute he is set down. Take him to the area you want him to use and let him sniff around for a preferred spot. Stay close by. The moment your dog relieves himself, praise him lavishly, then bring him inside. If nothing happens, try carrying the newspaper from his bed outside if it is wet. Set the paper on the ground, put the pup on it, and when he has performed properly, praise him and bring him in again. The soiled paper tells the puppy what to do and is a good temporary stimulant. There are also commercial preparations which you can sprinkle on the spot you wish your puppy to use, either indoors on paper, or outdoors. The odor is similar to dog urine. Do not hurry the youngster back inside, since he may have a bowel movement to make.

After his breakfast, take him out again. Either lead or carry him out the same door so he learns which door means *go out*. And as you walk toward the door, say "Want to go out? Go out?" This will help in teaching the pup to go to the door when he feels the need to go out.

Be a clock watcher. At least every two hours, especially after meals or drinks of water, after play periods, or after he wakes up from a nap, say "*go out*," and stay out until he relieves himself. Watch the puppy carefully in case your timing is not quite right. The moment you see him sniffing, acting restless, or going around in circles, rush him outside. You may be going outside frequently the first few days, but once your puppy settles into a routine, you'll need to take him out only four to six times a day, depending on his age.

Until your dog is housebroken, keep his diet consistent and nutritious. Set his feeding dish down for about 15 to 20 minutes, then remove it (with any uneaten food) and give nothing until the next scheduled meal. Most dogs relieve themselves shortly after eating and drinking, and doing this will facilitate housebreaking. Giving a dog unlimited access to food and treats at this time causes constant elimination, and possibly diarrhea, which will slow down the training schedule.

Mistakes and Corrections

There will be mistakes at first, perhaps many of them, until your dog learns control. To correct him properly you must be right there *at the time*, not five minutes or even two minutes later. Stoop down, look him in the eye, and scold "Shame!" "Shame!" Take him out at once, even though this particular visit may not bring results.

Do not spank the puppy for mistakes. Do not rub his nose in his urine or bowel movements. Do not mishandle him in any manner whatsoever except perhaps to grasp him by the collar or back of the neck to hold him still as you look him in the eye. Spanking will frighten the puppy and he may hide his excrement next time in a dark corner or beneath a chair. To terrify him by spanking makes him think his waste matter is wrong, or at least that would seem to be the way he figures it out. Puppies spanked while being house-trained will continue this unpleasant behavior.

Remember that very young puppies do not have full control over their bladder or bowel movements. Petting or an unexpected motion on your part may cause instant dribbling. This is an act associated with submissive behavior. Never scold the puppy at a time like this. Instead, try to avoid actions that trigger the dribbling. For instance, if the puppy urinates when you come home after an absence or when you bend down to pet him, don't make a fuss over the dog when you come in the door, and crouch down, instead of bending over, to pet him. Obedience training will help build a submissive dog's confidence level.

Clean away all mistakes, using soap and water and a commercial odor neutralizer until the spot cannot be recognized for what it was. A solution of equal parts ammonia or white vinegar and water can be used on rugs. Careless cleaning is a strike against the pupil, since he will always want to visit a spot that has been visited before, either his own or that of another dog.

Vary the Procedure

Once the dog is fairly well housebroken, use a different door to get to the yard. Also, change the place the dog is expected to use. If a particular spot becomes too firmly fixed in his mind, he may refuse to go anywhere else.

Attach his leash and walk him around to another section of the yard or along the street. Lead him over grass, gravel, dirt, pavement, anywhere at all so long as the footing differs. Variety of terrain is very important. Dogs broken only in grassy yards have to be taught to use the highway; and city dogs, knowing only pavements and streets, have refused to use natural ground until trained to it.

Some dogs become so dependent on their owners that they will not listen to anyone else. When taken out by a person other than his owner, such a dog may make himself sick rather than relieve himself. Once the dog is housebroken, let a neighbor or a responsible child walk him occasionally. This will teach the dog that *going out* is more important than *who takes him out*.

Curb Training

Curb training is done in the public interest to keep the sidewalks clean. "Curb Your Dog" signs are found in many towns and cities, and owners who do not do so are fined. Whether or not your town goes this far, remember that at some time or another your dog may have to be walked in a city where such laws are enforced.

Watch the dog closely as you lead him along and, just as he gets ready to squat or lift his leg, pull him gently but firmly toward the curb and down into the street. It is not difficult; most dogs take to the idea quite readily. The same effort can be made when crossing the graveled paths of parks and other public places. And don't forget to scoop up fecal matter and deposit it in the nearest receptacle. Those who try to keep all such areas free from fouling can do much to further the cause of dog-owning everywhere.

Housebreaking a Grown Dog

More difficult to housebreak is the dog that grows up without regular lessons in cleanliness or whose training has been slipshod. Cases of this kind are often the fault of owners who are too lazy to housebreak or who have left the dog alone for long periods of time.

Confinement in a closed crate night and day is useful. If you know the dog will not urinate or defecate while you are at home, you can let him out of his crate but keep him under close surveillance at all times. Or the dog may be leashed to a kitchen table leg or any firm support and taken out when relief is needed. Since the dog dislikes to soil his own quarters, he will be more likely to control himself when crated or tied up short than when allowed to roam the house freely. Take him out *faithfully* at regular intervals: the very first thing in the morning, and the last thing at night, and several times during the day. When he does what is expected of him outside, praise him lavishly. You may offer a reward of some relished tidbit. As for mistakes, clean them thoroughly with soap and water and a commercial odor neutralizer. And scold but do not spank.

Let one person do the training, if possible the one who feeds him. Let that person be on hand all day and every day as long as needed. And let the teacher give the dog a great deal of affection. Many of these hard-to-housebreak dogs have had no one to love, no one to please. Every dog wants to please his master; and if given a master, he will want to please him as soon as he understands how.

When housebreaking is delayed beyond one year of age, the dog may be very stubborn; on the other hand, he may catch on very quickly. In either case, housebreaking can be done, and is well worth doing. Many a so-called "dirty dog" has been sold for a song simply because it was claimed he could not be trusted in the house. Training an older dog does take time, since bad habits must be broken as new ones are learned.

The dog sold as "guaranteed housebroken" may be a problem for a while. Strange voices, a new bed, and an unfamiliar house and yard can result in a very homesick animal. Give this dog time to get acquainted. A dog rarely forgets his house manners but he is understandably confused when moved to a new home. Don't rush the training; your first job is to gain the dog's confidence.

The Reason for Mistakes

Even a perfectly house-trained dog will misbehave upon occasion, such mistakes being caused by changes in diet, illness, or the call of scent. Illnesses and other conditions that can delay or affect housebreaking include intestinal upsets, bladder or kidney infections, cold, and the beginning of a female's "season." In such cases, neither scolding nor punishment will help; instead, they add to the dog's discomfort by making him nervous. The housebroken dog has a sense of shame for mistakes. To punish him for an act he already knows is wrong is to worry and confuse him unnecessarily. When a dog is ill, seek veterinary help as soon as possible. Take him out more often, or give him an indoor spread of newspapers.

The age-old call of scent is powerful and may cause mistakes. Food and urine are the two smells to which the dog reacts most quickly. Whenever and wherever he finds the scent of urine, whether on trees or posts along his line of march, or previously soiled spots within the home, it is natural for him to leave his own mark.

This is what may happen. A neighbor and his dog come to see you. The visiting dog leaves his "calling card" on your carpet. Immediately your perfectly housebroken dog forgets he ever was housebroken; maybe for two or three days he has to be confined in his crate or tied up. This was not his fault. It could have been prevented. In fairness to *your* dog it can be avoided. Speak plainly to the visitor. Ask him to hold his dog on his lap or to keep him leashed. When the visitor leaves, watch your dog carefully; when he sniffs around, speak sharply to him and hustle him outside. Even a single mistake at such a time may encourage a return of habits you have tried hard to break.

Eternal watchfulness is the price you must pay when your dog meets another dog indoors. Lifting the leg is the characteristic greeting of dog with dog, a form of territory marking that he will never outgrow. Be on the alert with a sharp *"Stop that!"* or a quick slap at the offender.

Another annoyance is the dog that decorates your porch as well as your choice shrubbery. If your female is in season, all the males for miles around will know it, especially if you let her go outdoors. They may come into your yard and stay there around the clock for the duration of the heat period. The male dogs are not to blame, of course, since leg-lifting is their natural method of announcing their willingness to call. To avoid unwanted pregnancy, confine the female indoors during her season. Always take her outside on leash to relieve herself and do not let her run free until the heat cycle is finished.

Keeping the Yard Clean

Cleaning the yard is one of the responsibilities of dog-keeping. In its way it is just as important as cleanliness inside the house. Yard cleanliness means: disposing of fecal matter and watching for overacidity in the soil, which can be caused by too much urination in one small area.

If fecal matter is left in the yard, flies collect instantly, then leave to spread germs far and wide. Neglected piles of feces not only are foul-smelling but also can produce disease. They, as well as the soil underneath, can be infested with various kinds of canine-worm larvae and the highly contagious canine parvovirus. Droppings, therefore, should be picked up daily and thrown into a covered receptacle or buried. This will help stop the spread of disease and prevent reinfection of a dog that has been wormed.

To keep the lawn clean, dog-owners frequently use the one-spot method of housebreaking. That is, they teach the dog to go to one corner of the yard. The advantages of this method are obvious, but the small section of ground becomes sour, moldy, and foul-smelling from urine. Grass is quickly burned out and the soil is hard-packed.

If you do limit your dog's toilet to a small section of fenced yard, the soil will have to be refreshed from time to time. Cover the surface with lime and mix it in thoroughly. Rake the dirt over fine and level, leave it alone for a while, then plant grass or clover. Meantime assign the dog to a different section of the yard. Where lack of space makes this impractical, floor the dog's yard with gravel or sand. Concrete areas are good, too, for they can be hosed down frequently; however, they must be properly graded to throw off the water, or equipped with drains.

10
General Care and Grooming

Given proper attention, the dog's coat, teeth, eyes, ears, nose, and feet can be kept in good condition. Regular care and grooming may seem bothersome, but it will save time and money in the long run. Many minor disorders of the skin, teeth, and feet may be avoided completely; others will be caught in their earliest stages, when cure will be fairly simple.

Care of the Coat

Brushing a dog's hair every day, or every second or third day, depending on the length and texture of his coat, is one of the most important phases of grooming. It is the best way to help prevent tangles from forming and to keep the skin clean and healthy and free from irritation.

Ideally, a fixed pattern of hair care is best established while a dog is young, especially if he will eventually have long hair. Learning correct brushing techniques while the hair is still short is a good way for an owner to gain confidence. And it's very easy and pleasant to train a young puppy to accept brushing by making a game of the first few sessions. You can put the puppy in your lap or stand him on a firm surface and place your hand under his stomach (to give both support and confidence) as you quickly brush through the coat.

As your dog grows older, gradually increase the length of

the sessions. By this time his puppy coat has been replaced by a stronger, tougher kind of hair which, according to breed, may be short, medium, or long. Most coats are two-ply. The long-haired and the medium-haired kinds, especially, have an outer coat varying in coarseness, and a soft undercoat that is thick and dense.

The short, smooth-haired dogs have a double coat also. However, it is less noticeable because the undercoat is neither downy nor flat-lying. Thus, it is almost impossible to tell the top coat from the undercoat. When the undercoat sheds in warm weather, the chief change observed is the thinner covering of the whole.

The coat is the dog's complexion. A rich, full, glossy coat usually means that all is well within; whereas a dry, lifeless coat with hair constantly shedding means that something is wrong. Normally, the coat sheds twice each year, spring and fall, although some shedding goes on all the time. Heavy shedding between seasons may be caused by a lack of strength, following an illness, for instance, whereas dryness may result from too many baths with harsh shampoos, or an overheated apartment. A temporary faded look may merely mean that the old coat is on the wane, since the hair tends to lose its vigor and color just before it is cast.

Brushing

Regular brushing helps to keep the hair in good condition by removing dirt, by spreading the natural oils evenly throughout the coat, by preventing tangles and mats, and by stimulating the skin. It also keeps the dog comfortable by removing loosened, dead hair before it can cause the dog to scratch (or before it sheds all over your rugs or upholstery!). When you see your dog rolling vigorously in the grass or pulling himself back and forth under the sofa edge, you can be fairly sure he is shedding his coat and is trying to get rid of it himself.

Regular brushing involves a time commitment from a pet's owner. Five to ten minutes every second or third day may be sufficient for smooth-coated breeds, but at least a half-hour *every* day may be necessary for longer coats.

Different brushing techniques are necessary to care for the various types of hair, as are different kinds of brushes and combs. The type of brush, the length and kind of bristle or pin, the length and spacing of the teeth of a comb, all play an important role in correct grooming. The kind you need depends on your dog's coat texture. Your pet-supplies dealer can show you the right tools.

Brush the hair as if you meant it, going over every single part of the head, body, legs, and tail. Brush always in the direction you wish the hair to lie. In other words, if yours is a short, smooth-coated dog, brush from head to tail and down the legs to keep the hair trained down tight to the skin. If your pet has a stand-off type of coat, then brush against the grain, from the skin outward, to bring the hair up and away from the body. If your dog has a long and flowing coat, use a long and sweeping brush stroke that goes beyond the ends of the hair.

Take it slowly; do not neglect one inch. Brush out the ear fringes, the mane on the neck, the frill or apron on the chest, the skirts on the hindparts. Either sit on the floor beside him or stand him on a firm surface. So long as the dog enjoys it, keep at it as long as you wish, but if he grows tired or restless, stop for a while.

Removing the coat by faithful brushing as it is shed will go a long way toward keeping the rugs and upholstery free of hairs. However, a few hairs on the furniture is not the worst of evils—gentle rubbing with dampened sandpaper or with Scotch tape will pick them up, while a dry sponge will serve to scrape them off clothing.

Mats and Tangles

Along with a brush and comb, you should also purchase a canine coat conditioner, a specially formulated product with conditioning oils that is sprayed lightly onto the hair before brushing it. It will add a shine to the hair that will deepen and enrich the natural coat color, but more important, it will help remove any tangles. Spray the conditioner into any matted clumps, then ease them apart gently, holding the tuft close to the skin with your thumb and forefingers. Don't hurt the dog by pulling.

Mats of tar or chewing gum can be removed by rubbing them with peanut butter and easing them gently out of the hair. Another method is to rub an ice cube over the gum or tar. It will become brittle and pull out of the hair. Tangles of burrs can be worked out of the coat without harm by saturating them with mineral oil.

Excessive Shedding

It may seem as though some dogs are continually shedding. Those quartered out-of-doors shed more definitely in the spring and fall, whereas those kept in the house may cast their coats more or less constantly. Experts believe that the natural light cycle has something to do with it. At any rate, to control continual shedding, try mixing into the food a spoonful of vegetable oil per pound of dry food, or add a food supplement for the skin and coat containing linoleic acid, such as Linatone.

You might also try sponging the coat with a mixture of equal parts bay rum and water, then dry thoroughly. Brush the dog daily as usual, and massage the skin with your fingers to loosen as much dead hair as possible. Do not bathe unless absolutely necessary, since overbathing (especially with the wrong shampoo) could dry the skin and cause itchiness. Worms, too, may cause brittleness and shedding of the hair. So have the dog checked for worms. (See page 144.)

Bathing and Dry Cleaning

Those who believed in bathing their dogs and those who did not used to be quite determined in their opposition to the theories of the other. However, modern research has taught us that if you use a pH-balanced mild shampoo formulated for dogs, you can bathe as often as necessary.

How often you bathe your dog, though, will depend on his type of skin and hair, how often he gets dirty, and the climate of your area. For the average dog, a bath every few weeks or so keeps him really clean, stimulates his skin without drying his coat, and makes him feel "top-of-the-morning."

The exceptions to this rule, however, are the harsh double-coated breeds. They are bathed less often because shampooing softens the coat texture.

In cold weather, be sure the room is warm so the wet dog won't get chilled. Use your own bathtub or, if your dog is small, one side of a laundry tub. You can press a little ball of steel wool in the drain to hold back and collect the hairs. Have the water comfortably warm, *not hot*, and the shampoo mild.

To prepare the dog for his bath, first plug his ears loosely with cotton and put a drop of mineral oil in each eye to prevent irritation. When the dog has learned to enjoy his bath and cooperates with you, these steps can be skipped; but if he resists or is in any way hard to handle, his eyes and ears must be protected or he will fight harder the next time.

Stand him in water up to the middle of his legs, leaving enough free space to hand-scrub him well underneath. Wet him all over, thoroughly but gently, to avoid fright. Squeeze shampoo on the hair, and work from the top of his head down over the neck, back, and around the tail, underbody, legs, and feet, paying particular attention to the undersides of the legs, the base of the tail, and between the toes.

Massage the shampoo in thoroughly with your fingers so that it reaches the skin. Use a washcloth to go over the face last, taking care not to get shampoo into his eyes. Rinse quickly, then shampoo again. The first sudsing loosens the dirt, the second removes it. Rinsing is important, for even a light amount of soap left to dry in the hair causes dandruff and itching. A few drops of vinegar added to the rinse water helps to remove the soap. A creme rinse (applied after the shampoo) will make long hair glossier and more manageable.

Now lift the dog out of the tub and blot the excess moisture from his coat with a terry towel. Keep changing towels and blotting the hair until it is dry, or use a hair dryer, pointing the nozzle at a section of wet hair, as you brush at the same time. In winter or unseasonably cold wather, confine the dog to a warm, draft-free room for two hours or more. The coat may appear to be dry, yet is damp near the skin. Be sure the dog is absolutely dry before letting him go outdoors.

The way you give your dog his first few overall shampoos will do much toward making him like a bath, and once he does, he will save you time and trouble by lending himself willingly to the job. There are occasional dogs that battle their way through every bath, with two or more members of the family required to assist. For the most part, however, fear of a bath is unnecessary and can be avoided if the handling is gentle but firm and the water temperature moderate.

A dog can be dry-cleaned too—that is, washed without water—with a "no-rinse" shampoo. Such products are applied directly from the bottle onto the coat and worked into a lather; then the hair is towel-dried. They work equally well on short and long coats. Powder shampoos formulated for dogs, or cornstarch for light-colored coats and cornmeal for dark ones, may be sifted into the skin and then brushed vigorously out again. Much of the dirt and extra oils will be removed and the coat will be made soft and fluffy.

External Parasites

There are a number of external parasites which can cause problems for your dog. With proper preventive steps, however, you can control these irritating creatures.

Fleas—These small, black, fast-moving pests, about ⅛ inch long, feed on your dog's blood. They are extremely hardy and can live up to four months without a meal. They also have long legs that make it easy for them to jump from dog to dog or cat, searching for a host to feed on. Adult fleas live and breed on the dog. The females lay eggs which drop off the host, hatch into wormlike larvae, and complete their life cycle. Fleas especially like to hide in the dog's bedding, in carpets, and on chairs, sofas, and draperies. It has been said that for every flea found on a dog, a hundred or more are lurking nearby. Since they multiply at an amazing rate, lose no time in dealing with them.

What harm can fleas do? They transmit several viral and bacterial diseases and are the intermediate host for a species of dog tapeworm. They irritate the dog by constant jumping; they keep him awake nights with their biting. Their blood-sucking also causes anemia in young or sick dogs. They can cause flea-allergy dermatitis, a skin disease that is characterized by pruritus and lesions. And last but not least, fleas can ruin a good coat by inflaming and irritating the skin. Dogs that are kept free of fleas seldom have skin problems.

If your dog is infested with fleas, control involves not only treating the animal but also his environment. Begin by washing the dog's bedding and all other washable doggy articles in hot water. Thoroughly vacuum the carpets, floors, and crevices, then remove the vacuum bag from the house as soon as possible. Fumigate your premises: do it yourself or hire a professional exterminator. A second fumigation within fourteen days may be necessary. If your dog spends a great deal of time outdoors, spray the patio, the lawn, and other areas he frequents with a yard and kennel spray.

While you are meticulously treating the environment, it is also necessary to attend to every pet in your house. Use a fine comb and powder the hair thoroughly with flea powder. Then go over each pet, inch by inch. The powder will numb the fleas so they are more easily removed. The pests will be found mostly around the root of the tail, the ears and neck, and under the legs. These are favorite hiding places, but because fleas move like lightning, they may be found anywhere at all. The black, grainy deposits that you may notice on the skin are flea excrement that can be dissolved by washing. If flea powder is not used, you should bathe each pet with an insecticidal shampoo. Once fleas are removed, the use of flea collars (a solid mixture of plastic and highly concentrated, time-released pesticide), in combination with sprays and powders, will help prevent reinfestation.

Always check with your veterinarian before selecting a flea-killer. Be sure all products are safe for use on dogs (or cats) and that they are used according to package directions.

Flea eradication is difficult and time-consuming, and special vigilance is required in "flea season," when these pesky creatures flourish. Flea season usually extends from late spring until the first frost in some parts of the country; in hot climates it lasts year-round.

Lice—These small wingless pests are equally annoying. They do not move about like fleas but hook into the skin, hold fast, and suck the dog's blood. In fact they suck so closely beneath the hair as to almost defy detection. One sure way to confirm the presence of lice is to look for the eggs or "nits" that are laid by the female. These hatch on the dog and will be attached to the hairs. They can be seen with the naked eye, but unless you look carefully or use a magnifying glass, you might miss them. They are ash-colored and no larger than the head of a pin. Adult lice may be missed at a casual glance, too, but if your dog is scratching, and you find signs of dirt but no fleas, look thoroughly. The skin will usually be reddened in spots where the lice suck. Dips and shampoos formulated to kill fleas on dogs will also kill lice.

Ticks—These eight-legged pests are the hardiest and most dangerous of the bloodsucking parasites. Ticks can transmit several diseases, including Rocky Mountain spotted fever and tularemia. They are found in warm, moist places: woods, high grass, beaches, and bushes. When a tick bites, its barbed proboscis pierces the dog's skin, and as it sucks the blood, it grows to about one-third of an inch. Mating takes place on the host, then the female drops off and looks for a concealed place to lay her eggs. Inside your house, this could be in the carpets, the baseboards, under the furniture, or behind the drapes.

Ticks cannot be removed by combing but must be pulled off by tweezers or, if you don't mind, with your hand. Soak the ticks in alcohol to help paralyze them and loosen their grip. Then grasp each tick as close to the skin as possible and pull it straight out, making sure that no part of the head remains in the skin to cause infection. Protect your fingers with paper if you don't use tweezers. Once the tick is removed, swab the area with an antiseptic, then wash your hands thoroughly with soap and water. Eradication involves treating the dog and his environment. Tick dips will help prevent reinfestation.

Clipping

When the temperature goes up, we pity the dog with the heavy coat. He's so hot, we think, perhaps we should have him clipped. Don't do it! Mother Nature knew what she was doing when she provided the dog's sensitive skin with a good covering of hair to shield it from the sun's hot rays, and to screen it from the bites of gnats, mosquitoes, and flies. In preparation for the summer's heat, the undercoat sheds—this underlayer is what holds in the body's heat—leaving most of the outer coat intact to prevent sunburn. If we clip the dog in summer, we may make him more uncomfortable than he was before.

Special Hairstyles

The wiry-coated terriers will require periodic stripping or plucking, probably two or three times a year, to keep the coat free from tangles and hard in texture. Left untrimmed, the hair grows long and thick, making the dog quite uncomfortable. Also, he looks rather like a stray instead of a stylish, well-tended pet.

With a stripping knife or dull penknife held between thumb and forefinger, you can pluck out loosening hairs as the terrier coat is cast. You might do better, however, to take a few lessons in the art or to let a professional pet groomer do the job. If you wish to take care of the coat yourself, you can purchase trimming guides and charts containing excellent directions for each breed at your pet-supply store. You can also buy the right tools to do the job properly.

Certain breeds—Poodles, Cocker Spaniels, and Bichons Frises especially—require clipping and scissoring expertise, and an amateur may have a difficult time making his dog look right. There are hundreds of hairdos for Poodles—the English Saddle, the Continental, the Dutch, the Sweetheart, for example—each one finishing off the dog with a radically different outline. It is a big job, to be sure; the Poodle has a wealth of coat which must be taken off in some places, left on in others, and shaped according to the particular pattern preferred. Better have this done at the canine beauty shop, then later, perhaps, take a few lessons from a professional in the accepted manner of doing the work yourself.

Tooth Troubles

Early adulthood is a good time to have the teeth examined to make sure that the permanent ones are straight, not crowded too closely together, free from disease, and not worn by gnawing. The amount of actual tooth decay among dogs is negligible. However, the dog's teeth cannot repair themselves; once the enamel is worn off, they remain damaged and may need treatment or extraction.

Guard against tartar, that hard brownish deposit on one or more teeth. The least of its harm is its unsightly color; the real danger is that it menaces the life of the tooth to which it clings. It is most serious as it pushes into the gum, breaking the membrane which is the tooth's main brace. With this support gone, the tooth may loosen and fall out. The condition may not be painful. On the other hand, if food particles work down into gum cavities and decompose to cause abscesses, there will be considerable suffering. When tartar is noticed, take the dog to the veterinarian, who can scrape the teeth expertly before any damage has been done. It is also helpful to feed some dry meal or biscuits that require chewing.

Bones and hard substances are, in a manner of speaking, the dog's toothbrush. Not that they actually clean the teeth; they perform an even better service than that. They stimulate the blood supply as they rub over the gums. Therefore, the gnawing of bones and the chewing of coarse, hard food helps keep the entire mouth healthy. That is why as the puppy grows we gradually discontinue very moist foods and instead feed drier, more crumbly mixtures. And then, when the second teeth are in, we give hard-baked biscuits occasionally.

All through the dog's life you may keep his teeth clean by wiping them regularly with a damp cloth dipped in salt or baking soda, or with a canine toothpaste. A gentle rotating motion will stimulate the gums as well as actually clean the teeth. The dog accustomed to this attention from puppyhood does not object. He rather enjoys being fussed over.

Do not expect the dog to announce dental troubles by crying. He suffers in silence, while rubbing the affected side of his jaw along the floor or perhaps pawing it. He eats gingerly, mouthing his food with his lips rather than with his teeth. He may drool, too. All of which may indicate a decayed, broken, or otherwise sensitive tooth, or possibly a piece of something wedged between two teeth. At any rate, it means an uncomfortable mouth requiring professional aid.

Care of the Eyes

The dog's eyes are his most attractive feature. They are the "tie that binds" him to mankind. Let him look at us just once with that expression of entire trust, and he lifts himself up and away from all his kind and becomes our best friend among all animals.

Sight is not one of the dog's strong points. It need not be, since his hearing and power of scent are so phenomenal. He cannot see colors very well; on the other hand, he can differentiate degrees of brightness better than we can. He sees motion in a flash because, as an animal of the chase, he had to get his food on the run. Although he has an eye very much like ours, the eye-white surrounding the iris or color portion does not show as much. A lid covers the white except perhaps for a tiny speck at the inner corner.

The expression of the normal dog is bright, intelligent, knowing: his eyes in health are clear and clean. The moment the eyes appear at all different, we suspect that something is wrong. A staring, dazed expression, with white showing, may mean overexcitement and the possibility of a fit. Watery, weeping, squinting, or heavy-lidded eyes alert us to watch for distemper or some other infection.

Departure from the normal is not always serious. Weeping and pus discharge may be caused by a cold, by a blow on the eyeball, by weed seeds caught beneath the lids. Serious or slight, however, eye troubles require prompt attention to prevent the sight from being endangered.

A dull, heavy expression may be caused by an enlarged haw, the triangular stretch of reddened membrane across the eye's inner corner. This enlargement is sometimes so small that it escapes attention; at other times it may be raised halfway across the eye and highly inflamed. The swelling can be treated with cotton pads dipped in warm boric-acid solution; but since it will occur again, minor surgery may be required.

Weeping eyes should be attended to without waiting for them to cure themselves. Bathe the eyes very gently with cotton dipped in boric-acid solution to remove any dirt or pus. Then use a simple eye ointment like mercuric oxide, and as you finish, roll the lashes up and off the eyeball. Mineral oil can help soothe the eyes of field dogs. Place a drop in each eye before taking the dog out for a run in woods and fields. Doing this will help ensure against the scratching and discomfort caused by dust, pollen, and weed seeds.

Entropion, or inversion of the eyelids (and with them the lashes), and ectropion, an eversion of the eyelids, are both congenital and acquired conditions. They cause blepharitis and pawing of the eye. Don't procrastinate. Let your veterinarian try to correct the condition before the eye is damaged.

Care of the Ears

The dog's sense of hearing is better than ours; actually he hears twice as well as man. And though he has an ear very much like our own, its flap or leather is quite different from the ear shell of man. Made to catch the sound, it also moves to find the direction from which sound comes.

Selective breeding has resulted in a wide variety of ear types. In certain breeds the flap stands erect or pricked; in others it rises halfway and then tips over. In still others it is "buttoned" or turned down though slightly raised at the base, while in many breeds it falls flat to the head, when it is said to be dropped. The kind of ear flap seems to have no bearing upon the dog's hearing but it does influence the amount of care required. The drop ear or turned-down flap interferes with ventilation, and must be watched more closely.

When a puppy is born, the ears lie flat to the head. In breeds whose ears stand up at maturity, ear-cartilage strength changes so much during the process of growth that the exact age when the ears should come up cannot be stated. They may begin to stand quite early in life, and then, while the teeth are changing, drop again or flare around uncertainly for weeks or months, after which they finally stand strong and straight.

During play a puppy may injure an ear tendon. The upright ear may then drop and never recover. Some people have helped weak or injured ears to stand by bracing them with surgical adhesive tape or moleskin. Cut the material you are using into the desired shape and length, then apply it to the inside of the ear in order to stiffen it. Most puppies won't mind this very much, while others will give you a hard time. The first few hours usually are the worst, and if you can get through this initial stage, a big part of the battle is won. How long you should leave the ears set depends on the individual dog. Faulty ear carriage is sometimes rectified within a few days; others require several weeks and a number of resettings. Apply an antiseptic when you take off the tape.

Ear flaps that stand when they should drop are fastened down lightly with surgical tape for short periods. But do not attempt to shape the ears in any manner without first checking the breed section, which begins on page 204. Make sure you know exactly how your dog's ears should be carried when he is fully grown.

Scratched or Fly-bitten Ears

Diseased-ear conditions may cause deafness if not treated. Trouble should be suspected if the dog shakes his head constantly or carries it sidewise, or if he rubs an ear against the floor or attempts to massage it with his paw. Cuts, scratches, and fly bites can injure the flap so that it becomes scabby and perhaps infected. A gentle soap-and-water cleansing will remove the crusts, after which a light dusting with antiseptic powder will soothe the irritation.

For fly-bitten ear tips, you might try bathing the flaps with the following: oil of clove, 3 parts; bay oil, 5 parts; tincture of eucalyptus, 5 parts; alcohol, 15 parts; water, 200 parts. Your druggist can make this up for you.

Ear Canker

Canker of the ear is often serious. Caused by mites, wax accumulations, dirt, eczema, and even by a generally weakened condition, it can be suspected when your dog constantly scratches at his ears, shakes his head, or rubs it on the floor. Look for inflammation inside the cup or base and leading down into the canal where debris and pus of brownish color can be seen and a foul odor can be smelled. The debris and pus can be cleaned out with a medicated ear lotion formulated to loosen excess wax accumulation and float it to the surface. But never probe deeply into the ear! You may injure the delicate interior or push down material which should be brought up. Simply let the debris float to the surface and carefully wipe it away with a cotton ball.

Dogs with drop or hairy ears which prevent air from reaching the ear canal need special attention. Air is important in all cases of ear treatment. Severe canker is a task for the veterinarian and should be attended to promptly. Ear mites so tiny that they cannot be seen by the naked eye can cause deafness if not removed before the inner ear becomes involved.

These ear mites are the most frequent cause of a dog shaking his head and scratching at his ears.

The Nose

So keen is the dog's sense of smell that his world is full of scents, some soothing, others exciting, each with a definite message to influence his behavior. Take your dog out to walk and watch him closely—to him, half the fun is sniffing places where other dogs, other animals, have passed.

Scenting ability differs in certain kinds of dogs. It seems to be sharpest in those with long noses, long ears, and pendulous lips, such as the hounds and sporting breeds. Shape and color of the nostrils also may be important. The keenest noses are usually those whose nostrils are large, black, and wide open. Exceptions to the color rule are the brown-nosed hunting dogs. A temporary fading of the nostrils from black to brown is usually caused by some "off" condition; it happens frequently to females in season.

The dog around the house, be his nose long or short, can recognize smells to an amazing degree. He feels safe and at home on his blankets because they carry *his* scent. He likes your old sweater or coat to lie on because it carries *your* scent. When he rides in the car, head out the window, he knows you've turned homeward because he recognizes *neighborhood* scents. It is almost unbelievable, but true. A dog can smell formic acid, for instance, in a solution containing only one part of the acid in ten million parts of water; and he can recognize your scent on an object you have held in your hand for a mere two seconds.

Since the nose is also the organ of breathing, it does its best work when the nostrils are cool, clean, and mucus-free. The cold nose, by the way, as a sign of a healthy dog has been overrated. A snooze under blankets or a huddle beside a radiator can warm the nose of an animal in the best of health. Dryness, however, usually indicates fever rather than warmth. When in any doubt, take the temperature. (See page 166.)

Watery or mucus discharge is more serious. It suggests distemper or bronchial ailment, but may also result from a simple cold. Clean off the nose with a soft cloth, remove the mucus within the nostrils with a swab, and then lightly grease them with Vaseline or olive oil to keep them soft. This is important in illness since mucus makes breathing difficult and prevents the smelling and tasting of food.

Care of the Feet

When a dog's nails are trimmed regularly, they stay short and neat and help the dog grip the ground. But when the nails are neglected, they keep growing and eventually make the feet spread and cause serious damage to the legs and feet. Walking and running become uncomfortable, even painful, and eventually, the dog may become lame.

Long nails are not always the result of deliberate neglect. It's surprising how many owners believe that normal exercise will wear the toenails down to comfortable length. Wild animals may wear down their nails in the course of daily activities, but things are a little different with domesticated dogs. Yes, those that walk or exercise a great deal on concrete or hard ground may wear down their nails, but they are in the minority. The average pet spends most of his time indoors, and when he does go outside, usually it's to a grassy lawn or other surface too soft to shorten the nails.

It's up to you, therefore, to establish a regular schedule for trimming your dog's nails. The job can be done by a groomer or veterinarian, or you can learn to trim your dog's nails yourself. You will need dog nail clippers sized to the breed (ordinary scissors will not do), and a file to smooth the rough edges after trimming. Insert the tip of a nail into the trimmer opening and cut it back a little at a time. Don't cut into the quick—the fleshy area inside the nail that contains the nerves and blood supply—which is very sensitive and may cause bleeding and fright. Nip off little sections at a time, especially when you cannot see the line of the quick in dark-colored nails. If you do snip the quick, press a little nail-clotting powder on the spot for a few seconds. Nail-clotting powder is available at most pet stores.

Pay special attention to the upper inside nails or dewclaws. Since these do not touch the ground they continue to grow, sometimes curling around to pierce the flesh and cause infection. This is a problem that requires immediate veterinary attention. The dewclaws may be removed by your veterinarian. (See page 26.)

Thorns in or between the pads, usually indicated by limping, should be taken out with tweezers. Cuts and abrasions will need thorough washing in soap and water. Then apply an antiseptic. Until healed, protect the foot with a bandage or baby's stocking to prevent infection. Also watch out for possible fungus infection of the toes which dogs occasionally pick up from the ground. This is a case for the veterinarian, not the amateur.

11

Practical Home Care

A healthy dog begins as a healthy pup. When you bring home a new dog, especially if he is a puppy, schedule a visit to the veterinarian for a thorough going-over as soon as possible. The veterinarian can get acquainted with you and your dog and plan an annual health and immunization program. Thereafter, you should take your dog for regular checkups at least once a year—preferably twice annually—because preventive care is the key to good health.

Every dog is an individual entity with peculiar characteristics that distinguish him from others. Help your veterinarian by learning the signs of good health. Then, as you get to know your dog, you'll be able to tell if something is not quite right.

10 Signs of a Healthy Dog

1. General appearance: alert, active, lively; good muscle tone.
2. Coat: glossy and unbroken.
3. Skin: smooth and supple.
4. Gait: smooth and effortless movement.
5. Eyes: clear and shining.
6. Nose: moist and cool with no secretions.
7. Mouth: pink gums and lips, not bluish or ash-colored; firmly implanted teeth with no tartar buildup; pleasant-smelling breath.

8. Body: no lumps or masses, especially around the nipples.
9. Urination: clear yellow, not orange, although color may be altered temporarily by certain drugs.
10. Defecation: stools should be well-formed and eliminated regularly.

15 Warning Signs

Call your veterinarian if any of the following develop:
1. Behavior changes: lethargy; lack of normal energy or playfulness; reduced tolerance for exercise; viciousness.
2. Changes in eating habits; excessive weight gain or loss.
3. Changes in water intake and urination: unquenchable thirst; changes in urinating habits; straining or inability to urinate.
4. Changes in defecation: frequent, bloody, uncontrolled, or forced stools; constipation or inability to defecate.
5. Vomiting: short periods or continual episodes over a long period, especially if vomitus is bloody or accompanied by weakness, pain, or fever.
6. Eye abnormalities: redness, excessive tearing, mucus discharge, frequent squinting, film over eye, sensitivity to light.
7. Pain and limping: pain in getting up or lying down or when touched or lifted; difficulty in walking.
8. Coughing: prolonged coughing (other than single episodes) and sneezing; nasal discharge or dry, scaly nose.
9. Ear abnormalities: foul odor, excessive wax, unusual discharge, shaking or tilting of the head, hematoma (an accumulation of blood beneath the skin) on ear flap.
10. Fever: temperature over 102.5° F.
11. Lumps or masses: swellings or lumps on or beneath the skin, particularly those that are growing rap-

      idly or bleeding; abdominal swelling; tumors of the breasts or testicles.

12.   Skin abnormalities: hair loss, baldness, open sores, pustules, lesions, excessive external parasite infestation or any other skin problem, intense biting or scratching at the skin and coat.

13.   Bleeding or discharges: bleeding from any body part; abnormal discharges from any body opening.

14.   Changes in respiration: difficult or shallow breathing.

15.   Convulsions: stiffening and jerking of the legs, chomping, facial twitching, dazed expression.

When you do take your dog to the veterinarian, be prepared to give an accurate account of the symptoms, the time of the problem's onset, and any other important observations. The more information you can give, the better the veterinarian can diagnose and treat the problem.

Immunization

All puppies and adult dogs must be immunized against the following viral and bacterial diseases: canine distemper, infectious canine hepatitis, leptospirosis, parainfluenza, canine parvovirus, and rabies. Immunization involves a series of vaccine injections to safeguard a dog's health. Vaccination types and schedules vary among veterinarians, and are affected by statutes and local conditions.

A puppy born to a dam that is immune receives fluids from his mother's colostrum (milk produced the first few days after birth) which help him produce disease-fighting antibodies until he is weaned. The amount of protection a puppy receives depends on the amount of antibodies his mother has, and this immunity diminishes rapidly. A puppy loses about half of it by the time he is two weeks old. Vaccinations pick up where the mother's colostrum leaves off, by inducing the pup to produce his own antibodies.

Most veterinarians like to give a puppy his first vaccinations when he's 6 to 8 weeks old. A second series of inoculations generally takes place at 9 to 11 weeks, then a third sequence is given after the puppy reaches 12 weeks of age.

Your veterinarian will decide on a specific schedule for your dog. *Vaccinations are not permanent.* Thereafter, you'll need to take your dog to the veterinarian at least once a year for booster shots.

Canine Distemper

Although great progress has been made, canine distemper remains the greatest single disease threat to the world's dog population. It strikes principally at young dogs, usually affecting those under one year of age. Among puppies the death rate from distemper often reaches 80 percent. The disease also strikes unvaccinated older dogs. More than 50 percent of the adult dogs that contract the disease die from it. And even if a dog does not die from the disease, its health may be permanently impaired. Blindness in one or both eyes may result from discharges affecting the cornea. The same discharges sometimes leave the dog deaf or without the sense of smell. Permanent damage to the nervous system may cause chorea (muscle twitching), convulsions, partial or total paralysis.

Distemper is caused by an airborne virus. It may be picked up by the dog that comes in contact with mucus and watery secretions from the eyes and noses of infected dogs, and also from contact with their urine and fecal matter. A healthy dog can become affected without direct contact with an infected animal. Kennels, runs, bedding and in fact everything used by a distemper-sick dog may spread the infection—even the feet, hands, and clothing of the person caring for such a dog.

Symptoms appear within four to ten days after exposure and include listlessness and loss of appetite, eye and nose discharges—at first watery, later thickened with pus—coughing, vomiting, fever, thirst, and diarrhea with black, foul-smelling stools. In later stages the virus often attacks the nervous system and there may be partial or complete paralysis, as well as fits or twitching. Occasionally the virus causes rapid growth of tough keratin cells on the footpads, resulting in a hardened pad.

To avoid infecting others, a distemper patient should be isolated for at least three weeks following his recovery. If there is a case of distemper in your neighborhood, steer clear of the house in which the sick dog lives and of every member of his family. Do not let them visit you! Remember: they can bring the disease to your dog even though they leave their dog at home.

There is no drug that will cure distemper, although antibiotics, serums, and fluid therapy are helpful, particularly against the secondary infections which often do the greatest damage. Good nursing is vital to bring a dog through. The patient should be isolated in clean, warm, dry, well-ventilated quarters. Give simple foods in small amounts three or four times daily: beef broth, cooked egg, custard. Keep the eyes and nose free of mucus. Flush out the eyes with sterile cotton dipped in boric-acid solution. Clean out the nostrils gently with a cotton swab, and use Vaseline to prevent cracking.

Follow your veterinarian's advice about medications. Above all, keep the patient quiet. His nerves are on edge, so no sudden bright lights, no door slamming, no confusion, no loud talking. Dim the lights in his room, since his eyes are sensitive throughout the course of the disease.

Following recovery, burn any dog blankets, beds, and bedding that are not too valuable to discard. Otherwise thoroughly disinfect everything the patient has used or come in contact with. If the dog dies, do not bring another puppy into the house for at least a month, and be sure to have him properly immunized.

Infectious Canine Hepatitis

Hepatitis in dogs is a highly contagious disease of the liver that is also caused by a virus. Like distemper, it affects young dogs most often, though it can strike unvaccinated dogs of all ages. It is not the same virus that causes infectious hepatitis or epidemic jaundice in humans. The virus is not airborn, but is spread by contact with saliva or with the urine and fecal material of infected animals. In fact, the urine of an infected animal is dangerous for some time following recovery.

Symptoms appear within six to nine days after exposure and include listlessness with high fever and thirst, a watery discharge from the eyes that becomes thickened, sensitivity to light, vomiting, diarrhea (often bloody), and abdominal tenderness. The throat, particularly the tonsils, becomes red, and the glands swell.

Hepatitis works fast, so fast in fact that a puppy may die before the seriousness of his illness is realized. It may follow distemper or may be present along with it. Consult your veterinarian immediately. Treatment consists of hospitalization and supportive measures. The prognosis is poor in young dogs.

Leptospirosis

Leptospirosis is not a virus like canine distemper and infectious hepatitis, but a highly contagious bacterial spirochete infection that primarily attacks the kidneys. It is spread in the urine of infected animals, mainly rats, and can affect humans as well as canines. Unvaccinated dogs of all ages are susceptible, although the disease is more likely to strike male rather than female dogs.

Signs of leptospirosis appear within five to fifteen days after exposure, and include fever, loss of appetite, depression, jaundice, vomiting, dark-colored urine, and abdominal tenderness from kidney pain. Treatment involves the use of antibiotics and fluid therapy.

Infectious Tracheobronchitis, or "Kennel Cough"

This is a highly contagious viral tracheal disease complex that affects unvaccinated dogs of all ages. It is caused by one or several microorganisms that infect a dog's respiratory system, among them the canine parainfluenza virus, at the same time. The parainfluenza virus causes small lung lesions and produces a persistent hacking cough which may cause the dog to gag or sometimes vomit. The dog sounds as though he has something caught in his throat.

Symptoms last from one to three weeks, and in some cases, secondary infections can cause pneumonia. Treatment involves the use of antibiotics and cough suppressants, plus little or no exercise for a week or so.

This disease complex is also called "kennel cough," because unvaccinated dogs that congregate together or are housed in kennels, shelters, and pet stores are frequently infected. In addition to parainfluenza immunization, your veterinarian may also want to vaccinate your dog against Bordetella Bronchiseptica and Canine Adenovirus-2, which are also responsible for the "kennel-cough" syndrome.

Canine Parvovirus

Canine parvovirus is a highly contagious viral infection that first appeared "out of the blue" in 1978. A series of epidemics swept through the United States, Canada, Australia, and many European countries, causing a tremendous mortality rate. It was especially severe in young puppies, and spread rapidly at dog shows and in areas where dogs were housed together, such as kennels and pet stores. There is proof today that parvovirus did not exist before the 1978 epidemic.

Parvovirus is spread primarily through contact with the feces of an infected animal. A susceptible dog can become infected by ingesting less than a thousandth of a gram of infected fecal material. The virus can also be carried on the hair and feet of infected dogs, and on the shoes and clothing of people who handle them. It can contaminate cages and other objects as well.

Symptoms appear within three to twelve days and include fever, pale gums, vomiting, and bloody diarrhea. The onset of the disease is sudden and may be preceded by a listlessness and loss of appetite. Death can occur in dogs of all ages, although it is more likely in young puppies.

Success in treatment depends on early and accurate diagnosis made by a veterinarian, as death can occur within two to four days after the onset of the disease. Treatment consists of intensive fluid and electrolyte replacement therapy with antibiotics and vitamins. Several days of intensive care is often required during the crisis period.

When this deadly virus swept the country, scientists began immediately to formulate vaccines. Today, thanks to the development of an effective vaccine, parvovirus is under control. However, it is vital that puppies be vaccinated at the proper time. Many puppies are exposed and most susceptible to the virus at a time when they have too few maternal antibodies to protect them but too many to allow successful vaccination. Decisions about how soon and how often to vaccinate, therefore, must be made on an individual basis by the veterinarian in charge of the dog.

The virus causing this disease is one of the most hardy and resistant known. It can live on many surfaces at room temperature and remain infectious for twelve months or longer. It is also resistant to most disinfectants. You can help reduce contamination, though, by cleaning kennels or other areas the dog frequents with a solution of Clorox or other chlorine bleach.

Rabies

Rabies seldom results in human fatalities in the United States today, but it remains a potentially serious public health problem. More than 20,000 Americans have to undergo rabies treatments each year as a result of exposure to potentially rabid animals. In the United States, Foxes, Skunks, Raccoons and Bats are the major wild hosts, although domestic dogs and cats are also sources of exposure.

Rabies is caused by a virus. It is spread through the saliva of an infected animal and in no other way. All warm-blooded animals can spread rabies. Rabid animals can infect other animals by biting them. This means that your dog will not get rabies *unless he is actually bitten by a rabid animal, or infected by the animal's saliva through an open wound.*

Rabies also can be transmitted from animals to man by a bite from a rabid animal. The wound is contaminated with the virus found in the saliva of the infected animal. The incubation period varies from ten days to several months, depending on the location of the bite and how long the virus takes to reach the brain.

There are two forms of rabies: furious and dumb. In the former the first symptom is usually a marked change in the dog's behavior, that is, from friendly to snappy and offish. The infected dog may become restless and wander off to hide in dark corners. His voice may undergo a change in pitch or he may howl. He grows excitable. Usually, he wanders far afield and eagerly attacks anything in his path, including people and other animals. Loud noises or bright lights may induce biting seizures. Finally, the disease progresses to the paralytic state. His throat muscles become so paralyzed that he cannot swallow and he salivates profusely. It is during this period that he appears to be frothing at the mouth. His legs and body become progressively paralyzed. There is a lack of coordination, then collapse, and finally coma and death. There is no cure for rabies.

If your dog should show any of these symptoms, or if you know he has been bitten by a strange dog, you must handle him with all possible care. Throw a blanket over him (to keep him from biting you if he has grown snappy), gather him up, and shut him in a room. Then call your veterinarian at once. If you are bitten, consult your physician *immediately* and follow his advice.

Many communities today are encouraging owners to immunize their dogs by sponsoring rabies-control programs, while others have made vaccination compulsory. This cannot wipe out the disease. Vaccination can reach only some of the dogs in any community. *Responsible* owners look after their dogs, but right in the same town or city live *irresponsible* owners who let their dogs run the streets and who would disown them rather than pay license and vaccination fees.

The free-roaming dog is the chief source of infection. To help wipe out rabies, fence your yard and exercise your pet only under control. And try to make your neighbor control his dog also. Licensing and vaccination do not entitle a dog to run free; any roaming dog can still be a neighborhood nuisance.

Internal Parasites

There are several kinds of worms which can infect a dog: roundworms, hookworms, whipworms, tapeworms, and heartworms, as well as the protozoan parasites Coccidia and Giardia. It is wise to know something about the different types of internal parasites and how they affect a dog's general health.

Roundworms—or ascarids—the most common canine internal parasites, have already been mentioned on page 48.

Hookworms—These parasites are also common. They live in a dog's intestines, where they "hook" onto the intestinal wall and suck the blood. They can be present in newborn puppies that have been infected in the womb from their mother. Most dogs become infected by hookworms, however, when they eat soil or feces contaminated with larvae from other dogs. Symptoms of infection include pale gums (due to anemia), vomiting, and intermittent bloody diarrhea.

Whipworms—These parasites live in a dog's colon and cecum (the junction of the large and small intestines). Dogs between six months and two years old are most susceptible to infection. They get whipworms by eating the egg-infested feces of an infected dog. Symptoms include loss of weight and anemia. As infection increases, the dog becomes emaciated and suffers from foul-smelling diarrhea. Whipworms are not easy to diagnose because their eggs don't often show up in stool samples.

Tapeworms—These live in a dog's intestines, where they attach their heads to the intestinal wall. Unlike the three previously mentioned parasites, tapeworms require an intermediate host to develop their growth and larval stages. For dogs, the most common host is the flea. Tapeworm larvae are often ingested when a dog, biting himself for relief, swallows a flea.

Although tapeworms are virtually impossible to detect by microscopic examination, they can often be determined with the naked eye as flat cream-colored segments when they leave the rectum. Then they become dry and brownish and look like grains of rice in the hair. You might find a few sticking around the dog's rectum or to his bed.

This parasite may become several feet long and continue to grow unless the head part is eliminated. Symptoms vary with severity of infection, age, and physical condition of the dog, but include a dull and brittle coat, listlessness, thinness, and diarrhea. Infection also causes irritation at the rectum, and the dog will often drag its rear along the floor.

Protozoan Diseases—Coccidia and Giardia are both protozoan parasites (small one-celled animals) that live in the intestinal tract. Coccidia most often infest puppies, while Giardia can also infest adult dogs. Transmission occurs when an infected dog eliminates the parasite and it is then ingested by a susceptible dog. Infestation causes the same symptoms as worms, especially loose and bloody stools. Giardia can be transferred to and from humans.

Treatment for intestinal worms and protozoan parasites. A veterinarian can determine if your dog has roundworms, hookworms, whipworms, or protozoan parasites by microscopic examination of a fresh stool sample. Tapeworms, as previously mentioned, are tough to detect in this manner. You can often tell when your dog has tapeworms because segments break off and pass out in the bowel movements.

Once the kind of parasite is identified, your veterinarian will dispense the correct anthelmintic. There are special medicines for each kind of intestinal parasite, but the specific type must be identified before the right drug can be given. Worm medicine is powerful stuff, irritating to the stomach and intestines, weakening to the patient, and often dangerous unless given in the proper amount, carefully measured by the age, size, strength, and condition of the individual dog.

It is safer to let your veterinarian worm your dog for you, and not advisable to try over-the-counter remedies. And be sure to follow your veterinarian's instructions to the letter. If he states that the dog should not eat for a certain number of hours before giving the medicine, make sure the dog fasts, with no tidbits or even milk to "tide him over."

Heartworm Disease

Heartworms are dangerous internal parasites that live in the right ventricle and pulmonary artery of the heart. Adult worms can grow up to fourteen inches long, and a dog may have several hundred of them in his system.

Heartworm is transmitted by the bite of a mosquito (about sixty species are capable of carrying the disease). The cycle works something like this: when a mosquito feeds on an infected dog, it ingests blood which contains an immature form of heartworm called *microfilariae*. These incubate in the mosquito and, in as little as two weeks, become infective larvae. Then when the mosquito bites another dog, the infective larvae pass into the second dog. There, they migrate through its body tissues and enter the heart, where they mature and begin to produce *microfilariae*, which enter the bloodstream. The complete cycle can take up to six months.

Signs of heartworm disease include frequent coughing, listlessness, fatigue, lowered tolerance to exercise, labored breathing, and faintness. Most symptoms, however, are usually not apparent until the disease has reached a serious stage. By this time the damage to the dog's vital organs may be so severe that he cannot be saved. Therefore, early diagnosis is important.

To determine if your dog has heartworm, your veterinarian can examine a blood sample to see if any *microfilariae* are present. A dog occasionally may have adult heartworms but no *microfilariae*. In this case, X ray and other tests are necessary to confirm infection. If the dog has heartworm, the veterinarian may be able to treat him if the disease is detected early.

Fifteen years ago, heartworm disease was prevalent mainly in the eastern and southern coastal areas of the United States, but now it is found throughout North America. No vaccine is available, but veterinarians have developed a method of prevention. It consists of giving small daily doses of diethylcarbamazine, either in liquid or pill form, throughout the mosquito season. In areas of constant mosquito infestation, the daily medication must be given year-round. Dogs should be tested and show no signs of heartworm disease before the preventive program is started.

Skin Troubles

Skin diseases are some of the most perplexing health problems of dogs. When in normally good condition, the dog's skin is elastic. When you grasp it over the back, then let it go, it springs right back to its tight fit. In most breeds, the skin is a light pink color; in a few others, it is blue, dark, or spotted. Part the hair and look at your dog's skin just to make sure it is healthy.

The most common trouble sign is scratching, perhaps followed by the appearance of lesions, or a breaking out of blisters or bumps on the surface of the skin. Often the dog's furious scratching and biting to gain relief aggravates the condition.

It's best to consult your veterinarian at the first sign of any dermatological problem. The quicker problems are diagnosed and treated, the better the chances of curing them.

Dandruff—This common problem affects all areas of the dog's skin. One of the most common causes is dry heat. Most dogs like to sleep near a warm place. Indoors, that is frequently near a heat vent, where the constant flow of hot air can dry out his skin. Brushing often raises many little scales, too. A light spray of a coat conditioner containing mink oil or protein, brushed into the coat and massaged into the skin, usually helps get rid of scaliness.

Skin flakiness can also result from too little rinsing after the bath, when the remaining shampoo dries and irritates the skin. Lack of fat in the diet can also cause dandruff. The introduction to the diet of a nutritional supplement containing unsaturated fatty acids may help solve the problem.

Eczema—This troublesome condition can be caused by allergies, dietary deficiencies, digestive disturbances, external parasites, hormone imbalance, grooming neglect, or predisposition. Dogs do not inherit eczema, but some lines seem to be more inclined to develop it.

The condition manifests itself in two forms: dry and moist. Both types occur in smooth and long-coated purebreeds and mixed-breeds, especially those that have thick undercoats. Although eczema can occur at any time in any geographic locality, it seems to be more common in hot and damp climates.

In the dry form, the skin becomes scaly, with cracked and inflamed spots. In the moist form, ulcerated red spots form on the skin. In most cases, the affected areas are made worse by the dog's biting, scratching, licking, and chewing to gain relief. And this can quickly cause a relatively minor condition to mushroom into a serious one. If untreated, it can cause untold misery for a dog.

The best way to deal with eczema is to prevent the initial irritation by maintaining a regular brushing schedule to remove dead hair and dirt and to keep the skin clean, to keep the dog and his environment free of external parasites, and to be on the lookout for any signs of trouble, especially the dog's constant licking of certain areas. When eczema does develop in spite of preventive measures, however, it usually can be treated successfully in the early stages with antibiotics and corticosteriods.

Mange—This term is used to describe skin and coat damage caused by several types of external parasites. *Sarcoptic mange*, or scabies, caused by the sarcoptic-mange mite, is an extremely contagious condition that can spread from animal to animal and from animal to man. The mites live on and burrow into the skin, causing it to thicken and become inflamed and intensely itchy. Diagnosis is confirmed by microscopic examination of deep skin scrapings. Treatment generally involves the use of an antiseborrheic shampoo, followed by insecticidal dips. Since sarcoptic mange is extremely contagious, all pets in the family should be treated at the same time. *Demodectic*, or "red" mange, is caused by the demodectic-mange mite, which lives in the hair follicles. The skin reddens, the hair falls out, and the follicles become infected, sometimes oozing blood and pus. The first signs are often small bare patches around the eyes and muzzle and on the forepaws. Diagnosis involves microscopic examination of hair roots and skin scrapings. Demodectic mange is usually treated by medicated baths or dips and possibly oral medication or injections. *Cheyletiella*, also called "walking dandruff," is caused by the cheyletiella mite, a large parasite that lives on the skin. It is a very unsightly condition characterized by mild itching and an abundance of yellowy-gray scales that resemble dandruff. Treatment involves a thorough cleansing with an antiseborrheic shampoo to remove the scales, followed by insecticidal dips at intervals that depend on the product used.

Ringworm—This condition is caused by a fungus which, like mange, can be identified only under a microscope or by culturing. The disease takes its name from the circular-shaped affected areas. It first may appear as round or irregular rough and scaly patches raised above the normal level of the skin. Some lesions can barely be seen, while others may be scaly or crusted formations which discharge pus.

Treatment involves shaving off the infected hair, the application of dips and fungicidal and fungistatic ointments, plus the drug Griseofulvin.

Ringworm can be transmitted from animal to animal and from animal to man. Wear gloves when handling an affected dog, and wash your hands thoroughly with antibacterial soap before touching any parts of your body. Infected

animals should be isolated from contact with people and
other pets. It is also necessary to sterilize or destroy bedding,
collars, leashes, and other contaminated articles.

Flea-allergy dermatitis—The most common allergic skin
disease in dogs is caused by a hypersensitivity to flea bites, and
is characterized by intense itching and acute moist dermatitis. The allergic agent is found in the saliva of fleas and is
injected into the dog when fleas bite. Some dogs are so sensitive that they will break out from the bite of one flea.

The lesions are concentrated on the top and underside of
the lower back, near the base of the tail and on the rump, and
on the inside surfaces of the hind legs. The dog will scratch or
bite these areas intensely, causing the hair to fall out, and pustules and crusts to form. Although the disease occurs more
often in warm months, many dogs suffer constantly through
the year.

Treatment is based on keeping the dog and his environment free of fleas through the use of dips, powders, sprays,
and flea collars. Corticosteroids will help relieve the symptoms of the allergic reaction.

Other allergies—In addition to allergic reactions to the
bites of fleas and mites, skin lesions and other reactions can be
caused by allergy to weed, tree, and grass pollens; to the
stings of bees, wasps, and hornets; to antibiotics, hormones,
and other drugs; and even to certain foods. Suspected allergies should be handled by a veterinarian because a complete
history of the dog is necessary to determine correct treatment.
Often these cases respond well to antihistamine and corticos-
teriod therapy.

Vomiting

Vomiting often occurs in dogs of all ages because the dog
can vomit at will. Dose him with a foul-tasting medicine and
he might throw it up because he does not like the flavor. Feed
him a piece of candy and possibly he will throw this up, too.
Occasional vomiting, therefore, may merely show dislike. It is
often caused by grass which the dog eats when his stomach
feels uncomfortable.

Frequent vomiting, however, can be a symptom of many

diseases, among them kidney and liver disease, canine distemper, canine parvovirus, pancreatitis, and bloat (gastric dilation/torsion complex), as well as digestive upsets. Overloading the stomach is a common cause; the cure, less food fed at more frequent intervals. Persistent vomiting of just a little food may mean a change in diet is needed. Worms can also be responsible; getting rid of them solves the problem. Then there are what may be called mechanical causes, among them poisoning and drug intoxication (see pages 153–154).

To treat routine vomiting, withhold food and water for 12 to 24 hours to rest the stomach. After a period, let the dog lick a few ice cubes if he is thirsty, then water or Gatorade can be given gradually in small amounts. During the fast, an antacid product with a protective coating action, such as Pepto-Bismol or Maalox, will help sooth stomach irritation. Give one to two teaspoons per 20 pounds of body weight every 4 to 6 hours. After twenty-four hours, give small amounts of bland food: two parts whole-grain rice combined with one part lean chopped beef or chicken that has been boiled to remove the fat; cooked egg; cottage cheese; or baby cereal.

Do not experiment with the persistent vomiter too long, however. Better see your veterinarian if it doesn't clear up within twenty-four hours. And if blood is vomited, especially a profuse amount, or if blood clots are present in the vomitus, seek veterinary assistance immediately.

Diarrhea

Diarrhea often results from a number of systemic and other problems. It is sometimes caused by bad feeding. If it happens only once or twice, it may be nothing more than a slight intestinal upset. A sudden change in diet can bring it on; a switch from one brand of food to another is best done over a period of several days, the new food gradually mixed in increasing amounts with the old. Often diarrhea results from nervousness or fright brought on by unaccustomed journeys or excitement. Spoiled food, too, will cause it.

Diarrhea can be an indication of canine distemper or canine parvovirus, in which case the stools emit an especially foul odor. Intestinal parasites such as hookworms and whipworms are also a major cause. Serious diarrhea involving several daily evacuations, evil-smelling or blood-streaked stools, should be treated immediately by a veterinarian.

Mild or occasional cases may be relieved by the same treatment as for vomiting: withholding food and water for 12 to 24 hours, giving only ice cubes to lick, then offering water gradually, after a period of time. Simultaneously, Kaopectate or Donnagel, given according to your veterinarian's instructions, will help to stop the diarrhea and calm the stomach. Start bland food after twenty-four hours.

Constipation

Constipation, which is more common than supposed, can be dealt with easily, but its cause should be eliminated or it will happen again. Eating bones or a diet composed largely of meat is a frequent cause. When evacuation is difficult, a single dose of mineral oil may be enough. Mineral oil should always be added to the dog's food (1 to 2 teaspoonfuls per 10 pounds of body weight) and never given separately, for it can cause pneumonia if inhaled.

If the system has been poisoned by long-standing constipation, a purgative dose of milk of magnesia (a teaspoonful for small dogs, 1 to 2 tablespoonfuls for medium-size dogs, and 2 to 3 tablespoonfuls for large dogs) will help clear the intestines. For quicker action, use a soap-and-water enema (see pages 170–171).

Except in the case of very old dogs, persistent constipation can usually be avoided by balanced feeding and additional exercise. Dietary changes, such as the addition of roughage and bulkier foods, will help stimulate the colon and add form to the stools.

Flatulence or Excessive Gas

Indigestion is often suspected when a dog passes foul-smelling gases, but this is sometimes the result of a diet consisting largely of meat or many eggs and from eating highly spiced foods or table scraps.

This unpleasant condition can usually be corrected by feeding a meal-type or biscuit-type dog food and by avoiding large quantities of gas-producing foods. Adding small amounts of charcoal to the food also helps correct flatulence.

Seizures or "Fits"

Seizures, or involuntary paroxysmal disturbances of brain function characterized by violent spasms or contractions of muscles, are common among many breeds of dogs. They may result from a variety of causes, including hereditary predisposition, epilepsy, hypoglycemia, hypocalcemia, and exposure to certain drugs and poisons.

An attack may last for only a few moments as the dog becomes restless, shakes, stiffens, stares glassy-eyed, chomps his jaws, and froths at the mouth. Or he may stagger and roll over on his side as his legs continue to contract, lose control of his bladder or bowels, and become unconscious. Remove the sufferer to a quiet, semidark room or place him in a crate where he can't injure himself. After the seizure the dog can exhibit a number of behavioral changes, including confusion, depression, and fatigue.

Repeated or prolonged seizures should be considered a serious emergency requiring immediate veterinary attention. Whether the seizure is mild or severe, however, it should be followed by a complete physical checkup and perhaps a neurological evaluation. Anticonvulsants are often prescribed.

Lameness

Lameness, limping, and a stiff gait may result from a variety of causes, including foot injuries, limb fractures or dislocations, muscle strains and sprains, degenerative joint diseases, and musculoskeletal diseases and disorders. Lameness is frequently associated with footpad irritations, and this, of course, can account for uncertain and faulty gait. Inspect the feet for thorns, cuts, splinters, embedded foreign objects, and the like (see pages 155–160).

Rheumatism often develops from lying on cold ground, concrete, or damp bedding. A dry play yard, a warm bed, and moderate exercise are recommended. Older dogs can develop arthritis, in which the joints stiffen with prolonged rest, causing lameness. As the joints loosen up, much of the stiffness and pain diminish. If the dog is suffering from no other, more serious disease, a veterinarian can prescribe medication to relieve the pain and discomfort of stiff joints.

Burns and Scalds

Most animal burns and scalds result from contact with direct heat; with hot water, grease, or other liquids; with chemical agents; or from chewing wires. A burn is caused by dry heat, such as flames, while a scald is caused by moist heat—hot liquids spilled on the body, for instance. Emergency treatment includes the following:

Thermal—For heat burns, help cool the area by applying cold water or an ice pack for 20–30 minutes. Apply an antibacterial ointment. Do not apply butter, margarine, grease, salad oil, or other home remedies; these will trap the heat and delay healing.

Chemical—For burns from corrosive chemicals, *flush the skin with quantities of cool water*. If the substance contained an alkali, follow with a rinse of equal parts vinegar and water. If the substance contained an acid, follow with a baking-soda rinse (2 to 3 tablespoons per quart of warm water).

Electrical—Disconnect the wire from its power source if it is touching the dog's body. If you can't unplug the cord, wrap a heavy towel around your hand or use a ruler, broom handle, or other nonconductor of electricity to push the wire out of the mouth or away from the body. Keep the dog warm and get veterinary attention at once.

Extensive external burns from fire and scalding liquids can be a very serious emergency. Keep the dog warm and quiet and get immediate veterinary treatment.

Coughing

A cough is serious, whether or not breathing is difficult. It can be a sign of several different illnesses and diseases, including pneumonia, canine distemper, tracheobronchitis or other bronchial disease, diseases and disorders of the respiratory tract, cardiac disease. and congestive heart failure.

A cough may be no more than a barely audible hack, or it may be severe enough to choke the animal temporarily, and it may be accompanied by fever and labored breathing. Consult your veterinarian immediately. For temporary relief, you will not go wrong dosing with honey and lemon. Into the juice of a lemon mix enough honey to make a thick syrup, and give this to the dog several times daily to ease the irritation. Do not give human cough suppressant medicines.

Poisoning

We frequently think of poison as a dose planted by a fiend to kill the dog next door. Such cases are rare. More often someone's ignorance or carelessness causes the dog to poison himself. The garbage can, too, so attractive to all dogs, must bear its share of blame for such tragedies. It is here that a dog often finds old pills and powders. Occasionally a dog comes to grief when, with the best of intentions, he is doctored with remedies from the family medicine chest. Never give your dog "people" medicine without first checking with your veterinarian.

Poisoning can floor a dog suddenly when large doses are swallowed, or it can sicken him gradually if taken in small amounts. While ingestion of different toxins produces various symptoms, some of the most visible signs of poisoning include trembling, excessive thirst, increased salivation, dilated pupils, frequent swallowing, mouth odor, vomiting, staggering gait, cramps, panting, diarrhea, paralysis, convulsions, and coma.

The most common household danger for dogs is poisoning. They can become poisoned by chewing, tasting, or swallowing toxic substances out of boredom or curiosity, or when they are teething or hungry. Every room in the house, including the garage, contains items that are potentially dangerous to pets. Prevent accidental poisoning by keeping such substances out of your dog's reach.

For instance, ethylene glycol, the active ingredient in antifreeze, Sterno, and windshield de-icers, is one of the most deadly substances for dogs. They are attracted to its sweet, syrupy taste. Symptoms of ingestion include vomiting, mental confusion, progressive depression, and eventual collapse. If treatment is not started early, the dog will usually experience kidney failure and die. When products containing ethylene glycol are stored in the garage, they should be tightly sealed and placed out of the pet's reach.

First aid for swallowed poisons. First aid depends on the kind of poison ingested. When a noncaustic substance is ingested, an emetic is given like any liquid medicine (see pages 169–170) to make the dog vomit. Giving hydrogen peroxide is an efficient and safe way to make a dog vomit in an emergency situation. Give undiluted or mix with an equal amount of water, 1–2 tablespoonsfuls peroxide per 10 pounds of body weight. Table salt is another good emetic. Give one tablespoon dissolved in one cup of warm water. Vomiting should follow in a few moments.

If the dog has swallowed corrosive acid or alkali, gasoline or other petroleum distillates, or strychnine, do not attempt to make the animal throw up. Instead, dilute the poison by giving milk, whipped egg whites, vegetable oil, or water to help delay further absorption.

The veterinarian within easy reach is a godsend, for there is no time to be lost. Act with all speed if your dog is to be saved. If you know the particular kind of poison your dog has eaten, take along the package. This will help the veterinarian choose the right antidote. Packages containing poisonous materials clearly state the correct antidotes on the labels. If you cannot reach your veterinarian immediately, call the nearest Poison Control Center to learn the correct emergency treatment—the number for your area should be listed on the inside front cover of the telephone directory.

Snakebite

Snakebite is not uncommon among dogs given free run in country where poisonous snakes abound. Immobilize the dog immediately—any movement spreads the venom throughout the system. If the bite is on a limb, apply a tourniquet to the leg above the bite, that is, between the bite and the heart. Use a handkerchief, necktie, stocking, or anything of the kind that is handy.

With a razor blade or sharp knife, make two linear cuts (*not crisscross incisions*) over the wound to start bleeding. Don't cut too deeply or you can sever muscles, nerves, and tendons. Squeeze out the blood. If you have brought along a snakebite suction cup, keep suctioning the wound with this. If not, suck with your mouth (provided it is not cut or injured) and spit out the blood. Apply antiseptic to the area and get the dog to a veterinarian as soon as possible. Carry him; do not let him walk even if he can.

Hunters who take their dogs into snake country should carry a snakebite kit of anti-venom for use in an emergency. If you live or travel in a snake-infested area, ask your veterinarian about this.

Encounters with Skunks

If your dog has had an argument with a skunk, you will want to take immediate steps to get rid of the odor, for your own sake as well as the dog's. Skunk spray can be very irritating and you may see your dog pawing his eyes in misery. In such cases, flush the eyes with lukewarm water or a sterile eyewash, then place a small amount of ophthalmic ointment in each eye. Then shampoo the dog as thoroughly as possible, rinse thoroughly, and towel the excess moisture from the coat. To remove the skunk odor, mix about 5–6 ounces of Massengill douche powder or liquid (available at most pharmacies) with a gallon of warm water. Pour the mixture over the coat. Don't rinse it off; let it dry on the hair. Two or three treatments may be necessary.

Porcupine Quills

The dog that tangles with a porcupine is going to be stuck with a lot of quills, particularly around the head and face. The quills are barbed and will become more deeply embedded if not removed promptly by a veterinarian or yourself. Since this is painful for the dog, give him a sedative first. A couple of aspirin will do if you have nothing better.

Grasp each quill close to the skin with long-nosed pliers and twist it out carefully with a steady pull. Pull straight backward, not at an angle, or the quills will break apart. Work slowly and be sure to remove the entire quill, disinfect the site with Hydrogen Peroxide, then apply antiseptic to each wound. Check the inside of the mouth carefully; usually these and any other deeply embedded quills will have to be removed under anesthesia.

Insect Stings

Stings by bees, wasps, and hornets are common. Those on the body are not so serious since the coat serves as a protection, but those on the head, where the hair is often shorter, can cause pain and swelling. The latter are especially dangerous for short-nosed breeds such as Pugs, Pekingese, Bulldogs, and others, because swelling around the throat can cause additional respiratory stress.

Extract the stinger with tweezers if you can see it. Apply a paste of baking soda and water or of boric-acid powder and water to help relieve itching. Cold compresses will help to reduce swelling, which may not go down for twenty-four hours.

Insect stings usually are not considered dangerous unless the eyes or nearby tissues are involved. Here, the pain is so intense that the dog scratches and frequently tears the eye with his nails. Your veterinarian can inject a local anesthetic to relieve the pain.

Cuts, Scratches, and Bites

Superficial cuts and scratches of the type a dog gets from slithering through fences or from thorns in heavy wood cover are sometimes so slight that they need no treatment other than the dog's own licking. However, all abrasions on any part of the body should be washed thoroughly with antiseptic soap and water to stop infection. Then apply antiseptic and a bandage. If the dog tries to bite off the bandage, put on a protective collar (see page 168).

Lacerations and wounds on the skin surface usually result in minimal bleeding. Deep wounds, however, that cause profuse bleeding or hemorrhaging from any part of the body should be considered an emergency. If an artery has been severed, bright red blood will spurt from the wound in time with the heartbeat. Blood escaping from a vein will be much darker in color and ooze. Use a pressure bandage: place a clean cloth or gauze bandage over the wound and apply manual pressure until the bleeding stops, then seek veterinary help immediately. It probably will require stitches.

If your dog is bitten by another dog, clip away the hair around the puncture, then wash the area thoroughly with antiseptic soap and water. Get the name and address of the attacking dog's owner and make sure of that dog's health. It is always wise to have your veterinarian inspect all animal bites.

Choking or Swallowing Foreign Objects

It is not unusual for a puppy to try to eat things he shouldn't—toys, bones, a piece of a glove, and other small things—which can become lodged in the esophagus or swallowed. If you can get to the veterinarian immediately, so much the better. He can look inside with an endoscope and see exactly what has been swallowed and where it is lodged. Surgery may be necessary.

If help is not available and the dog has swallowed a foreign object, feed soft food such as bread and milk, then give an emetic. The chances are that the dog will vomit the food and bring up the object at the same time. If the object is lodged deep in the throat, open the mouth and try to retrieve it with your fingers or long-nosed pliers. If you cannot, try the Heimlich maneuver: lay the dog on his side, then place the palms of your hands (one on top of the other) on his abdomen just below the rib cage. Press into the abdomen with a sharp upward thrust to expel the object. Repeat if necessary.

Drowning and Artificial Respiration

Most, but not all, dogs are good swimmers. Until you determine your dog's abilities in water, take precautions to protect him. Dogs have been known to drown in steep-sided pools that they cannot clamber out of, or by falling out of pleasure boats.

Remove the dog's collar and start first aid by lifting him up by his hind legs to drain the water from the lungs. If he's too large to lift, lay him on his side on a sloping surface, with his head lower than the rest of the body.

If he has stopped breathing, place him on his right side (with head and neck extended) and give artificial respiration. Clear any mucus or foreign objects from his mouth and draw his tongue forward. Place your hands over his ribs immediately behind the shoulder blades. Press down suddenly but gently, then immediately release the pressure. This should be repeated at five-second intervals. To keep the rhythm reasonably correct as you work, say "out goes the bad air" and press down; "in comes the good air" and release. Keep at it. Do not give up.

The moment breathing starts, let the dog inhale a little aromatic spirits of ammonia. When he is fully conscious and can swallow, give a few drops of whiskey well diluted with water. Wrap him in a warm blanket and get him to a veterinarian.

Automobile Accidents

No matter how careful you are to protect your dog from street traffic, there may come a time when he is hit by a car or truck. Always approach a hurt dog cautiously, reassuring him with your voice. His fear and pain may make him bite. For easier handling, use a bandage muzzle of a strip of gauze or cloth, or even a necktie if nothing else is available. (See pages 167–168).

Slide him carefully onto a plank or other hard object, a stretched blanket or coat (keeping it taut), and carry him to a quiet spot or into your car. If a leg seems to be broken, keep it as straight as possible. If the bone has broken through the skin, cover the punctured area with a gauze dressing or clean handkerchief and apply a temporary splint or support the leg with something soft to immobilize it. This will prevent the sharp point or edge from cutting a blood vessel should the dog move or struggle.

When there is a gash or cut, put a gauze dressing or piece of cloth over the wound and secure it in place with a bandage. In a leg injury, always start at the foot and work upward. Apply the bandage firmly but not too tightly, as this would stop the blood flow.

If the head must be bandaged, wrap the bandage across the forehead (maintaining the ears in regular position), down the side of the face, under the jaw, and up over the other side of the face, repeating until several layers have been applied. The bandage should be tucked here and there to keep it in place, making sure that breathing is not obstructed.

If blood from a wound is spurting, you can be fairly sure an artery has been cut. In that case, haste is essential, for a dog can lose a significant amount of blood if the hemorrhaging continues too long. Use a pressure bandage and get emergency veterinary aid as quickly as possible. Except in the case of snakebite, most first-aiders do not recommend the use of a tourniquet (a twist of cloth or whatever else is available to cut off circulation), even if the wound involves a limb. Tourniquets are not as effective as applying pressure and may cause the loss of a leg because of interruption of blood circulation.

After an accident a dog will suffer from shock. This is characterized by shivering, confusion, weak pulse, and pale and grayish lips and gums (normally they are bright pink). These signs may also indicate internal bleeding. First aid for shock is to wrap the dog in a coat or blanket to keep him warm; seek veterinary treatment immediately. Intravenous fluid therapy will usually be given.

Hunting Accidents

Accidents that happen to dogs in the home and on the street can also occur on hunting and camping trips, where you may be miles from the nearest veterinarian or even from your car. Broken glass and opened tin cans hidden in rock piles or brush where the dog is hunting may cut a pad or leg.

Sometimes a poorly directed shot or another hunter mistaking your moving dog for the quarry causes a gunshot wound. A dog that is severely wounded may go into shock, falling down, breathing shallowly, with eyes staring and glazed. In all such cases, keep your dog as quiet as possible, cover him with a blanket or your jacket, and put him in a comfortable place. Get to a veterinarian as soon as possible.

Heat prostration often occurs when dogs hunt in warm weather after a long layoff. Dogs suffering from the heat will often develop thick saliva and foam in their mouths. They will breathe noisily and their tongues will hang out.

First aid for heatstroke is to cool the animal down quickly. This can be done by immersing him up to the neck in cool water or by spraying cool water over his body. Use a rectal thermometer to take the dog's temperature every ten minutes; when it drops to 103° F., remove him from the water. If water is not available, rubbing alcohol sponged on the skin will help lower the temperature. Rinse the dog's mouth with water, if he is conscious, or give small quantities of water to drink. Get to a veterinarian immediately.

Cuts from barbed wire should be treated to prevent infection. In camp, close all discarded empty cans. This prevents not only the chance of a cut foot but also the chance of food poisoning, since the dog might otherwise lick the food still inside a long-discarded can. Especially in the summer months, food spoils quickly, so all garbage should be burned or buried and the spot covered with a heavy stone.

Your dog may get a foot caught in an animal trap. First apply an emergency muzzle. (See pages 167–168.) If you have nothing with which to make a muzzle, wrap your coat around the head to keep the dog from biting. Place the trap flat on the ground and step on the spring so the jaws open and you can pull out the dog's foot. Treat the cuts, and if the foot is broken, get to a veterinarian as soon as possible.

First-Aid Kit

A first-aid kit can help save your dog's life in an emergency. The following items should be kept at home, in a clearly labeled box or carton, in a location known to every family member. Replace them when they are used. Take them with you when you travel with your dog.

Sterile gauze dressings (generally in sizes 3-by-3 and 4-by-4): to protect wounds and help stop bleeding.

Gauze bandage: 1- or 2-inch-wide rolls.

Self-adhesive bandage: elastic wrap to hold dressings in place.

First-aid tape: to hold dressings and bandage in place.

Cotton/cotton balls/cotton swabs: for applying ointments, swabbing wounds, etc.

3% hydrogen peroxide: to clean wounds and to induce vomiting.

First-aid cream or antibacterial skin ointment: to soothe minor rashes and burns.

Antiseptic: for minor cuts.

Germicidal soap: for cleaning and disinfecting wounds.

Disposable enema: to relieve constipation.

Ophthalmic ointment/drops.

Activated-charcoal tablets or powder: to absorb poisons.

Motion-sickness preparation: to prevent car- or airsickness.

Any medication your dog takes.

Maalox or other coating-type antacid.

Kaopectate, Donnagel, or other antidiarrheal preparation.

Aspirin: for relief of pain. *Never give on an empty stomach;* add to food or milk. Dosage is based on body weight; your veterinarian will advise how much to give.

Children's medicine spoon or syringe (with needle removed): for administering liquids.

Rectal thermometer; petroleum jelly is a good lubricant for the thermometer.

Tweezers or forceps.

Eyedropper.

Blunt-tipped scissors: for cutting hair away from wounds, especially on hairy dogs.

In snake country, carry a snakebite kit of anti-venom. It may mean the difference between life and death for your dog. If you don't, at least carry a suction cup and a sealed packet of razor blades (these are more efficient than a pocketknife for opening snakebites).

12
Nursing and Special Care

You don't have to be an expert to know when your dog is sick. All you have to know is how he should look and act when he is well. The healthy dog is responsive and willing, runs and plays, is happy and reasonably fearless. His tail wags with enthusiastic messages. His face is expressive, his eyes bright and clear, his nostrils clean and slightly moist. His nose does not have to be cool, but it usually is. The insides of his ears are pale pink; a little wax is normal, but excessive amounts are not. His breath should smell pleasant, and the tissues inside his mouth should also be pink. His skin is smooth and supple, and his coat is glossy. There is a certain springiness about him that shows pleasure in all he does. He eats eagerly, drinks rather sparingly.

Signs of Illness

When a dog is too good, when suddenly he stops his mischievous ways, we begin to suspect that something may be wrong. Maybe he becomes listless, droops his tail, and doesn't care about cleaning up his dish. Or perhaps he eats as if he were starved, or drinks so much water that he vomits it right up again. His stomach may even be bloated.

You can help your veterinarian by learning the signs of good health. Every dog is a distinct being with peculiar characteristics that distinguish him from others. Once you learn what is normal for your dog, the subtle changes in general appearance, behavior, temperature, respiration, and pulse that precede illness will be readily apparent.

A dog's stools, for instance, should be medium brown in color and well-formed. A puppy may defecate four or five times a day, a grown dog once; don't worry as long as color and consistency are right. If the stools are black, watery, blood-streaked, or putrid-smelling, or if there are more movements than usual, then something is wrong. Fluctuations in a dog's urinary pattern may indicate changes in body chemistry. Urine should be clear yellow, not orange.

In a puppy, the eyes and nose are often first to show oncoming illness. The eyes may tear excessively, possibly with pus collecting at the inner corners; the nose may discharge either clear water or mucus. He may pant continuously, his breathing may be difficult or shallow, his expression strained.

Other signs of a sick dog include fever; prolonged vomiting; changes in appetite or water intake; excessive weight gain or loss; changes in behavior; swellings or lumps beneath the skin; abnormal discharges from body openings; hair loss, open sores, lesions, or other skin problems; limping or difficulty in moving; and prolonged coughing or sneezing. Not all of these will be noticed, of course, when a dog is getting sick; certain symptoms point to one ailment, others to another. However, they are signs that should be watched for. Any one of them is enough to tell the owner that something is wrong. Don't wait to see whether the condition will correct itself. Chances are that it won't. Don't experiment with remedies suggested by well-meaning friends. Get the advice of an expert—your veterinarian. Quick action at the first sign of illness is the best shortcut to its cure.

The Sickroom

When a dog is ill he needs a room or corner of his own in which to recuperate. Protect him from noise and confusion and from the well-meant attentions of children and unthinking adults. He will be comforted by the quiet presence of his owner, but don't talk too much. You'll tire him out.

He needs, first of all, peace and quiet. The dog recovering from a serious disease like distemper may be thrown into convulsions by nothing more than the slam of a door or the shrieks of children playing. Or a frenzy of fear may be caused by the raising of a window shade and the entrance of sudden, stabbing light. Use dark shades, and keep the light fairly dim. Over one side of his bed throw a blanket to further shield the light, which will pain him if his eyes are affected.

Remove rugs and carpets so the floor can be easily cleaned, and cover the floor with newspapers or plastic. Arrange for enough air without drafts, and moderate heat that will remain even. Hang up a thermometer so that you can watch room temperature. Have some water bottles or a heating pad handy in case the patient needs additional warmth.

A table or a chest for medicine, utensils, everything used in the course of treatment will be helpful. And do not forget a pad upon which you note each dose of medicine and the time of day it was given. Wash all utensils carefully whenever used. Wash your hands before and after tending a sick dog.

The Pet's Medicine Chest

The dog's own medicine chest will be helpful to him and to you. Put in it the things he needs or may need—no family remedies, no human medications, just the pet's very own remedies that can be found in a jiffy when required.

Things such as sterile cotton and gauze dressings and bandages, first-aid tape, rectal thermometer, three-percent solution of hydrogen peroxide to cleanse wounds, antiseptic for minor cuts, mild laxative, antidiarrhea tablets or liquid, germicidal soap, first-aid cream or antiseptic/antibacterial skin ointment (for burns and abrasions), Vaseline, aspirin (to help reduce fever and pain), emetic to induce vomiting in case of poisoning, activated-charcoal tablets to absorb poisons and milk of magnesia to help neutralize them, flea spray or powder, and a proper cough mixture. These are some of the things you may need from time to time. You will think of others. Your veterinarian can help. Ask him what sedative is best; when to use it and the dosage. Then in case of overexcitement or accidents, you will be prepared to give first aid. This may seem like a lot of unnecessary work, but the day may come when it pays off handsomely. Always remember: dogs cannot take some drugs that are helpful to people.

Keeping the Patient Clean

One of the chief problems of canine nursing is how to keep the patient clean. In mild illnesses, when the dog can go out-of-doors for relief, the problem is less acute; when he is too weak to stand or is paralyzed, his cleanliness is of real concern.

It is safe to assume that in serious illness the housebroken dog worries when he cannot perform his bodily functions outside. Also, the constant soiling of bedding causes odors in the sickroom. This may make the dog anxious and thus slow his recovery.

The weakened or paralyzed patient should be turned over often, not only to ease the strain of lying in one position but also to prevent bedsores. He needs a softer underbed than usual, and since it will be soiled often, it should be of washable material. Lightweight cotton flannel blankets, cut in yard squares, will do, and can be washed in the washing machine. Mattress pads are also excellent.

Make for the sickbed a canvas-covered, removable false bottom, raised two or three inches off the floor of the box itself. Air will circulate under the bed, keeping the floorboards dry. At least two canvas slides will be needed for each bed so one can be aired and sunned after scrubbing while the other is in use.

However soft the bedding upon which the patient lies, he will also need a wrapper or diaper. Lay under him a full-size terry towel, disposable baby diaper, or disposable pad for pets; bunch it up between the hind legs, across the inner thighs, and around the tail. Wipe him often with a soft cloth moistened with warm water, and then dust the skin lightly with antiseptic powder or baby powder. Long-haired dogs, lying helpless for any length of time, should be clipped around the hindquarters. Cut off the long feathering and the hair around the tail.

If the patient is able to go outside for relief, wipe him off when he returns. Not a trace of dirt should be brought in to his bed; also, he should not lie down wet or damp. Towel him dry; brush his coat gently, but don't take too long, since it may annoy him.

Pay special attention to the sick dog's eyes, ears, and mouth. If he vomits often, wipe out his mouth with a mild saltwater solution. Wipe away any discharge from the eyes and ears. (See pages 127–130.)

The Temperature

The dog's normal rectal temperature is within the range of 100.5° F. to 102.5° F. A few tenths one way or the other has little significance. It may be slightly higher under excitement or following rough play; therefore, take the temperature when your dog is quiet or has been resting. An elevation over 102.5° F. should not be ignored. This indicates that the body is fighting an infection of some sort. A subnormal temperature of below 100° F. is also cause for alarm, since it may indicate internal bleeding, shock, or collapse.

The time of day at which the temperature is taken may affect the reading. Ordinarily the temperature rises in the afternoon and early evening and drops lower during the morning. When talking to your veterinarian, tell him the time of day the reading was made, as well as the day-to-day rise and fall.

Taking a dog's temperature is easy. Use a regular clinical rectal-type thermometer. Wash it carefully in tepid water, then shake down the mercury column with a quick flip of your wrist to below 95° F. Lubricate the bulb end with Vaseline. Lay the patient on his side or have an assistant steady him for you. Insert the bulb about two inches into the rectum, and hold it there for a minute or two. Remove the thermometer, wipe it off with a tissue, then determine the temperature. After use, wash the thermometer carefully with soap and tepid water, then immerse it in rubbing alcohol for a few minutes. Dry it and shut it up in its case.

Phoning the Veterinarian

Many illnesses do not require daily visits to the veterinarian, yet he may ask to be kept informed of his patient's progress by phone. This means he will want *facts* about the animal's day-to-day condition. It is not enough to say that the dog "is about the same" or that "he seems better than he was yesterday." *Give facts.* In other words, keep a record.

Take the temperature twice daily, at ten in the morning and four in the afternoon. Watch the breathing—is it quick, strained, shallow, with pinched nostrils, or is it deep, relaxed, easy? Are there muscular spasms or jerky movements, coughing, strangling, clouded eyes, unusual bowel movements, and so on? These things can be reported accurately only when written down as you see them. So have the record at hand when you phone the doctor. You will save him a lot of time, and you will stand a better chance of saving your dog.

When the veterinarian tells you what to do, do it to the letter! When medicine is to be given every two hours, that means every two hours, and in the exact amount, no more, no less. If it is a case for twenty-four-hour medication, that is, night as well as day, see that it is done. Faithful nursing has pulled many a dog through.

Bandaging and Restraint

Bandage muzzle—A muzzle made of gauze bandage is used when a dog may be tempted to bite from fright or pain during the trimming of nails, the treatment of wounds, or when in shock or hurt from an accident. The width of the gauze bandage will depend on the length of the dog's nose, but ordinarily the one-and-a-half- or two-inch size will be correct, even if it has to be folded over for the shorter faces.

Depending on the size of the dog, cut a 24- or 36-inch-long strip. With the ends of the bandage hanging down over the sides of the muzzle, place the center over the nose. Bring the bandage down around the muzzle under the chin, form a loop, and tie with a fairly loose knot, then bring the ends back on each side of the face behind the head and tie with a bow-knot. Adjust the bandage tightly enough to hold the jaws closed but not so tight as to make breathing uncomfortable. Put on a muzzle of this kind once in a while just for practice; it will teach you how to do it, and your dog will learn not to mind it.

A bandage muzzle has many uses. If, for example, your

dog has been struck by a car, he may be in such pain that he doesn't recognize you and must be restrained before you can handle him.

Jacket bandage—This bandage is used to hold throat compresses and poultices in place, in pneumonia where chest rubbing may be indicated, and for drying up lactating females whose breasts have been daubed with camphorated oil. Such coverings are helpful when fresh air is important but when drafts may be deadly. They also protect furniture and bedding from being smeared with salves and oils.

Fit the jacket from belly to back. For the front legs cut two holes in a square of freshly laundered cloth which is brought up around the throat and ribs, then sewn or taped across the back. A few minutes and a bit of ingenuity will produce a jacket that will be comfortable and reasonably wrinkle-free. The cold or pneumonia jacket is usually made of lightweight flannel, while one for greasy salves or dressings is made of cotton material.

Protective collar—An Elizabethan collar is standard equipment to keep a dog from licking wounds, tearing off bandages, and biting sores or stitches. You can buy a prefabricated vinyl Elizabethan collar from most veterinary hospitals, or you can make your own by cutting a semicircular piece of heavy cardboard, the inner circumference fitted to the dog's neck. Make it wide enough to reach about to the tip of the muzzle. In the two straight sides puncture eyelets, and through the eyelets run a cord or shoelace to pull the collar together. When tied, it looks something like a lampshade worn around the neck. It is very effective and, being light in weight, rarely annoys the dog. In fact, most dogs feel "dressed up" in it and wear it proudly.

Nail taping—It's a good idea to tape the nails of dogs suffering from eye disease or injury to prevent further tearing of the eye by the upper inside toenail. Even when this nail is trimmed and filed, it can scratch the eye because the dog uses considerable force as he paws it.

The toenail on the same side as the injured eye is the one that does the damage. With surgical or first-aid tape, wrap this paw completely, covering the nail. Keep the tape on until sometime after the eye has returned to normal. Boots can be purchased for the same purpose; here all the nails are covered, which is very good in cases of eczema and skin infections that cause constant scratching.

Administration of Medicines

Pills and capsules—If the dog is eating well, the easiest way to give a pill or capsule is to hide it in a piece of meat, cheese, or some other food he finds appetizing.

In cases where trickery doesn't work and the pill or capsule must be force-fed, coat it with butter, margarine, or honey to make it slippery. Seat the dog on a sturdy surface and tilt his head upward. Place the palm of one hand on top of his muzzle. Open the mouth by pressing inward behind the canine teeth with your index finger on one side and your thumb on the other. Holding the pill in your other hand, place it on the dog's tongue toward the back of his throat and push gently downward. Close the jaws and hold them together as you stroke his throat with a downward motion. The dog should swallow; if he does not, hold your thumb against his nostrils for an instant.

Liquids—Bitter-tasting liquids should be put into capsules and given as previously described. The dog can vomit at will, and thus can reject what he does not like. Mild-tasting or tasteless liquids are best poured into the mouth from a small bottle, a syringe with the needle removed, or a plastic medicine dropper. If no one is helping you, back the dog into a corner so he cannot draw away. Put your left-hand index finger in the right-hand corner of the dog's lips, drawing out his lower lip to form a pocket. Pour the liquid slowly into the pouch. Hold fast to the lip and keep the dog's head up until he swallows. When a large dog is handled without help, the attendant usually straddles the animal to control him with his knees, then pours the dose into the left pouch.

Tasteless powders and liquids can often be concealed by serving them with the dog's regular food or by mixing them with honey.

Eye medicine—Medication for the eyes usually comes in liquid or ointment form. To apply liquid, tilt the dog's head upward. Hold the container between your thumb and index finger, steadying the palm of this hand on the dog's head. The prescribed amount of medication can then be dropped into the corner of the eye(s). To apply ointment, lift the dog's head upward. Pull his lower lid downward and squeeze a little ointment on the inside. Let the lid go back into place and, as the dog blinks his eyelids, the medication will coat the entire eye.

Ear medication—This also comes in liquid or ointment form. Hold the ear flap carefully (if the dog's ear hangs down, draw the flap back, close to the head). Insert the required amount of liquid or ointment into the ear canal. Steady the dog's head with your hand to keep him from shaking while you massage the base of the ear to spread the medication inside. Release your hold on the head.

Hypodermic injections—While it is unusual for a pet owner to give medication by injection, in the case of diabetes, for instance, you might be required to give insulin to your dog subcutaneously at home. A subcutaneous injection is one that is given under the skin, and when it is necessary, the procedure *must* be done under the supervision and instruction of your veterinarian. He will demonstrate the necessary procedures involved so that you become familiar with the correct techniques. Injections that are given incorrectly can seriously harm a dog.

How to Give an Enema

An enema may be needed to empty the bowels of impacted matter when a mild laxative might be too slow-acting. Generally, two people are needed to give an enema. An assistant holds the dog in a standing position while steadying his hindquarters, or else the dog can lie stretched out on his side. The disposable enema with prelubricated tip for humans— Fleet, for instance—is quite effective for dogs and easy to administer. It can be purchased at pharmacies in either adult or pediatric size.

Bring the Fleet to room temperature or warmer, then remove the protective shield. Insert the tip into the dog's rectum and squeeze the contents slowly, inserting about one to one and a half ounces per ten pounds of body weight. Steady the dog on papers. Results should be obtained quickly.

You can also prepare your own enema solution, using castile or a mild soap that does not contain detergent to mix some warm soap-and-water suds. For a very little dog, a plastic syringe or even a rubber syringe is sometimes used. On the whole, however, a regular quart-sized enema bag with rubber hose and shut-off valve is preferred.

Fill the bag with the soapy water mixture and hang it on a hook higher than the dog's body. Coat the nozzle with Vaseline, but don't clog the opening. Before inserting the nozzle, open the valve. This clears the nozzle and forces air from the tube. Close the clamp again, insert the nozzle tip into the rectum, unclamp the hose, and slowly begin to administer the liquid. Give about three to four ounces of water to small breeds or puppies, up to one pint to medium-size dogs, and about a quart to large and giant breeds.

Collecting Fecal Samples

Your veterinarian may want to examine a fresh sample of your dog's feces to diagnose certain diseases or to determine the presence of internal-parasite eggs. Collecting a fresh fecal sample is easy. Once the dog has a bowel movement, pick up a sample (try not to include dirt, grass, or other objects) and transfer it to a clean, airtight container or seal it in a plastic bag. Print your name and address on a label and attach it to the sample for proper identification.

Separating Fighters

If a strange dog attacks your dog on the street, you are going to need help to separate the two. If someone can bring some water to dash on the fighters, or better still, douse them with a water hose, that is probably the easiest way.

One dog is usually the attacker. If he can be grabbed by the tail and pulled hard, he will turn around to see what is happening and thus lose his hold. Or if you can get help, have another person grab him firmly and quickly beneath his stomach and raise his hind legs off the ground, while you do the same with your dog, to break their leverage and separate them. To prevent the dog from being able to turn and bite you, hold him as high off the ground as possible until he cools down.

There are a number of actions that will cause fighting dogs to break apart; try to get an object like a stick, a trash-can lid, your jacket or coat between the two animals. They often will become frustrated and stop biting each other. Loud noises also work well. They can create a momentary stunning effect that allows you to take control of the situation. If the dogs are males and you have no assistance, as a last resort try to get in a position where you can pinch the testicles. That usually takes the fight out of them for the moment. When the fight is stopped and you grab your dog, have a helper ready to shield you. The still-infuriated attacker could try to reach your dog and may strike you. The nosy dog that bothers your dog when you go for a walk is often a cause for great annoyance. Your dog is on leash, the other dog is not, so you have a difficult time snubbing him. He may not be a fighter, perhaps he merely wants to sniff your dog and follow along after the two of you. Carry a water pistol in your pocket. A squirt or two in the face will dampen his enthusiasm.

Dog Bites

If you are bitten by a dog, wash the area thoroughly with germicidal soap and water and cover the wound with sterile gauze. Wash and redress the wound every day. The bite of a clean and healthy dog need be no more serious than any other minor cut. However, if the dog is vicious and/or unknown to you, as in the case of a stray dog, the wise course is to consult your veterinarian immediately.

13
A Few Simple Tricks

Tricks can be a lot of fun for the dog and for the family. More than this, they give the dog something to do and keep him from becoming bored. The trained dog is a busy dog and is less likely to be mischievous and destructive. And the more you train, the more you *can* train, since ability to learn usually grows as it is used.

Trainers say that one year is a favorite age at which to begin. If your dog is older, don't despair! You *can* teach an old dog new tricks! Some puppies, too, can learn simple tricks at a fairly early age, but do not expect too much of the very young.

Rewards get results because the dog understands them. When he obeys and gets a tidbit as a reward, he is happy because he has pleased you and he'll want to do it again. Show him that doing the right thing and a pleasant reward go together. Repeat this lesson often enough and he will learn.

Be cheerful, happy, sociable in all your teaching, and your dog will just about fall all over himself to do what you want. If you can arrange it, teach before mealtime, when he is hungry. Use a dog biscuit or other food as the tidbit. When the lesson has been learned, you can skip the "eats" but never forget the pat on the head or the spoken "Good dog."

Short, regular lessons which will not overtire the pupil are best. Two or possibly three daily lessons of ten minutes will be enough. Work on one trick at a time, and do not go on to a second trick until the first has been mastered. When beginning a new trick, review the tricks he already knows; this gives your dog confidence in himself. Do not smoke while teaching, for the fumes will bother the dog's nose and eyes.

And do not keep your dog repeating a trick—or obeying a command—until he is weary and bored.

Shake Hands!

Even a young puppy can learn to "shake hands" because it takes no special strength or skill. It is natural for any dog to lift a paw in greeting or to attract attention. The point is to make him put out one paw when you *tell* him to do so.

We will now stress the importance of the *Sit* and the *Sit-Stay* exercises. (See pages 71–72 and 84–85.) If your puppy has not learned these, teach them first. You will have to use them constantly. In the *Sit*, of course, the dog sits beside you facing straight ahead, while in the *Sit-Stay* he sits and remains seated as you walk away from him.

Order the leashed pup to *Sit-Stay*, as you stand facing him. Now stand quite close and a little to one side. Lean toward him. This will make him draw back and raise one foot. If he does not raise his foot, tap it lightly. Whichever paw he raises as you lean over him, take that paw in your hand and shake it gently as you say *"Shake hands!"*

There seem to be right-handed and left-handed dogs, so at the start you never know which "hand" you are going to shake. Take the one offered, then later you can teach the pup to shake first with one and then the other. After you shake the first, say *"Now the other one!"* If he keeps offering the same paw, just nudge the other one and he will give it to you. Remember the phrase *"Good Rover"* as you give him a tidbit. As this trick is mastered—it won't take long—stand away from the dog rather than close to him, and finally do it without the leash.

Speak!

In some ways the *Speak* is like *Shake hands* because you are telling the dog to do something he does anyway. Notice when the pupil barks readily—perhaps when the doorbell rings, when a stranger comes in, or when you are preparing his dinner.

Make him bark. If yours is one of those very quiet dogs,

you may have to "bark" yourself to start him off. At any rate, be ready. When he barks, order *"Speak!"* Do not shout; don't be nasty about it. Use an encouraging tone of voice—you and the dog both are having a good time. When the bark answers your command, pet him and feed the tidbit.

The *Speak*, however, should be one or two yips and no more. If barking continues, pick the dog up and fondle him, or if he has learned the meaning of *No!* or *Quiet!*, use one of these words to stop him.

Beg!

Most beloved of all tricks is sitting up. However, since we use the word *Sit* for another exercise, we had better use the word *Beg* so that the dog will not be confused. In all orders we must avoid words which sound the same.

Use a corner of the room where a rug or carpet will keep him from slipping. Have the dog *Sit-Stay*, his back close to the corner. Hold a tidbit in one hand and give him a chance to smell it. He will follow it with his eyes and straighten up as you slowly raise this hand above his eye level. At the same instant, with your other hand raise his forelegs off the ground as you order *"Beg!"*

Holding his head up to sniff the tidbit will help him to stiffen his back and maintain the unnatural upright position. The moment he stiffens his back, hold your hand under his chin instead of under his legs. The first few times, he may stay upright for a second or two. This is enough. Praise him and give him a nibble of the tidbit.

This trick is not hard for the dog to learn, but it is very hard for him to master before four or five months of age. A young puppy's weak back muscles and poor sense of balance make "sitting up" practically impossible. The wall close behind him, of course, helps to support his back. After a few lessons he may not need it, and then the lessons can be given anywhere at all so long as the footing is good. If he rears on his hind feet as you lift his forelegs, take your hands away, order *"Sit!"*, then start over. Some breeds and shapes of dogs find it easier than others. If your dog cannot sit up, do not try to make him do it, but choose some trick for which he is better suited.

Steady!

Steady is an interesting outgrowth of *Beg*. When the dog has learned to sit up and beg without wobbling around, try to make him hold a piece of the tidbit on his nose while sitting up.

When he is in the *Beg* position, put the tidbit on his nose as you point a finger at him and say *"Steady!"* You will have to speak firmly now since all he wants to do is eat the tidbit. He must hold it on his nose and remain still until you say *"All right!"* or *"You can have it!"* which means he may flip the tidbit off and swallow it.

This may take a little time, but sooner or later he will learn that he may eat the tidbit only when you tell him to. Until then he must keep absolutely still. If he moves his nose and drops the piece on the floor, do not give it to him. Start over. Dogs like this trick because they know that in the end they always get the prize. They will learn to hold the pose for several moments.

Dance!

When the dog's back is strong enough for him to learn begging, he is ready to learn dancing. Put him on leash and work up a little excitement by letting him sniff the tidbit in your hand. Hold the hand fairly high above his head but not too close or you will throw him off balance.

As he rears up on his hind legs, slowly move your hand in a circle so that he can follow its direction. As you do this, order *"Dance!"*

At first, he may need the taut leash to keep him on his hind legs as he twirls around. As soon as he learns to balance himself upright, skip the leash. Do not give him the tidbit if he jumps to get it. In this case, order *"Sit!"* and start over.

Catch!

The game of *Catch!* is the delight of dogs big and little, since it also means something to eat. You will throw a piece of biscuit or other food to the dog, who must catch it in his mouth without fumbling. This may be difficult because you must aim the biscuit correctly. In fact, the timing and direction of the teacher's cast are as important as the pupil's ability to catch the object. Use a smaller tidbit than usual.

Stand well away from the dog. With a slow, underhand movement throw the tidbit in the direction of the dog but slightly higher. The dog can then follow it with his eyes and try to catch it as it comes down toward him. If he misses it, remove it; let him eat it only when he makes a clean catch.

This trick leads to ball playing. Take care to use a ball large enough to be grasped but not swallowed, and soft enough to avoid injury to the teeth.

Lie Down!

Have your dog on leash and order him to *Sit-Stay*. He is facing you, sitting about three feet away. With the leash in your left hand, crouch or kneel, and as you say *"Lie down!"* or *"Down!"* pull down on the leash. If he goes down flat, with forelegs stretched out before him, praise him for a job well done.

The chances are he will not drop at first. Try again. Repeat the order, pulling down on the leash. At the very same instant, run your right hand under his forelegs and with one quick motion slide both forelegs out from under him. Both legs must be pulled at once; if you pull one at a time, he will pull back, using the other leg for support.

Once he is in the down position, forelegs outstretched, praise and reward him. With practice he will stay down until you tell him to rise by saying *"All right!"* But while he stays down, you too must kneel. If you stand, he will also, at least until the trick is thoroughly mastered.

Roll Over!

When the dog has learned the *Down*, you may go on to *Roll over*. Order *"Down!"* first. Then with your hand push him over on his side as you say *"Roll over!"* If he resists, as he may at first, hold a bit of food in front of his nose to signal the direction his body should take. Crouch closely over him so he will not get up. How fast he learns will depend upon whether or not he is at ease in the *Down* position.

Retrieving

You may not have a retriever which you use for duck hunting, but if you want your dog to fetch and carry, whether a ball in play or your newspaper from the front lawn, the same steps in training are used.

First, you teach him to accept or take an object. Use a favorite toy that he enjoys carrying around—a burlap roll, a rawhide bone, or an ordinary small dumbbell.

Stoop low or get down on the floor and waggle the dumbbell to attract the dog's attention. If he picks it up, say *"Hold it!"* If he doesn't, stand over him; with your left hand hold his muzzle from above, and press with your thumb on one side and middle finger on the other into the corners of the mouth between the lips and teeth. This makes him open up.

Slip the dumbbell between the teeth just far enough back for him to hold it. He may resist. There is no telling how he will react at first. When he holds it for even a few seconds, praise and reward him. If he drops it, correct with *"No!"* and start over.

When he gets the idea of holding for a moment or two, tell him to release it. Kneel down before him, gently take the toy out of his mouth, and say *"Out!"* or *"Drop it!"* If he won't let go, force the mouth open as described above. He must learn to let go of the object only when you tell him to.

Carrying an object comes next. But make sure the pupil knows *Hold it* first. Snap on the leash. With the toy in his mouth, lead the dog around the room or out in the yard. Since holding a hard object is a strain on teeth and jaws, you may want to use a newspaper or an old shoe or anything soft. The dog usually enjoys this, he'll walk as far as you like. But do not overdo it. Every so often say *"Sit!"* and *"Out!"* Remove the object and wait awhile before you give it back.

The next step after holding and carrying is to teach the dog to get an object, pick it up, bring it back, sit, and drop it. This may be difficult, since the pupil will want to run and play with the object instead of bringing it back. Therefore, it is best not to try this trick until the dog has learned to come when called. (See pages 85–86.)

With the dog on a fairly long leash, take the object in your hand and waggle it before him to attract his attention. Throw the object a short distance away. Then run with him to it and order *"Hold it!"* Wait until you are sure he has it firmly in his teeth—he may mouth it and play with it, so you must insist on the hold before giving the next command.

Now say *"Fetch!"* as you crouch down and slap your knee exactly as you did when teaching the *Come.* When he gets fairly close to you, order *"Sit!"* and then *"Out!"* You may skip the *Sit,* but it may be helpful in teaching control.

Hold, *Carry*, and *Fetch* should be taught in just that order, but use the same command so as to simplify things for the dog. Each should be thoroughly mastered before the next is attempted. Actually, they are one trick, taught in three stages to avoid confusion. You will use the *Fetch* around the house as well as out in the yard as the dog learns to bring your slippers, his leash, his bone, a ball, or the newspaper.

Climb Up!

If yours is a tiny dog or one so short-legged he cannot jump into your lap, teach him to climb up. This seems to give little dogs a great deal of pleasure and it can be learned in about one minute. As your dog rests his forepaws on your knee, asking to be picked up, place the palm of your hand against the back of his head and say *"Climb up!"* Stiffen your hand as he braces his head against it and he will walk right up into your lap.

Jumping

Jumping is a favorite pastime. It is a rather showy trick at which some dogs are very good and others no good at all. But don't let your dog jump unless he is full-grown, strong, and sturdy. By nature the dog is a broad jumper rather than a high jumper. He can go across a ditch more easily than he can go over a fence. If allowed to jump too young or too hard, he may seriously injure the tendons of his legs and feet.

A word of caution. The dog who learns to jump very high may be able to scale the very fence you built to keep him safely at home. However, if your dog is sturdy and enjoys doing tricks, you can teach him to jump over a stick or broom handle. First, hold the stick close to the ground; have an assistant help the dog over the stick as you say *"Jump!"* Holding a tidbit on the other side of the stick also helps in teaching this trick. The stick can be raised gradually, but do not try very high jumps.

The Forbidden Chair

To the tricks taught for pure amusement, you might add one aimed at better conduct around the house. In some homes there are sad little dogs tied up all the time because they refuse to stay away from the best furniture. Maybe they nap on your bed when they are not supposed to; maybe they prefer the best living-room chair! You have tried to discourage Rover from sitting in this chair but he cannot understand because he has been allowed to sit in other chairs.

A dog can usually learn to stay off all or certain chairs if he is told *"No!"* every time he starts to get up on them or is found there. If this doesn't work, stack a few metal pie pans or baking dishes on the arm of the forbidden chair. Place them so that they will fall off with a great clatter when he jumps up. The loud noise should discourage him. He'll soon learn which chairs, couches, and beds mean unpleasant sounds, and he will be sure to stay away. Your dog will be less likely to jump on the furniture if he has his own comfortable bed or rug.

How to Talk to the Dog

The average house pet understands more words than most people realize, and if you talk to him in the right way, an amazing increase in his understanding is possible.

In the first place, use a friendly, conversational tone, not too loud and not too soft. The sharp, quick manner of speaking is for correction, whereas the softer, slower manner of speaking is for teaching. Talk clearly, using as few words as possible. Short sentences are the rule. Use the same words each time for the same idea. For instance, do not send him to *Bed* one time and to *Box* the next. Decide on one word and stick to it.

Talk to your dog as you would to the child whose understanding of words is limited. When you say to the child *box* and then show him a box, he learns to connect the sound with the object. The dog will also. Say *shoe* every time you show him a shoe or give him a shoe; he'll soon learn what the sound means.

If you keep this up with many objects, he will become so smart you may have to spell out certain words when you don't want him to catch on. In time, you may even have to spell backwards!

14
Traveling with Your Dog

Today's dog is quite a traveler. In former years he was boarded in a kennel or cared for by a friend or neighbor when the family went away. Today he goes right along in the car or on a plane, often touring great distances to vacation spots. Vacations can be more fun with dogs along. They make wonderful companions on trips, and they also serve as good protectors. But whether your dog is well-behaved or something of a nuisance depends largely upon his training for the open road.

These days, most owners travel by car or plane with their pets. A few regional railway lines allow dogs in passenger cars. Amtrak, which provides nationwide service, once permitted dogs in both passenger and baggage compartments, but now accepts only Seeing Eye dogs as passengers. And guide dogs are the only canines permitted to ride interstate buses.

Lessons in Riding in the Car

The best way to help your dog become a seasoned car traveler is to start with short drives to get him used to the motion. Do not feed him or give him a drink of water for at least two hours before riding. A few short rides will probably be enough to get him used to the movement of the car. Hold him on your lap at first, or set him on the seat beside you. Keep your arm around him for confidence and support, as well as to guard him against being thrown to the floor in case of a sudden stop.

If your dog is large and you want him on the floor, order *Sit* and see that he remains there. Many dogs like to lean out the window to enjoy passing scents. The constant rush of wind, however, may cause cold in his eyes and ears, not to mention resulting in a serious eye injury.

If you have trained your dog to stay quietly in a crate or carrier, this is an excellent way to confine him in the car, too. His carrier will also serve as a comfortable bed in hotels and motels. Always prepare a special place for your dog in the car. Give him enough room. Don't wedge his carrier between luggage that restricts air flow as well as space, and keep the luggage secure from unexpected shifting during sudden stops.

Car Sickness

While it is not unusual for dogs to become carsick when riding, it is less likely among those trained to ride while young. The car vomiter can frequently be cured by taking him for short drives each day. As soon as you notice him beginning to swallow a great deal or to drool excessively, stop the car and let in some fresh air. Take along a damp washcloth and paper towels to clean up if the dog becomes sick. After a few drives, the dog should begin to adjust to being in the car; his fears and anxieties should pass and he should enjoy riding.

If this fails, however, speak to your veterinarian. He may prescribe something like Dramamine or Bonamine to overcome motion sickness, or possibly a sedative, given before starting, that may help to control drooling and nausea. A dog that is nervous and sick in a car often can be "cured" by merely sitting with him in a standing car and petting him there for short periods each day. In some cases, the nervousness often disappears after the dog has been fed a meal or two inside the motionless car. Letting him see out helps, too.

Planning the Trip

The trip will be more enjoyable for both you and your dog with a little advance planning. Take along your pet's own food and water bowls. Pack a few containers of his favorite food (plus can opener and spoon, if needed), since you may not be able to buy it in out-of-the-way places. Also take along a thermos or gallon jug of drinking water. A dog can be affected by changes in food and water and may develop an upset stomach or diarrhea as a result.

Be sure his collar is attached, complete with license and identification tags. Take a sturdy chain leash as well as an extra leash, for you will need this for exercising along the way. No matter how warm it is when you start, pack a sweater, too, if your dog is used to wearing one in cool weather.

Take a few bath towels and also a roll of paper towels to clean up in case of accidents. And don't forget a pooper-scooper and some plastic bags to dispose of feces. You should also pack an adequate supply of necessary medications that your dog will need, such as heartworm preventive, and something to control diarrhea or upset stomach, plus a few of his favorite toys.

Before starting out, make sure you have in the glove compartment of your car a copy of the "Touring with Towser" booklet published by the Gaines Dog Research Center, which lists hotels and motels throughout the United States that accept travelers with dogs. You can order a copy by sending $1.50 to Gaines T.W.T., P.O. Box 8172, Kankakee, IL 60902.

Travel by Air

When a dog travels by air with his owner, he rides either in the passenger cabin or in the baggage section. In either case, it is wise to make your reservations well in advance, as shipping dogs is big business for the airlines today.

Most major airlines allow one pet to ride in the first-class passenger section and one in tourist class per flight. The pet must be small enough, however, to fit into a carrier that can be stored under the seat. And you *may not* remove the dog from the crate during the flight.

Larger dogs must ride in the baggage compartment in a shipping crate that you can buy or rent from the airline. Riding in this manner is comfortable; jet airliners have pressurized cargo holds that are both heated and ventilated.

The choice of a shipping crate is important. It should be

large enough for your dog to stand up and turn around, but not so big that he can't brace himself when necessary. It must also be strong enough to withstand shipping, and it should be adequately ventilated on at least two opposite sides so that air can flow through. The door should have metal bars to let the dog see out.

The most popular type of airline shipping crate is the Vari-Kennel, made of molded fiberglass. It is very sturdy yet light in weight, and has plenty of ventilation slots, a latch that a dog cannot open, and a protective rim around the outside to prevent baggage from shifting against it. When not used for travel, the lower half can be detached and used as a bed.

Most airlines have different sizes of this shipping crate available to accommodate almost any breed of dog. If you wish to rent one, you can reserve the carrier when you make your own reservation. There is, however, one important advantage to owning your own crate: you can condition your dog weeks before the trip to accept the enclosure as his "security blanket."

Prepare the carrier for travel by attaching clearly printed identification labels on top. Mark the sides of the kennel prominently with the words "LIVE DOG." Arrows should indicate the top of the carrier.

On the day of departure, feed your dog a light meal about four hours before flight time, then encourage him to drink some water just before you leave for the airport. Be sure the dog is wearing his collar with an identification tag. A calm dog probably won't need a tranquilizer, but a nervous one may have to be mildly sedated before leaving. When you arrive at the airport, snap a leash to the dog's collar and take him for a walk so he can relieve himself. Put him inside the carrier at the last moment before check-in.

The Health Certificate

Look into the laws affecting dogs for the various states you plan to visit or drive through. Most states require a health certificate signed by a veterinarian. This is a statement saying that he or she has recently examined your dog and finds him to be in good health. Most states honor a health certificate for thirty days. Some states also require current proof of the dog's vaccination against rabies. A rabies certificate should state the dog's name, breed, and age, the date of vaccination, the type of vaccine used, and its serial number.

If you are traveling by air or by rail, these certificates are absolutely necessary. When traveling by car, you and your dog may never be stopped, then again you may be. Dog regulations change from time to time, so before you go you might check with the health departments in the capitals of the states you plan to visit.

National Parks and Campgrounds

Many national parks, mobile-home parks, and campgrounds in the United States accept dogs, as do many popular tourist attractions, including Disneyland in California and Disney World in Florida.

Be very careful in national parks, since they may have special laws. There usually are areas where dogs are allowed if they are on leash or under control of the owner. You can write to the National Park Service, Department of the Interior, Washington, D.C., to learn which national parks accept dogs and exactly what their rules are. Most bookstores carry a variety of directories and guidebooks which list campgrounds, trailer parks, public and private parks in the United States and Canada that accept dogs.

Dogs in Parked Cars

There probably will be times when you will have to leave your dog in the car while you eat, shop, or sightsee. Park the car in the shade, of course, but more than that, be sure that the sun cannot get to it before your return. Sun on glass makes a furnace of the car, and your dog may easily suffocate.

Be sure to allow for enough air. Lower a window a few inches on either side, but not so low that the dog can squeeze through and escape. It's best to check the car every thirty minutes, especially in hot weather. Always place a pan of water on the car floor if you will be gone any length of time. *Do not leash the dog*. He might hang himself. Besides, only when he is free inside the car can he protect it against theft.

Traveling in Hot Weather

Owners rightly fear for their pets when traveling in hot weather, especially when driving across the desert. Dogs probably suffer from the heat even more than humans. They don't perspire through the pores of their skin as do humans, but release heat less efficiently through their footpads and by panting. When dogs are confined in poorly ventilated enclosures, they are subject to heat prostration.

This is where your bath towel comes in handy if your car is not air-conditioned. Place a damp towel on the car floor for the dog to lie on; then place another damp towel over him. These will help to keep him as cool as possible. Your supply of cool water, too, may be a lifesaver. Offer the dog a drink often, and feed lightly.

Conduct in Public Places

Not all hotels and motels accept dogs. The number of those that do, however, is increasing because dog-owners are learning the importance of making their dogs behave.

Exercise your pet where you are told he may be exercised, and nowhere else. Guard the bushes and greenery against damage by your dog; keep the paths clean by curbing him (see pages 113–114). Stay away from gardens, swimming pools, or the beach. Scoop all droppings into a plastic bag, then deposit it in the nearest receptacle.

Insist that your dog be clean indoors also, and spread newspapers thickly on the floor in case you are not positive of his house-training. Do not bathe the dog in the hotel bathtub and do not use the management's towels to freshen him up. Such actions have made enemies of friendly hotelkeepers.

You may have to leave your dog alone in the room at times. This is where trouble often starts because even the best-behaved dogs often become noisy or destructive when they are left alone. Confine him to his carrier, or else he may escape and try to find you when the maid enters the room. If he will not be crated, inform the maids or place a "Do Not Disturb" sign on the door when you go out. Watch the windows, too. Never leave a window open wide, since this is where the dog may try to escape, even through a screen.

Leave the room as clean as when you found it and you and your dog will be welcomed again. If furniture or bedding is damaged, pay willingly for the damage. Do not try to hide it, or the next fellow and his dog may be turned away.

Foreign Travel

Traveling with your dog abroad, of course, is more complicated. International travel requirements vary considerably from country to country. Readers who plan to travel overseas with a dog should arrange their itineraries well in advance, and should contact the embassy (in Washington, D.C.) or nearest consulate of the country they plan to visit for specific entry requirements.

Almost every foreign country requires a health certificate and current proof of rabies vaccination. Check with your veterinarian well ahead of departure date about these. Once you obtain the documents, take them along to be examined by customs officials when you enter a foreign country. Certain countries, however, may require that these certificates be validated beforehand by a veterinarian from the United States Department of Agriculture, and then legalized by the consulate of the nation you are planning to enter.

A few countries do not admit dogs, and a few others— including Great Britain, Australia, New Zealand, Sweden, Denmark, Finland, and certain Caribbean islands—impose quarantines on dogs ranging up to six months, during which time the dog will be confined before entering the country.

Some but not all steamship companies offer kennels for dogs. Be sure to ask, before booking passage, which ships carry dogs and which do not. All of the major airlines carry dogs to Europe and the Far East. Here, too, it's best to get in touch with each air carrier about special regulations. Or you can obtain the services of a kennel or pet-shipping service which specializes in the boarding and shipping of animals to and from almost anywhere in the world. They will arrange for the necessary documents, make travel reservations, and provide special traveling carriers. Such agents are listed under "Pet Transportation" in the classified section of the phone directory.

15

Dogs as a Hobby

Whatever breed of dog you have chosen, you are going to be proud of him. You take him with you wherever you go, and put him through his paces for visitors to see how smart he is. Sooner or later somebody says: "Why don't you put him in a show? I'll bet he could win!" At once your curiosity is aroused. What about this place where dogs are shown?

Dog shows are competitions for purebred dogs involving prizes, ribbons, trophies, and championships. There are hundreds of such shows held yearly throughout the country, some in big buildings like armories, amphitheaters, and Madison Square Garden, others under canvas on outdoor grounds. There may be 3,000 or more dogs competing at a time; there may be a hundred or two.

If you want to enter your dog in a competition, you should first register him.

How to Register

Of the several agencies which register dogs, the American Kennel Club (AKC) is the oldest and largest in the United States. Their records list the majority of purebred dogs in this country. When you get your puppy, if he is a purebreed, you should have received a partially filled-in printed form from the seller. This is an application for registration issued by the AKC. It indicates that your puppy was a product of a registered purebred sire and dam of the same breed, in a litter that was registered. If the seller does not provide a registration application, however, but guarantees that the puppy is AKC-registered, get a written statement or bill of sale listing the pup's breed, sex, color, date of birth, registered name of sire and dam, and the breeder's name and address. *Don't accept a promise of later identification.*

Let's consider, then, that you have been given the AKC registration form with your puppy. You sign it and send it with the required fee to the American Kennel Club, 51 Madison Avenue, New York, NY 10010. If the form is correct, within a few weeks you will receive a certificate of registration in your name. This contains your dog's official registration number, which must be used, along with his name, when he is entered in a show.

In the United States, there are two kinds of dog shows governed by American Kennel Club rules and regulations: all-breed shows, open to all the recognized breeds (sponsored by all-breed clubs) and specialty shows, limited to a single breed or a related group of breeds (sponsored by clubs whose members are dedicated to the advancement of a particular breed). These competitions are managed by AKC-licensed dog-show superintendents or, occasionally, by club members themselves.

There are many local dog clubs, both all-breed organizations and specialty clubs for one breed, throughout the country. Many of these also hold informal sanction "match" shows, which are excellent training grounds for both puppies and novice exhibitors. No advance entry is required, and fees are low. Local newspapers sometimes carry announcements of matches, or you can write to the AKC for the names of any breed clubs or dog-show superintendents near you.

It is a good idea to go to a match or attend a dog show without your dog, so you will know what is going on. Watch particularly how your breed is groomed and shown in the ring, then practice at home. If your dog has learned how to heel on leash and to stand when told to, you will have little trouble.

To learn the dates of forthcoming shows in your area, contact your local kennel club or consult *Pure-Bred Dogs— American Kennel Gazette*. If you are planning to show your dog, write to the various dog-show superintendents and ask to have your name placed on their mailing list to receive information about future shows.

Several weeks before a show, the managing superintendent or club secretary will send you a "premium list." This is a booklet which gives advance information about the show—the date, location, judging panel, list of prizes—and contains an entry form which you fill out and return with a fee as directed. In order to compete, your dog must be over six months of age, must be registered (or listed), and must not be neutered.

The entry form will tell you to indicate the class in which your dog is to be shown. Dogs and bitches may be entered in the Puppy, Novice, Bred-by-Exhibitor, American-Bred, or Open class. If this is your first experience, you had best enter one of the easier classes, that is, the puppy class if your puppy is between six and twelve months old, or the novice class if he is more than one year old. To learn more about class requirements and show procedures, you should write to the AKC and request a copy of *Rules Applying to Registration and Dog Shows*.

Competing in Dog Shows

When you take your dog to a show for the first time, this is what you do. At the entrance gate, show your ticket, which admits you and your dog. Today most shows are "unbenched," which means that the dogs can arrive anytime before their scheduled classes and leave immediately after, provided they are not needed for additional judging. Some other shows are "benched," which means that the dogs have to stay in assigned stalls all day long, except when they are being groomed or judged. If the show is benched, the number on your ticket is your dog's bench number.

Be alert to take your dog into the ring at the right time. You received a timetable in the mail with your ticket, and it gives the starting time for judging of your breed. Be prepared in plenty of time, but let your dog relax until just before his class, so he will be clean and fresh. You will receive a numbered armband at the ring entrance, and then you are in the ring.

A dog show is a series of competitions, each more difficult than the last. Judging always begins with the Puppy dog class. Once the class has assembled, the judge usually stands in the center and watches the handlers gait their dogs counterclockwise two or three times around the ring. He then motions them to stop. The handlers then pose their dogs at one side of the ring and the judge goes over the dogs individually. Afterward he asks each handler to move his dog in various patterns, so that he can evaluate the animal's gait. As the judge examines each dog, he is determining how closely it compares, in his opinion, with the breed standard. The judge awards first, second, third, and fourth places.

The Novice dog class is judged next in the same manner, and after that the Bred-by-Exhibitor dog, American-Bred dog, and Open dog classes. When the dog classes are finished, the first-place winners come back into the ring and the judge picks the Winner's Dog.

The same class procedure is repeated for the bitches, ending with the judge's selection of Winner's Bitch. The dogs that are named Winner's Dog and Winner's Bitch earn points toward their championship. When the regular classes are finished, additional competition continues between Winner's Dog, Winner's Bitch, and the male and female Champions of Record. From these, the judge selects Best of Breed, Best of Winners, and Best of Opposite Sex to Best of Breed.

At an all-breed show, there is additional competition resulting in one dog being named as the best in the show. Each Best of Breed winner competes within his group: Sporting, Hound, Working, Terrier, Toy, Non-sporting, and Herding. The seven group winners then compete for the grand prize, Best in Show.

Now, this may seem complicated. Don't be discouraged. You do not have to understand it all straight off. In fact, if your dog wins first in his class, or even second, third, or fourth, you have every right to be happy about it. You can take the ribbon home and proudly show it to your friends. If you win nothing, never mind; there will be other days, other shows where you and your dog can try again. But you do not have to keep showing him if you do not want to. Just one show alone will be an interesting experience. Later you can exhibit again if you wish, and learn step by step as you go along.

If there is a dog club in your neighborhood, get in touch with the secretary, who will tell you something about the meetings of the group. You will be welcome to attend, and can learn a lot about dogs, shows, grooming and general care, and dog breeding.

Learning About Dogs

All such meetings can be quite educational, because, like you, all the others are interested in purebred dogs or they would not be there! You will be excited by other people's enthusiasms, sympathize with their troubles, and you will learn a great deal by getting to know folks who admire the same kind of dog that you do.

The subject of purebred dogs is fascinating. Once interested, you will want to learn more and more. Visit your nearest public library. You will find many volumes telling the histories of the dogs of all nations, from pole to pole.

Veterinary Care Available

There are about 38,000 men and women engaged in veterinary medicine care in the United States. The majority of them handle dogs as part of their general practice. There are more than 10,000 small-animal hospitals for the treatment of dog ailments. Canine blood banks and X ray, medical care and surgery on a par with that for humans, are all available to dogs today. Many of the new drugs developed for man, the serums, vaccines, hormones and antibiotics, also serve dogs.

Today's veterinarian has long and intensive preparation for his profession. A student must first complete at least two years of college preveterinary medical study. Then he has to study four more years at one of the twenty-seven veterinary colleges in the United States. These are the only schools where a Doctor of Veterinary Medicine (DVM) degree can be earned. Although veterinarians are not required to complete an internship before going into practice, many residency programs exist and graduates do take advantage of them. Before a veterinarian can practice in any state, he must pass rigid state board examinations to get a license.

Graduates of colleges of veterinary medicine are in great demand. They can work in various professional areas: private practice, teaching and research, regulatory medicine, public health, private industry, Peace Corps or World Health Organization programs, for the military, and for zoos, animal shelters, and wildlife preserves. Enrollment of women in veterinary medical schools has tripled in recent years, and today they practice in every field of professional activity.

More and more veterinarians are specializing in a particular species or specific phase of animal medicine. According to the American Veterinary Medical Association, today a veterinarian can specialize in more than fifteen different fields, including toxicology, biochemistry, parasitology, reproduction, anesthesiology, internal medicine, microbiology, pathology, surgery, radiology, preventive medicine, and diseases of the eyes, skin, heart, and nervous system.

Much research for dogs is being done in college laboratories, as well as in private laboratories of pharmaceutical companies and dog-food manufacturers. The result is that dogs live longer and healthier lives today than ever before. Thousands of dogs that would have died twenty years ago now recover from serious illnesses.

Obedience Schools and Training Centers

There are even obedience schools and "colleges" where dogs are prepared for AKC degrees of Companion Dog (C.D.), Companion Dog Excellent (C.D.X.), Utility Dog (U.D.), and Tracking Dog (T.D.). These are degrees awarded at obedience trials which are held in conjunction with regular dog shows or independently.

While developing dogs mentally, obedience instruction also teaches good canine citizenship. There are several hundred training organizations for dogs and their owners in states across the nation. So if you are not getting good results in training your dog at home, you might join one of these classes. For a free list of such classes, write to the Gaines Professional Services, 660 White Plains Road, Tarrytown, NY 10591.

Breeding Your Dog

You do not have to become a professional dog breeder, but you may consider mating your female once or twice, especially if she has a good temperament, is healthy, free from serious hereditary faults, and is from a fine bloodline. Whelping and raising a litter of pups is quite an experience that will teach you a good deal about the ways and wonders of nature.

First, be sure that your female is normal, average-sized for her breed, not too thin or too fat, and in top physical condition. You might have her examined by a veterinarian one to two months before her heat period is expected. Ask him whether he considers her fit for mating. The chances are that she is, but it is wise to get an expert's opinion. If the veterinarian gives her a clean bill of health, then go ahead.

The female's ability to reproduce is determined by a heat cycle which lasts about twenty-one days and may start sometime after the age of six months. However, many bitches—particularly the giant breeds—reach the age of twelve months or more before they have their first heat cycle.

The age at the first mating is important. With age, the bones become more set and rigid, hence a female bred for the first time at four or five years of age might have difficulty in delivering the pups. Therefore, if you plan to breed your female, do it while she is young. Not too young, though. It is unwise to breed a female that is between 6 and 12 months old when she has her first season. Most females are not mature enough to handle a litter at this age, and it becomes a strain on them both physically and mentally. It's better to wait for the second or third season. If you are confused, seek your veterinarian's advice about the correct age to breed, particularly with large and giant breeds, where it may be wise to wait until the third season (about two years of age) or later, when the female will be fully grown and sexually mature.

Selecting a Stud Dog

Well in advance, decide on the male to which your female is to be mated. If possible, select a dog offered at stud by a regular breeder rather than some unknown, untried dog in the neighborhood. For this service you will be asked to pay a stud fee, but it is well worth it. Occasionally a stud's owner will mate his dog without fee, instead taking first choice of one or two puppies in the litter. If such an arrangement is agreeable to both parties, record all the facts in a contract signed by each owner. A signed agreement protects against misunderstandings, before problems arise.

If you cannot find a stud of your breed, contact your local all-breed kennel or specialty club; most local groups publish a directory of area breeders, from which you can select one near your home. Go and see several stud dogs if you can, then select the one you like. Some pedigrees combine better than others, so take your female's pedigree along and be guided by the breeder's advice.

Having decided on the dog you will use, make a reservation for his services then and there. You should know the approximate date when your female is due in season.

The Female's Heat Cycle

The female's heat period usually occurs twice a year, but it can vary. Large and giant breeds may cycle only once every 9 to 12 months.

The heat cycle lasts about twenty-one days and has several stages. The first signs are swelling of the vulva, usually followed by a blood-tinged discharge several days later. This first stage is called proestrus and lasts about nine days after the blood discharge begins. Males are attracted to the female, but she is not yet receptive and will not permit mounting.

The second stage, called estrus, starts around the ninth day of the cycle and continues for the next 7 to 10 days, during which time ovulation occurs. During this period the female usually will permit a male to mount and breed her. The best time for mating is from the ninth to the twelfth day, when her vulva becomes less swollen and spongy to the touch and her discharge changes from red to a light pink or straw color. To help guarantee success, most breeders like to mate a bitch two or three times between the ninth and twelfth day.

There are exceptions, and not all females will breed on the same days. Some are ready for mating before the ninth day, while others may not be ready until after the twelfth day. Keep a close check on your female to help determine when she is ready. Besides noticing vulva sponginess and discharge color, you can lightly touch her vulva with your index finger. If she flips her tail to one side, she probably is eager to be bred. You can also ask your veterinarian to take a vaginal smear to determine the female's optimum time for breeding.

Care of the Pregnant Female

When you bring your female home after breeding, be sure to *guard her carefully* until she has gone completely out of season and has returned to normal. Then let her live her life as usual for the next three weeks, exercising her every day without fail. Have her examined by a veterinarian around the twenty-eighth day to determine if she is pregnant. At this stage, a veterinarian can palpate her abdomen and feel the slightest enlargements in her uterus. If she is pregnant, ask the veterinarian's advice about diet and the addition of a vitamin-and-mineral supplement.

During the fourth week, gradually increase the female's food intake. Canine nutritionists agree that pregnancy and lactation are the most critical stress periods in a female dog's life. She requires increased levels of vitamins, minerals, amino acids, and energy, and if she does not receive adequate nourishment for herself and her developing puppies, she will deplete her body reserves.

As your female's appetite and food intake increase, offer two meals a day instead of one. As her uterus enlarges, you may want to further divide her daily rations into three or four meals to avoid overloading her stomach.

In the last half of pregnancy, exercise is important, but it must not be too strenuous. Guard her against jumping and roughhousing, for as the size of the litter increases, she may injure herself or her puppies. If you must pick her up, be very careful. Support her hindquarters and set her down gently. Don't let her squeeze through swing doors. If in any doubt about her condition, let the veterinarian look her over.

Dogs usually deliver sixty-three days after the mating; often, however, it is a day or two more or less. Keep a record of the date of mating. Figure the probable delivery or whelping date and be ready for it.

The Whelping Box

Choose a draft-free room where the temperature can be held at about 72 degrees. Prepare a comfortable box and let your female sleep in it for two weeks or so before the whelping date. If she objects to new sleeping quarters, give her one of your old blankets or sweaters to lie on. A box of oblong shape is best. It should be as deep as the female is long, and about twice as long. You might attach upright posts in the corners so you can throw a blanket over the box, in case the room grows chilly. The best flooring is a removable canvas-covered slide. Make two, so one can be washed and sunned while the other is in use.

If you do not care to go to all this trouble, and your female is a little one, you can use ordinary cardboard cartons. Get several since, once damp, they are useless. The hardy female of larger size, used to living outdoors, can use a stall set up in the basement; but it must be arranged to keep the puppies in a limited space. Young puppies need warmth and protection from drafts—do not forget that when preparing the whelping bed. Finally, place in the box a piece of rug or quilt which the female can dig into and pull on during labor.

The Whelping

As the due date draws near, the carried litter sags. The nipples swell and a watery fluid may be expressed from them. As long as the mother-to-be eats, she is probably all right; if she refuses food, then she will probably whelp very soon. About twenty-four hours before whelping, her normal temperature of about 101 degrees will drop to below 99 degrees. Her vulva may become swollen, and there may be a mucous discharge from the vagina. She will be quite restless, pacing back and forth and perhaps crawling under tables and chairs, where she will lie panting. Now and then she scratches vigorously, rearranging the bedding in her whelping box and tearing papers or anything she can dig her claws into. Do not leave her alone; she may want you nearby.

Watch carefully for the first signs of labor pains. She will pant heavily, with her tongue out, lick her vulva, and strain as though trying to have a bowel movement. When she lies on her side, you will be able to see and feel the abdominal contractions. Look at the clock and determine the time. More than two hours of straining without the birth of a puppy will mean that your female needs a veterinarian.

When the whelping is normal, you may see a lump between the anus and vulva. With a few more painful strains a dark fluid-filled bag or sac begins to come out. It may be expelled without assistance; if not, use a rough-textured washcloth to grip on its slippery surface. Hold the sac to prevent its going back, and with each succeeding labor pain pull gently but firmly down.

Each puppy should come in its own enclosing sac—the afterbirth or placenta attached to the umbilical cord should come right along with the puppy. Should the connecting cord break, never mind for the moment—it will probably come out later. However, keep track because if any placentas are retained, they may cause an infection. A hormone shot must be given by the veterinarian if any afterbirths are retained, or if he thinks there may be another puppy left.

Ordinarily the mother takes care of the whelping without help. Don't be too eager, and in any case, there should never be too many people around. She will usually tear open the sac with her teeth, but sometimes she just sits and waits, not knowing what to do. In this case, you must work fast to get the puppy's head out or it will smother. Tear the sac down and around the head and off the body. If the umbilical cord is still attached, tie it firmly with cotton thread or dental floss about two inches from the puppy's body, being careful not to pull its stomach wall. Then cut the umbilical cord (on the placenta side of the tie) with sterilized blunt-tipped scissors, and swab the end with liquid antiseptic. The rest of the cord will dry up and fall off within a few days.

Give the puppy to the mother to wash. If she is the old-fashioned sort, she will lick the little one and tumble it about roughly to start the infant breathing. If she is an ultramodern "just-sit-and-watch" kind, do this for her. With a dry towel rub the baby all over. Wipe any mucus from the mouth with your index finger. Don't be too gentle; really rub and rub. When you hear a tiny squeal you will know the puppy is breathing; otherwise keep rubbing it until it shows some sign of life; then place it on the matron's breast.

If the afterbirth does not follow the puppy, it should come out with the next puppy. There is one for each pup and each must be accounted for. Let the matron eat one or two. They contain healthful substances and it is natural for the mother to clean the nest by eating them, but too many will make her nauseous and cause lack of appetite when she needs to eat food.

The puppies will continue to arrive—perhaps ten minutes apart, perhaps a full hour or more. The same digging, scratching, straining will go on for each one, or she may hardly know she has them. While straining for the next birth, the mother may injure an earlier puppy; in any case, it will get cold and wet if kept with her. You may remove the little ones to a basket nearby (be sure they are warm) until the whelping is completed. Then give the puppies back to the mother to nurse.

Feeding the Puppies and the Matron

During the first few hours after delivery, check to see that the matron has a sufficient milk supply for the puppies. The nursing period starts with the secretion of a watery-milky fluid called colostrum. During the first twenty-four hours of life, newborn puppies receive antibodies from their mother's colostrum which protect them against certain diseases for the first few weeks of life. If the mother does not have enough milk, or if there is too large a litter for her to take care of, then you must give extra bottle feedings.

You may use a commercial bitch's milk replacer such as Esbilac, or you can make your own formula with two teaspoons Karo syrup, two cups whole milk, and two egg yolks. Or use two parts of evaporated milk to one of water, adding a small amount of Karo syrup and the yolk of an egg. Mix thoroughly and keep the formula in the refrigerator, warming whatever amount is used at each feeding. A puppy nursing bottle or small doll's nursing bottle can be used for hand-feeding. A baby lamb nipple or the anticolic nipple used for premature babies is the best type for puppies. Make sure that the hole allows the formula to pass through readily but not too fast. For puppies raised solely by hand, the feedings should be given every four to five hours around the clock.

For hand-fed puppies, it is important after each nursing to take a swab of cotton, dip it in warm water, and massage the puppy between its hind legs until it has urinated and had a bowel movement. This takes the place of the mother's washing, which keeps the pup clean and the bowels open.

For the first day or two following the whelping, feed the mother meat, milk, egg, and other soft foods. She will refuse bulkier food, which would make her have to leave the puppies more often. Soon dog meal can be added. She needs even more food now than when she was in whelp. Ask your veterinarian about extra vitamins and minerals that may be needed. As time goes on, the matron will need more food during lactation; she is feeding her growing litter as well as herself, and she must be well-nourished if she is to make enough milk for her brood. Feed her a minimum of three times daily plus a bedtime snack if she wants it.

The Matron's Job

The matron takes entire care of her puppies throughout the nursing period, feeding, cleaning, warming, and otherwise making them comfortable. She should not, however, be expected to lie with her brood constantly. Gradually she will leave them for longer and longer periods to stretch her legs and perhaps lie in the sun. Arrange the box so the dam (but not the puppies) can come and go as she likes.

By the third week the mother will be getting good and tired of her brood. Their toenails will scratch her breasts, so nip off just the tips with manicure scissors or a dog nail trimmer. Then, every day, offer the puppies baby cereal and milk to lap; the commercially prepared bitch's milk substitutes for orphan puppies are excellent. Pups learn to eat strained baby beef almost immediately. Shortly they will also lap cow's milk or slightly thinned evaporated milk with only a little cereal, and then soaked puppy meal added. But stick to one type of milk. And see that each pup gets his share.

Gradually begin to add puppy meal as thickening for the milk. Or give beef broth and meal occasionally. You may notice that the matron vomits her partially digested meal for her puppies to eat. It won't hurt them—in the wild state it was the natural way for the mother to feed her pups—but on the other hand, the mother herself needs nourishment, so take this as a sign that the puppies need more food.

Weaning Schedules

The following program is one weaning method. You need not follow it exactly since there are other methods just as satis-

factory. Remember that new foods are introduced gradually
to avoid upsetting the puppy's digestion.

3-4 WEEKS

Twice daily: milk and baby cereal or soupy puppy meal
     lapped from a dish.
Once daily: strained baby beef.
Nursing as usual.

4-6 WEEKS

Three times daily: milk with puppy meal—very moist.
Twice daily: beef broth and puppy meal.
Nursing twice daily, then only at night.

6-8 WEEKS

Three times daily: milk thickened with puppy meal.
Twice daily: puppy meal, moistened with beef broth, perhaps
     adding raw or cooked beef.
Nursing only during the night through the sixth week but no
     longer, except perhaps for a backward puppy.

The following program is recommended as the best
method for weaning puppies to self-feeding.

3 WEEKS

Make a mixture of baby cereal or dry puppy meal and
milk to the consistency of a malted milk shake and put this
before the puppies for a three-hour period while the mother is
away from the litter. Nursing as usual after the feeding period.

4 WEEKS

Feed a thickened version of the above mixture for a six-hour period while the mother is away. Nursing as usual after the feeding period.

5 WEEKS

Feed a thick gruel of puppy meal and strained baby beef with water over a twelve-hour period while the mother is away. Feed two batches a day to eliminate spoilage and contamination. Nursing as usual after the feeding period.

6 WEEKS

Feed the same mixture on a self-feeding basis. The pups are now totally weaned. Make the mixture as crumbly as possible, deciding on the proper moisture based on the size of the puppies and the ease they have in eating. Until you are feeding the foods dry, prepare several batches of the mixture a day to eliminate spoilage and contamination.

7-8 WEEKS AND ON

Use the self-feeding method and gradually eliminate the liquid until the food is served dry. Be sure to keep drinking water available at all times.

Gradually cut down on the amount of food given the matron during weaning, to reduce her milk supply. Her milk should dry up of its own accord when she is removed entirely from her puppies. If she still produces ample amounts of milk, however, consult your veterinarian. For weaning to the self-feeding method, see pages 24–25.

16
The Story of the Breeds

The American Kennel Club, the oldest and largest registration organization for purebreed dogs in the United States, recognizes 130 breeds. The breeds eligible for AKC registration are classified into seven groups, based primarily on their common ancestry, the function for which they were originally developed, or physical characteristics. These are:

Sporting Group: Hunting breeds that point, retrieve, and flush feathered game.

Hound Group: Hunting hounds that trail by sight or scent.

Working Group: Guard dogs, watchdogs, war dogs, sled dogs, guide dogs for the blind, and other breeds that serve man.

Terrier Group: Breeds originally developed to ferret out badgers, rabbits, and vermin that burrow underground. "Terrier" derives from *terra*, the Latin word for "earth."

Toy Group: Small breeds, as their name implies, that make charming pets and lapdogs.

Non-Sporting Group: Various breeds that do not fit into any of the other groups. Mostly companion dogs, although some can still perform the tasks for which they were originally developed.

Herding Group: Dogs that herd cattle and sheep.

All of the breeds recognized by the AKC, plus several popular breeds that lack club recognition, are described on the next pages.

Affenpinscher

This pert little fellow is often called the "monkey dog" because of his big bright eyes, bushy eyebrows, prominent chin, and hair tufts about the face. His shaggy coat is hard and wiry. His tail is docked and carried straight up. The ears stand erect when cropped. The breed has been known in Europe since the seventeenth century.

WEIGHT: about 7–8 pounds. HEIGHT: under 10¼ inches. COLOR: black, black and tan, red, or gray.
GROUP: Toy.

Afghan Hound

Thought to have originated in Afghanistan about 3000 B.C., this lithe, slender, but very powerful coursing hound pursued his quarry by sight. He was swift enough to hunt gazelle, leopard, and hare in his native land. Shepherds prized him as a herder and watchdog. He has an aristocratic and distinctive look, with a heavy, silky coat, upcurved tail, and long feathered ears. The striking characteristics of the breed—exotic or "Eastern" expression, with eyes gazing into the distance, long silky topknot, peculiar coat pattern, prominent hipbones, large feet—stand out clearly.

WEIGHT: males 60 pounds; females 50 pounds. HEIGHT: males about 27 inches; females about 25 inches. COLOR: any color.
GROUP: Hound.

Airedale Terrier

The Airedale originated about a century ago in England's Valley of the Aire. Produced by Yorkshire sportsmen by crossing the now-extinct English Black-and-Tan Terrier with the Otterhound, he hunted otter, fox, badger, rats, and small game. He is used for hunting large game in this country, as well as in Canada, Africa, and India, and was one of the first breeds recruited for police and war duties by the British and Germans. He is upstanding and squarely built, with a long head, deep and strong foreface, a powerful jaw with a viselike bite, and a hard, wiry coat.
WEIGHT: 40–60 pounds. HEIGHT: 22–23 inches. COLOR: rich tan with black or dark grizzle markings.
GROUP: Terrier.

Akita

A robust Spitz-type dog from northern Japan, the Akita was bred to hunt deer, wild boar, and bear. He is designated as a national monument in his native country and prized as a protector of the home and a symbol of good health. Helen Keller introduced the breed to the United States. He is a large and powerful dog with much substance and heavy bone. His broad head, forming a blunt triangle, with broad and full muzzle, small dark eyes, and triangular-shaped erect ears, is characteristic of the breed. Balancing the head is a large and full high-set tail carried over the back.
WEIGHT: 75–100 pounds. HEIGHT: males 26–28 inches; females 24–26 inches. COLOR: any color, including white, brindle, or pinto.
GROUP: Working.

Alaskan Malamute

The Malamute, one of the oldest of Arctic sled dogs, was named after the native Innuit tribe, called Mahlemuts, who settled in the northwestern part of Alaska. Originally bred to hunt polar bears and wolves, and to haul sledges, in recent years he has been used for sled-dog racing and in polar expeditions. He is big and sturdy, with a broad and powerful head, erect triangular-shaped ears, slanting eyes, and distinguishing face markings consisting of a cap over the head, with the rest of the face a solid color—or a face marked with the appearance of a mask. His feet are the "snowshoe" type, tight and deep, with well-cushioned pads. His thick and coarse coat is fairly short.

WEIGHT: 75–85 pounds. HEIGHT: 23–25 inches. COLOR: light gray through intermediate shadings to black with white.

GROUP: Working.

American Staffordshire Terrier

Known here for some years as the Pit Bull Terrier, and later the Yankee Terrier, this muscular fellow was renamed the American Staffordshire Terrier in 1972. He comes from Staffordshire, England, where he was bred especially for pit fighting. Here is a well-put-together dog that gives the impression of great strength for his size. Stocky, with well-sprung ribs and well-muscled hindquarters, he has straight forelegs set rather wide apart to permit chest development. He has a broad skull and very pronounced cheek muscles. His tail is long, low, and tapering and his coat short and stiff.

WEIGHT: 40–60 pounds. HEIGHT: 17–19 inches. COLOR: any color. All white, more than 80% white, black and tan, and liver color not desirable.

GROUP: Terrier.

Australian Cattle Dog

Developed by Australian stockmen around the mid-nineteenth century as a dog with enough stamina to drive wild cattle over long distances. Ancestors were blue-merle Collie, Dingo, Dalmatian, and Australian Kelpie stock. Here is an energetic, sturdy, and compact dog with a strong back, muscular shoulders, deep chest, strong and straight forelegs, and broad and muscular hindquarters. The head is broad of jaw, cheeks muscular but not coarse, gradually tapering to a deep and powerful muzzle. The dark brown eyes express alertness and intelligence.
WEIGHT: 30–50 pounds. HEIGHT: males 18–20 inches; females 17–19 inches. COLOR: blue, blue-mottled, red speckle, with or without markings.
GROUP: Herding.

Australian Terrier

A sturdy, sprightly terrier of fairly recent origin, with a heritage as a hunter, farm dog, and companion in his native Australia. His ancestors were British Terrier stock: possibly Cairns, Dandie Dinmonts, Irish, Black-and-Tans, Yorkshires, and prick-eared Skyes. He first appeared at dog shows in his native land in the last part of the nineteenth century. One of the smallest working terriers, this sturdy and spirited dog is low-set and slightly longer than he is high. His harsh coat is good for any weather.
WEIGHT: about 12–14 pounds. HEIGHT: about 10 inches. COLOR: blue-black or silver-black with tan markings on head and legs, sandy, or clear red.
GROUP: Terrier.

Basenji

Tracing to the time of the pharaohs, the Basenji was used in his native Africa on various types of game. He was especially valuable as a hunting dog, for he did not bark. Even today he is known as the "barkless" dog, expressing himself with a sound that is halfway between a chortle and a yodel. He is smooth-coated, short-bodied, clean-limbed, and lithe. His rather large ears stand up straight, and his expression is puzzled due to the wrinkles over his forehead. His tail is set high and carried in a tight curl over to either side.

WEIGHT: 22–24 pounds. HEIGHT: 16–17 inches. COLOR: chestnut red or pure black, or black and tan, all with white feet, chest, and tail tip. GROUP: Hound.

Basset Hound

The Basset is a smooth-coated, slow-moving hound, possibly descended from the now-extinct St. Hubert and other strains of French hounds. He was developed in France and Belgium to follow deer, rabbits, hare, and other game that can be trailed on foot or taken to ground. A tireless hunter, he is noted for scenting ability. He stands low to the ground on heavily boned short legs with wrinkled skin, but is in no sense clumsy. His body is long and his tail is carried gaily in hound fashion. He's a sad-faced dog with a wrinkled brow, long ears, and pendulous lips.

WEIGHT: 40–45 pounds. HEIGHT: about 14 inches. COLOR: any recognized hound color. GROUP: Hound.

Beagle

A very old breed. The origins of the Beagle are mysterious; some authorities believe he originated in Greece. According to Xenophon, there were small scenting hounds that hunted in packs in his day. In Elizabethan England, hounds were divided into two classes, large and small. The small hounds were called "Beagles" and were hunted on hare. Here is a clean-limbed dog with a tight-fitting hound coat that feels quite hard, and a melodious bugle-like voice. His large, soft eyes have a gentle and pleading expression, and his moderately long tail is always wagging. WEIGHT: 15–25 pounds. HEIGHT: two sizes—under 13 inches, and from 13–15 inches. COLOR: any true hound color (usually white, tan, and black).
GROUP: Hound.

Bearded Collie

This shaggy-haired herder, one of Britain's oldest breeds, probably descends from the Magyar Komondorok of Central Europe. He was popular in Scotland as both a working and a show dog during the late Victorian era. The Bearded Collie is an attractive medium-size dog with a fairly long coat that falls naturally flat to either side of the body. His body is lean, slightly longer than it is high, with level back, deep chest, and well-sprung ribs. His large eyes are soft and expressive, and his medium-size drop ears covered with long hair. His coat increases in length from his cheeks, lower lips, and under the chin toward the chest to form the typical beard.

WEIGHT: 40–50 pounds. HEIGHT: males 21–22 inches; females 20–21 inches. COLOR: black, gray, blue, brown, or fawn, with or without markings.
GROUP: Herding.

Bedlington Terrier

The Bedlington is named for a mining region in Northumberland County in England, but was first called the Rothbury Terrier. His origins are mysterious. In 1825, however, a female named Phoebe, owned by Joseph Ainsley of Bedlington, was mated to a Rothbury dog and produced the first offspring to have been called a Bedlington Terrier. Here is a lithe, well-balanced dog, flat-ribbed, with deep brisket and a back naturally arched over the loin. His scimitar-shaped tail is set low. The narrow but deep and rounded head is covered with a profuse topknot. The inch-long coat is a mixture of hard and soft hair and, when trimmed, gives the dog its lamblike silhouette.
WEIGHT: 17–23 pounds. HEIGHT: 15½–16½ inches. COLOR: blue, sandy, liver, blue and tan, sandy and tan, liver and tan.
GROUP: Terrier.

Belgian Malinois

One of three Belgian sheepherding breeds, the Malinois is distinguished by its short easy-care coat. It shares a common background with the Belgian Sheepdog and Tervuren. Here is an agile, well-muscled square dog whose conformation gives the impression of depth and solidity. His head is strong and clean-cut, with top skull flat rather than round, muzzle somewhat tapered, dark brown eyes and erect ears. His tail, held low at rest, raises with a curl which is strongest at the tip.

WEIGHT: 55–70 pounds. HEIGHT: males 24–26 inches; females 22–24 inches. COLOR: rich fawn to mahogany with black overlay.
GROUP: Herding.

Belgian Sheepdog

This breed is also known as the Groenendael. Its origins date back to Brussels in the late nineteenth century. In addition to herding, Belgian Sheepdogs have also distinguished themselves on the battlefields during World War I, as police dogs, and in border-patrol work. Here is a handsome, strong, and well-muscled animal, square in appearance with an exceedingly proud carriage of head and neck. His black weather-resistant coat is especially long like a collarette around the neck, with abundant long fringes down the backs of the front legs and on the breeches and tail.
WEIGHT: 55–70 pounds. HEIGHT: males 24–26 inches; females 22–24 inches. COLOR: black.
GROUP: Herding.

Belgian Tervuren

Developed for herding abilities from the same European working stock as the Belgian Sheepdog and Malinois. Except for coat color, he is similar in conformation to the Belgian Sheepdog. He is an elegant, medium-size dog, square in appearance. He has a long, well-chiseled head, with strong and powerful jaws, dark brown eyes, and erect ears. In addition to his ability as a herder, he can protect his master's person and property without being overly aggressive.
WEIGHT: 55–70 pounds. HEIGHT: males 24–26 inches; females 22–24 inches. COLOR: rich fawn to russet mahogany, with black overlay.
GROUP: Herding.

Bernese Mountain Dog

The ancestors of this breed were brought into Switzerland more than 2,000 years ago by invading Roman soldiers. The dogs worked as drovers, drawing wagons for basket weavers, and acted as watchdogs on farms in the canton of Berne. A handsome, strong-boned dog, the Bernese has a long, silky jet-black coat with rust markings on the cheeks and spots over each eye, on all four legs, on each side of the chest, and under the tail. A white blaze embellishes the muzzle and forehead, white chest markings form an inverted cross, and there is white on the feet and the tip of the tail.

WEIGHT: 80–110 pounds. HEIGHT: males 24¹/₂–27¹/₂ inches; females 22¹/₂–25¹/₂ inches. COLOR: black with rich rust and clear white markings. GROUP: Working.

Bichon Frise

This white powder puff of a dog traveled a great deal through antiquity. Spanish sailors carried the Bichon Frise (pronounced Bee-*shawn* Free-*zay*) to the Canary Islands. They were rediscovered in the fourteenth century by Italian seamen, who returned them to the Continent, where they became great favorites of the nobility. This is a sturdy, squarely built dog whose merry temperament is evidenced by the plumed tail he carries jauntily over his back and by his dark-eyed inquisitive expression. His head is covered with a topknot of hair that blends into the long ear feathering, and when combined with the furnishings of the beard and mustache, creates an overall rounded impression.

WEIGHT: 14–20 pounds. HEIGHT: 9–12 inches. COLOR: white (may have buff, cream, or apricot shadings on ears or body). GROUP: Non-Sporting.

Bloodhound

Probably the world's first "police dog." The Bloodhound's history goes back to ancient times, where authorities believe he was known throughout the Mediterranean countries long before the Christian Era. His European descendants were St. Hubert hounds that crossed the English Channel with William the Conqueror. From that day to this, he has put his incomparable scenting ability to good use in trailing murderers, kidnappers, and lost children. The Bloodhound's skin is thin and extremely loose, this being more apparent around the head and neck, where it hangs in deep folds. His ears are long and drooping, his face wrinkled, his expression noble and dignified.

WEIGHT: 80–110 pounds. HEIGHT: males 25–27 inches; females 23–25 inches. COLOR: black and tan; red and tan; tawny.
GROUP: Hound.

Border Terrier

The Border, one of Britain's oldest terrier breeds, was raised in the Scottish borderland to kill powerful hill foxes. His conformation is such that he is small enough to run his quarry to ground, yet tall enough to follow a horse for long hours and long distances. He has a rather narrow but square-shaped body and an otterlike head. His small V-shaped ears are wide-set, dropping forward close to the cheeks. The coat is hard and wiry.

WEIGHT: 11½–15½ pounds. HEIGHT: 12–14 inches. COLOR: red, grizzle and tan, blue and tan, or wheaten.
GROUP: Terrier.

Borzoi

Once known as Russian Wolfhounds, Borzois were used centuries ago by Russian czars and aristocrats to chase wolves across the steppes. Extremely tall and agile, they hunt by sight. The Borzoi's body is slender and graceful, the head long and lean and inclined to be Roman-nosed, the ears small, and the eyes dark and slanting with an intelligent expression. The coat is long and silky, with a profuse neck frill, while the long tail is carried in a graceful curve.
WEIGHT: males 75–105 pounds; females 15–20 pounds less. HEIGHT: males at least 28 inches; females at least 26 inches. COLOR: any color or combination of colors.
GROUP: Hound.

Boston Terrier

A native American breed, the Boston Terrier is the outgrowth of a mating made about 1870 of a cross-bred Bulldog/white English Terrier named Hooper's Judge with a Bulldog-like white female named Gyp or Kate. The breed, actually developed in Boston, was first exhibited in 1889 as a Round Head or Bull Terrier. Square-headed, short-nosed, and square-bodied, he has erect ears, either cropped or natural bat, large round eyes, and a short, satiny coat marked with white.
WEIGHT: 15–25 pounds. HEIGHT: 15–16 inches. COLOR: brindle or black with white markings.
GROUP: Non-Sporting.

Bouvier des Flandres

First a cattle driver in Belgium, the Bouvier later gained fame as a police and army dog in his native land. The breed was nearly destroyed during World War I; those that survived helped to restore the Bouvier. Here is a powerful dog, upstanding, short in back, medium-long in head, with mustache, beard, and bushy eyebrows. The rough-coated ears are triangular-shaped when cropped. The tousled body coat is rough and hard, while the tail is docked.

WEIGHT: 60–90 pounds. HEIGHT: males 24 1/2–27 1/2 inches; females 23 1/2–26 1/2 inches. COLOR: fawn to black, passing through salt and pepper, gray and brindle.

GROUP: Herding.

Boxer

The present-day Boxer, a cousin to all the recognized Bulldog-type breeds, was perfected in Germany about a century ago. His ancestors were used for dog fighting and bull-baiting until the sport was outlawed in 1835. His name probably comes from the way he uses his forepaws when fighting or playing. Clean-limbed but muscular and rather stocky, he is a short-backed, medium-size dog with a smooth and shiny coat. He is rather square-headed—his forehead showing a slight furrow between the dark brown eyes—with black-masked muzzle and erect ears. He is normally undershot; his lower jaw protrudes beyond the upper and curves slightly upward.

WEIGHT: 55–70 pounds. HEIGHT: males 22¹/₂–25 inches; females 21–23¹/₂ inches. COLOR: fawn or brindle, often marked with white.
GROUP: Working.

Briard

Named for the province of Brie, the Briard is an ancient breed, dating back to the eighth century, when he was depicted in tapestries. He defended his charges against wolves and poachers in early times. He has been in America since the Revolution, having been brought to this continent by Thomas Jefferson and the Marquis de Lafayette. Square and powerful, the Briard has a short back, a rather large and long head, and heavy hair falling over the ears, eyes, and muzzle. His ears are semierect, while his tail is long, low, and well-feathered. The coat is long, slightly wavy, and coarse in texture. His hind legs have double dewclaws.
WEIGHT: 70–85 pounds. HEIGHT: males 23–27 inches; females 22–25¹/₂ inches. COLOR: uniform colors, except white. Dark colors—black, gray, tawny—preferred.
GROUP: Herding.

Brittany

Developed in France nearly 200 years ago, the Brittany is unique as a spaniel that points game. He is a vigorous, energetic worker, with a short body and straight back, deep chest, and well-rounded ribs. His skull is slightly wedge-shaped, with muzzle gradually tapered as it approaches the nostrils. His deep-set eyes are protected by heavy, expressive brows. His ears fall close to the head. He may be tailless, or is otherwise short-tailed, and his coat is flat or wavy with slight feathering.

WEIGHT: 30–40 pounds. HEIGHT: 17½–20½ inches. COLOR: orange and white, or liver and white, lightly ticked.
GROUP: Sporting.

Brussels Griffon

The Brussels Griffon was developed fairly recently from several breeds, among them the German Affenpinscher, the Belgian street dog, the Pug, and the Ruby Spaniel. He was an efficient ratter in his native Belgium, but here he is usually a pet and companion. He is short-backed and chunky, with an almost human expression. The domed forehead bulges over large, widely set eyes, and the ears stand semierect. The nose is extremely short and tipped up, the muzzle broad. Bushy eyebrows, whiskers, and cheek fringes complete a peculiar but appealing picture. There are two distinct types of coat: rough and smooth.
WEIGHT: 8–10 pounds. HEIGHT: about 8 inches. COLOR: reddish brown, black, or black with reddish-brown markings.
GROUP: Toy.

Bulldog

The Bulldog most likely originated centuries ago in the British Isles, and was used for bull-baiting until 1835, when the cruel sport was abolished by law. His low-slung body protected him from the thrusts of the bull, just as his short nose and long, heavy underjaw made possible the famous lock grip. He is a smooth-coated, massively made dog with a thick-set, low-slung body. His head is very large and broad, his face extremely short with thick, pendant chops, or lips that completely overhang the lower jaw at each side. His tail may be either straight or screwed. He moves in a rather loose-jointed, shuffling, sidewise motion, giving the characteristic "roll."

WEIGHT: 40–50 pounds. HEIGHT: 14–16 inches. COLOR: red brindle; all other brindles; solid white; solid red, fawn, or fallow; piebald.   .
GROUP: Non-Sporting.

Bullmastiff

A combination of 60% Mastiff and 40% Bulldog, the Bullmastiff was developed in England about 1860 to keep large estates and game preserves free from poachers. Fearless and obedient, they accompanied gamekeepers on their late-night rounds. Because they were less visible, the darker brindles were preferred to the more usual fawn colors. Here is a powerful-looking, short-backed, compact dog with a large, broad head, dark eyes, and a fair amount of wrinkle on the black-masked face. Ears are V-shaped and carried close to the cheeks. The tail, strong at the root and tapering to the end, may be short or curved. The coat is short and dense, giving good weather protection.
WEIGHT: males 110–130 pounds; females 100–120 pounds. HEIGHT: males 25–27 inches; females 24–26 inches. COLOR: red, fawn, or brindle.
GROUP: Working.

Bull Terrier (White)

The Bull Terrier resulted from a cross made about the year 1835 between the Bulldog and the now-extinct white English Terrier. The result was called the Bull and Terrier. Later crosses to the Spanish Pointer added size. Today he is a most friendly fellow unless provoked. His head is long and almost egg-shaped, with unbroken profile that curves gently downward—that is, without any step down from skull to muzzle—while his ears are erect and his dark eyes small and slanting. His body is short, strong, and muscular with big-boned legs. His thick, short coat fits like a glove, and his tail is straight, set low, and carried horizontally.

WEIGHT: 45–55 pounds. HEIGHT: 19–21 inches. COLOR: all white, though markings on head are permissible.
GROUP: Terrier.

Bull Terrier (Colored)

The Colored Bull Terrier, a separate variety since 1936, is exactly like the White Bull Terrier, except that his color may be anything other than white, or any color with white markings. The color most commonly seen is a rich, dark brindle, often with white markings.

Cairn Terrier

The modern Cairn is a descendant of a working terrier from the Isle of Skye, off the coast of Scotland. He was developed for bolting otter, fox, badger, and other game from the cairns or stone heaps on the shores of the isle. The Cairn is a hardy, short-legged working terrier with a well-muscled body, deep ribs, and strong hindquarters. The head, shorter and wider than all other terriers', has a rather pointed muzzle and is well furnished with hair—slightly softer than his body coat—giving him a rather foxy expression. His coat is hard and weather-resistant.
WEIGHT: 13–14 pounds. HEIGHT: 9½–10 inches. COLOR: any color except white.
GROUP: Terrier.

Chihuahua

The world's smallest breed of dog gets his name from the Mexican state of Chihuahua. His origins are mysterious, although relics from the ancient Toltec civilization in northern Mexico show small dogs with large ears that closely resemble modern Chihuahuas. He is all dog, alert and active. He has a well-rounded "apple-dome" skull, with lean cheeks and jaw, and slightly pointed nose. His ears are large, usually erect and flaring slightly outward; his eyes are full and shining. The back is short, the bones rather fine, the tail fairly long and carried away from the body. There are two coat types, smooth and long.

WEIGHT: under 6 pounds. HEIGHT: about 5 inches. COLOR: any color, solid, marked, or splashed.

GROUP: Toy.

Chow Chow

The Chow Chow dates back more than 2,000 years to the Han dynasty in China, where he was used as a hunting dog. His name derives from a Pidgin English term describing bric-a-brac sold by Oriental traders during the latter part of the eighteenth century. Aloof and scowling, he is a massive, squarely built dog with short back, well-rounded ribs, and deep, muscular chest. His head is massive in proportion to his size, with short muzzle, broad nose, deep-set dark eyes, small erect ears, and true blue-black tongue. He is clothed in a heavily furred offstanding coat, accentuated by a ruff around his neck.

WEIGHT: 50–70 pounds. HEIGHT: 18–20 inches. COLOR: any color (black, red, blue, and fawn most often seen).

GROUP: Non-Sporting.

Collie

Possibly named from the "colley," or black-faced sheep he guarded in the Scottish Highlands, the Collie comes in two varieties, rough and smooth, both of which are very old. He undoubtedly appears more often in literature than any other breed. With his long, heavy coat, mane, and frill, his proud carriage and lithe gait, the rough Collie is the perfect picture of grace. His head is long and slender, his eyes almond-shaped and slanting. His ears are half-raised, turning over to the front. His body is just a trifle longer than it is high, and his legs are straight and strong. His long tail is carried low with a slight upward twist or swirl. The smooth Collie is exactly like the rough variety except for the coat, which is short, dense, and flat, with an abundant undercoat.

WEIGHT: males 60–75 pounds; females 50–65 pounds. HEIGHT: males 24–26 inches; females 22–24 inches. COLOR: sable and white, tricolor, blue merle, and white.
GROUP: Herding.

Coonhound, Black and Tan

Probably descended from the now-extinct English Talbot Hound, and then through crosses of Bloodhounds and this country's Virginia Foxhounds. Coonhounds have been popular for years in certain sections of this country, where they are used for trailing and treeing raccoons. They also trail almost any kind of four-footed game, including bear and mountain lion. Quick and alert, these dogs cover ground easily. The body is slightly longer than it is high, the back level, powerful, and strong, the chest deep, and the ribs well sprung. The head is cleanly modeled, the flews or upper lips hang in true hound style, and the long ears drop in graceful folds. The coat is short and thick.

WEIGHT: 55–75 pounds. HEIGHT: males 25–27 inches; females 23–25 inches. COLOR: black with rich tan markings.

GROUP: Hound.

Dachshund

"Dachshund" is the German name for "badgerhound," a dog that follows its quarry to earth. Badger dogs with long bodies and short legs have been known since the fifteenth century. The breed comes in three coat varieties—smooth (or short-coated), longhaired, and wirehaired—and two sizes, standard and miniature. Exceptionally short-legged, long-bodied, and deep in chest, the Dachshund is sturdy, quick, and determined. His head is tapered and his drop ears are beautifully rounded. His forelegs are not quite straight and his feet turn just a trifle outward. The tail is fairly long and carried off from the body, but not high. The miniature Dachshund is smaller in size but otherwise exactly like the standard.

WEIGHT: standard 18–20 pounds; miniature 7–10 pounds. HEIGHT: standard to 9 inches; miniature about 5 inches. COLOR: Smooth—solid red; red-yellow; yellow; brindle; black, chocolate, gray (blue), and white, each with tan markings; and dappled. Wirehaired—any color. Longhaired—same as Smooth.

GROUP: Hound.

Dalmatian

Experts cannot pinpoint the origins of the spotted Dalmatian, named for the former Austrian province of Dalmatia, but there is no question he has been around a long time. Originally a hunting dog, although his love of running under carriages as guard and companion nicknamed him "Coach Dog." Also known as a firehouse dog, he will run beside or ride on engines. He has also served as war dog, drought dog, and shepherd. The Dalmatian is clean-limbed, with head of fair length. His sparkling eyes are rimmed with black or liver. His ears are wide at the base and taper gradually to a rounded point, while his tail is carried with a slight upward curve. His short coat is hard, dense, and glossy.

WEIGHT: 45–55 pounds. HEIGHT: 19–23 inches. COLOR: background of pure white marked with small and well-defined black or liver spots.

GROUP: Non-Sporting.

Dandie Dinmont Terrier

The Dandie Dinmont was bred from the rough-haired terriers of the border country between England and Scotland, where he was known for his gameness on badger, fox, otter, rats, and weasels. The breed gained popularity and its name from a leading character in Sir Walter Scott's novel *Guy Mannering*, published in 1814. He is a long-bodied dog, rather low at the shoulder, with an arch over the loin, a well-developed chest, and short legs with strong muscular development and bone. His large head is covered with soft, silky hair, and his luminous dark eyes are large and expressive. The moderately long tail curves upward like a scimitar. The body coat is a mixture of hard and soft hair.

WEIGHT: 18–24 pounds. HEIGHT: 8–11 inches. COLOR: pepper (bluish black to silvery gray) or mustard (reddish brown to pale fawn). GROUP: Terrier.

Deerhound, Scottish

Once called a rough Greyhound, the Deerhound is indeed a member of the Greyhound family. He was a sight-hunter of deer and stags in the Scottish Highlands in the seventeenth century, so valued that a lord condemned to death could purchase his reprieve with a leash of Deerhounds. One of our largest breeds, he has a deep chest and back line arched over the loin. His head is long, skull rather flat, muzzle pointed and covered with a silky mustache and beard. The ears are small, set high

and folded back, sometimes being raised semierect in excitement. The tail, which reaches almost to the ground, is carried dropped or curved. The harsh and wiry coat is three to four inches long.
WEIGHT: males 85–110 pounds; females 75–90 pounds. HEIGHT: males at least 30 inches; females at least 28 inches. COLOR: dark blue-gray preferred; darker or lighter grays or brindles; yellow; sandy red; red fawn. GROUP: Hound.

Doberman Pinscher

The Doberman Pinscher takes his name from Louis Doberman, a German tax collector who developed the breed about 1890 by crossing shorthaired Shepherd, Rottweiler, old English Black-and-Tan Terrier, and German Pinscher stock. Known far and wide as an outstanding guard dog, watchdog, police and war dog, he is very elegant-looking and clean of line throughout. His head is long and wedge-shaped, and his ears are normally cropped and carried erect. His eyes are almond-shaped rather than round, and his lips are tight. The back is short, and the tail docked, while the smooth, hard coat fits close to the skin.
WEIGHT: 55–75 pounds. HEIGHT: males 26–28 inches; females 24–26 inches. COLOR: black, red, blue, and fawn (Isabella) with rust markings. GROUP: Working.

English Toy Spaniel

English Toy Spaniels, probably native to Japan or China, have been known for four centuries in England, where they were pets and favorites of royalty. There are four varieties, similar in type but different in color.

They are compact and short-bodied dogs, rather broad in chest. The unusual skull is well-domed, with large, dark, widely set eyes. The stop, or indentation between the eyes, is unusually deep—deep enough on good specimens to bury a small marble in it—while the short nose is slightly turned up, as is the underjaw. The coat is long, silky, and wavy.
WEIGHT: 9–12 pounds. HEIGHT: about 10 inches. COLOR: King Charles—black and tan; Prince Charles—white, black, and tan; Blenheim—red and white; Ruby—solid red.
GROUP: Toy.

Foxhound, American

Descended from English stock owned by Robert Brooke, who sailed with his family and pack of hounds in 1650 to what is now the state of Maryland. Later crosses were made with other British and French hounds imported by early settlers. The Foxhound's head is fairly long with a straight and square-cut muzzle. The drop ears are set low and their tips are rounded. The large eyes are hazel or brown, with a gentle and pleading expression. The body is strong and muscular and the coat is smooth and hard.
WEIGHT: 55–70 pounds. HEIGHT: males 22–25 inches; females 21–24 inches. COLOR: any color (black, tan, and white most common).
GROUP: Hound.

Foxhound, English

The English Foxhound was bred primarily for the sport of fox hunting. Present type developed through select breeding over the past 150 years. In Britain today there are more than 250 packs of trained Foxhounds. Their breeding is controlled by the masters of hounds who lead fox hunts. The English Foxhound is similar to his American cousin but sturdier in build.

WEIGHT: 55–70 pounds. HEIGHT: 21–25 inches. COLOR: any hound color (black, tan, and white most popular).

GROUP: Hound.

Fox Terriers

Fox Terriers were developed late in the eighteenth century for fox hunting. Some say Smooths are older and descend from old English terrier stock, Greyhounds, and Beagles. Wires derive from rough-coated black-and-tan working terriers. Smooths and Wires were liberally crossed in early days. For nearly one hundred years in this country, Fox Terriers have been registered and shown as two varieties of the same breed. But as of June 1, 1985, separate breed standards became effective for the Smooth Fox Terrier and the Wire Fox Terrier. These are stylish dogs, short-backed, squarely built, straight of leg, and quick of movement. Their heads are long and lean with dark eyes that are full of fire and intelligence. The Smooth's coat is flat, hard, and dense. The Wire's coat is longer, broken, of wiry texture, with a softer undercoat.

WEIGHT: about 16–18 pounds. HEIGHT: 14$\frac{1}{2}$–15$\frac{1}{2}$ inches. COLOR: Smooth—predominantly white; brindle, red, or liver markings objectionable; Wire—predominantly white; brindle, red, liver, or slaty blue markings objectionable.

GROUP: Terrier.

French Bulldog

His ancestors were toy English Bulldogs, sent to France in large numbers. Crossed with various other breeds, their progeny were given the name Boule-Dogue Français. Here is a rather heavy-boned, compactly built little dog with a short, well-rounded body, broader at the front than at the back. His head is large and square with slightly rounded forehead, short, broad muzzle, and well-developed cheeks. His medium-size eyes are dark in color and set wide apart. His most unusual feature is perfect bat ears, broad at the base, long and rounded on top. They are set high on the head and carried erect, with their openings directly forward. The naturally short tail may be either straight or screw, while the coat is short and glossy.

WEIGHT: 18–28 pounds. HEIGHT: about 12 inches. COLOR: brindle, fawn, white, brindle and white.

GROUP: Non-Sporting.

German Shepherd Dog

Descending from Old World sheepherding types, the German Shepherd was developed as a breed in Germany late in the nineteenth century, and has been in America since the early part of the twentieth. Developed as a worker, he is a rugged animal of great courage and intelligence, an outstanding herder, guard dog, guide dog for the blind, police and army dog, as well as a companion. He is gracefully rounded, his body a trifle longer than it is tall, the chest deep, the forelegs straight with strong and springy pasterns, the hindquarters well-muscled and deeply angulated. The head is clean-cut, the muzzle wedge-shaped, the jaws strong. The large pointed ears stand erect, the eyes are almond-shaped and dark, while the coat is harsh and close-lying.

WEIGHT: 60–85 pounds. HEIGHT: males 24–26 inches; females 22–24 inches. COLOR: most colors permissible except white.
GROUP: Herding.

Great Dane

The Great Dane originated in Germany, not in Denmark as one might suppose, and has been known as a distinct type for over 400 years. Development of the modern type began in Germany in the nineteenth century, where he was used as a boarhound, and continued in England and the United States. He is a giant breed, dignified and majestic, with a powerful, well-formed body. His head is long, narrow, and finely chiseled, his muzzle deep and square with full flews. The eyes are usually dark and very bright; the ears should be well-pointed and carried erect when cropped, otherwise they drop forward close to the cheeks. The coat is short, thick, and glossy.

WEIGHT: 120–160 pounds. HEIGHT: males over 30 inches; females over 28 inches. COLOR: brindle, fawn, blue, black, harlequin (pure white with black patches).
GROUP: Working.

Great Pyrenees

An ancient breed that descends from the earliest-known Asian Mastiffs. He was named for the Pyrenees Mountains, where he worked as a shepherd dog and protected his flocks from wolves and bears. He was a

favorite of the French royal court in the seventeenth century. Immense size and a majestic air mark the Great Pyrenees. His head is large and wedge-shaped, measuring 10 to 12 inches from dome to nose; with slanting dark eyes and V-shaped ears. His body is powerful, his bushy tail long and low in repose, but curled high over the back and "making the wheel" when alert. His coat is his crowning glory—heavy and fine underneath, with a top layer of thick, coarser hair, straight or a trifle wavy.
WEIGHT: males 100–125 pounds; females 90–115 pounds. HEIGHT: males 27–32 inches; females 25–29 inches. COLOR: all white, or principally white with markings of badger, gray, or varying shades of tan.
GROUP: Working.

Greyhound

Known for several thousand years before the time of Christ, the Greyhound was used by Egyptian pharaohs to chase hare and gazelle. The first description of the breed was written by Ovid, the Roman poet, who lived from 43 B.C. to A.D. 17. The Greyhound is a typical sight-hunter, streamlined for speed, very tall and slender. His back is arched, his chest is deep, and his legs are straight. The head is long and narrow, ears small, thrown back and folded as if held down by the wind. His long and fine tail is carried in a slight curve, and his coat is short.
WEIGHT: males 65–70 pounds; females 60–65 pounds. HEIGHT: 26–28 inches. COLOR: any color.
GROUP: Hound.

Harrier

Believed to be brought into Great Britain by the Normans almost 800 years ago, the Harrier gets his name from the Norman-Saxon word for "hound." His ancestors were the now-extinct Talbot and St. Hubert Hounds and French Bassets. Known in the U.S. since colonial times, he was generally used in packs to hunt hare. He looks like a small Foxhound, although he is shorter in back. The Harrier is strong, with a deep chest, well-sprung ribs, straight legs, and round catlike feet. His head is medium in size and rather long, with closely hanging drop ears. His tail is carried off from the body. The coat is short and hard.

WEIGHT: 40–50 pounds. HEIGHT: 19–21 inches. COLOR: hound color—combinations of black, tan, and white.

GROUP: Hound.

Ibizan Hound

One of the oldest breeds; this regal hound's history traces back to 3400 B.C., when he was owned and used for hunting by the Egyptian pharaohs. Phoenician traders probably carried his ancestors to Ibiza, off the coast of Spain, from which he derives his name. He is a tall and agile dog used to hunt rabbits, hare, and other game. He has a level back and a narrow, deep chest. His head is long and narrow, with prominent muzzle and strong jaw. His small eyes range in color from clear amber to caramel. He has a short or wire-haired coat, both types being hard in texture.

WEIGHT: 42–50 pounds. HEIGHT: males 23¹/₂–27¹/₂ inches; females 22¹/₂–26 inches. COLOR: red and white; lion and white; solid white; solid red.

GROUP: Hound.

Irish Terrier

One of the oldest terriers, the Irish differs from the others in being slightly houndlike in outline; in fact, he looks very much like a small Wolfhound. His courage and disregard for danger, particularly as a messenger dog in wartime, earned him the nickname "daredevil." His body is fairly long, his back strong, his legs straight with plenty of bone and muscle, and his tail set high and docked. His head is rather long and narrow, with especially powerful jaws and teeth. The eyes are dark and full of fire, the ears small, V-shaped, and dropping forward close to the cheeks. The coat is dense and wiry.

WEIGHT: 25–27 pounds. HEIGHT: about 18 inches. COLOR: bright red, golden red, red wheaten, or wheaten.

GROUP: Terrier.

Irish Wolfhound

The Irish Wolfhound was Ireland's ancient pursuer of wolves and elk, and later a guard against the robber bands that rode by night. First written mention of the breed occurred in A.D. 391. He is the tallest of all dogs and possibly the most powerful. His back is rather long, his loins arched, chest very deep, forelegs straight, and thighs muscular and strong. His head is long; his muzzle is also long and slightly tapering. The ears are small, thrown back and folded like those of the Greyhound. His long tail is carried in a slight curve, and his coat is hard and wiry.

WEIGHT: minimum 105–120 pounds. HEIGHT: minimum 30–32 inches.
COLOR: gray, brindle, red, black, pure white, fawn.
GROUP: Hound.

Italian Greyhound

Thought to have originated in the Mediterranean basin more than
2,000 years ago, the Italian Greyhound was a favorite of European sover-
eigns, including Francis I of France, Frederick the Great of Prussia,
Catherine the Great of Russia, and Queen Victoria. He is slender, elegant, and graceful, a true Greyhound in miniature. The head is long and
narrow, the muzzle fine, the eyes dark and expressive. The small ears are
thrown back and folded. The body is arched over the loin, the chest is
deep, and the tail is long and carried low. The legs are finely boned, with
long feet like those of a hare. The hair is thin and glossy, satiny and soft to
the touch.
WEIGHT: 6–10 pounds. HEIGHT: 13–15 inches. COLOR: any color and markings, except brindle and tan markings.
GROUP: Toy.

Japanese Chin

The Japanese Chin was the pampered pet of Oriental royalty for
centuries and was permitted to associate only with those of noble birth.
Commodore Perry first introduced them to the West in 1853. A lively,
well-mannered fellow, the Chin spells quality from nose to tail. His head
is large for his size, with a broad skull rounded in front. His dark lustrous

eyes are prominent and set wide apart, while his small V-shaped ears fall slightly forward. His muzzle is broad, full, and very short. The body is square and compact, legs finely boned and tail heavily feathered and carried up over the back. The long and silky coat has a tendency to stand out, especially around the neck, so as to create a thick mane or ruff.

WEIGHT: 5–7 pounds. HEIGHT: about 10 inches. COLOR: black and white or red and white.

GROUP: Toy.

Keeshond

Developed from the same strains of Arctic stock that produced the Chow Chow, Samoyed, Pomeranian, and Norwegian Elkhound. The Keeshond (pronounced Kayze-hawnd) was Holland's barge dog, named for Kees de Gyselaer, leader of the patriots' party during the political strife of the eighteenth century. True to Arctic type, he is short-coupled and compact, with strong chest and straight legs. His head is wedge-shaped, with strong muzzle of medium length, and triangular ears that stand erect. The dark, slightly slanting eyes have unusual penciled lines running upward from the outer corners to the ears. The body is abundantly covered with long, straight hair that stands out from a downy undercoat.

WEIGHT: 35–45 pounds. HEIGHT: 17–18 inches. COLOR: mixture of gray and black (outer coat black-tipped, with gray or cream undercoat).

GROUP: Non-Sporting.

Kerry Blue Terrier

Born in the mountains of County Kerry, the Kerry Blue has been known as a sporting terrier for more than a century in Ireland, where he

was used for farmwork and all manner of hunting and retrieving. Puppies are usually born black, then clear to their blue color by eighteen months of age. The head is long, with flat cheeks and powerful jaw, and small dark eyes that are very keen in expression. The back is short, the legs fairly heavy in bone, the tail docked and upstanding. The coat is soft and wavy. WEIGHT: 30–40 pounds. HEIGHT: 17–20 inches. COLOR: deep slate to light blue-gray.
GROUP: Terrier.

Komondor

Imposing in size and strength, the Komondor guarded sheep in Hungary for a thousand years or more, and fought courageously against wolves, bears, and other animals larger than himself. He's rather shaggy and unkempt-looking, but that is the way he should be. His slightly long body has a deep and powerful chest, wide, sloping rump, and well-boned and muscular legs. His head is fairly broad, his blocky muzzle somewhat shorter than his skull, and his eyes are brown. His head and body are covered with an unusually heavy white coat, in which the coarser hairs of the outer coat trap the softer undercoat and naturally form permanent strong cords. Grown dogs are covered with these tassellike cords.
WEIGHT: 80–110 pounds. HEIGHT: males at least 25½ inches; females at least 23½ inches. COLOR: white.
GROUP: Working.

Kuvasz

The Kuvasz is an ancient breed whose ancestors came from Tibet. Named from the Turkish *Kwaz*, meaning "armed guard of the nobility," he was developed to his present form in Hungary and reached great prominence during the reign of King Matthias I in the fifteenth century. There he served as a sheep herder and protected noblemen against attacks by the populace. He is characterized by a sturdy build. His body is deep-chested, broad in back, heavy-boned and muscular, and is covered with luxurious white hair. His head, considered to be the most beautiful part of the breed, is complemented by beautiful dark brown, somewhat slanted eyes and V-shaped ears.

WEIGHT: males 100–115 pounds; females 70–90 pounds. HEIGHT: males 28–30 inches; females 26–28 inches. COLOR: white.
GROUP: Working.

Lakeland Terrier

First known as the Patterdale, the Lakeland Terrier was later named for the Lake District of England, which, like so many northern counties, developed its own special sporting terrier to guard against foxes and other vermin that raided farmers' sheepfolds. The Lakeland is a workmanlike dog of square, sturdy build, with strong-boned straight legs and muscular hindquarters. The head is well-balanced, with almost straight-sided cheeks, broad muzzle, and dark, moderately small eyes. The V-shaped ears fold just above the top of the skull. The weather-resistant coat is hard and wiry.

WEIGHT: about 17 pounds. HEIGHT: about 13½–14½ inches. COLOR: blue, black, liver, black and tan, blue and tan, red, red grizzle, grizzle and tan, or wheaten.
GROUP: Terrier.

Lhasa Apso

The Lhasa Apso, native to the lamaseries around the sacred city of Tibet, was valued as a watchdog inside the homes of the nobles and in monasteries. He is an ancient breed, dating back, say some authorities, to 800 B.C. Once cherished as a talisman to bring good luck and drive away evil spirits. Longer than he is high, the Lhasa is covered with a long, straight, heavy coat, with abundant facial hair. His short, muscular legs are covered with hair right down to and including the round, catlike feet. The head is narrow, muzzle fairly short, eyes medium in size, ears hanging and fringed. The tail is well-feathered, and carried up over the back in a screw, sometimes with a kink at the end.

WEIGHT: 13–20 pounds. HEIGHT: 8–11 inches. COLOR: all colors, with or without dark tips to ears and beard.
GROUP: Non-Sporting.

Maltese

Named for the Isle of Malta in the Mediterranean Sea, the Maltese was the favorite lapdog of highborn ladies of ancient Greece and Rome. Many ancient authors, including Strabo and Pliny the Elder, described the breed's beauty and intelligence. He is a sprightly little dog, covered with a mantle of silky white hair, which is parted down the back and hangs long on either side. The head is fairly long, the muzzle tapered but not snippy, the feathered ears dropped. The eyes are round and dark, preferably black-rimmed. The plumed tail is carried gracefully over the back.

WEIGHT: under 7 pounds. HEIGHT: 6–9 inches. COLOR: white.
GROUP: Toy.

Manchester Terrier (Standard)

The Manchester Terrier, a descendant of the old Black-and Tan Terrier, comes from England's Manchester district, where rat catching and rabbit coursing were the principal sports. A very fast and alert dog, he is sleek and streamlined, with narrow chest, short back, and slightly arched loin. His head is narrow, slightly wedge-shaped, and tapering to tight-lipped jaws. His dark eyes are small and sparkling; the thin ears erect when cropped; the short, fine coat tight to the skin. The moderately short tail tapers to a fine point.

WEIGHT: 12–22 pounds. HEIGHT: 15–17 inches. COLOR: black and tan. GROUP: Terrier.

Manchester Terrier (Toy)

Like his big brother the Manchester Terrier, the Toy variety can trace his ancestry back to the now-extinct Black-and-Tan Terrier, one of the oldest British breeds. He is a smaller replica of the Standard except for the ears. Cropped ears, acceptable for the Standard, are disqualifications for the Toy. He has a long, narrow head, tapering to the nose, with clean-sided cheeks and tight lips. His eyes are black and sparkling. His body is short, the legs straight, feet compact and well-arched, the tail tapering to a point. The coat is smooth and glossy.

WEIGHT: under 12 pounds. HEIGHT: about 7–9 inches. COLOR: black and tan.

GROUP: Toy.

Mastiff

Probably of Asiatic origin, the Mastiff descends from ancient fighting dogs. In 55 B.C. he fought beside his masters in Britain against Caesar's Roman legions, and later at the Circus in Rome, when dogs were pitted against bulls, bears, lions, and tigers. So useful was he as a guard against wild animals that Anglo-Saxon law required him on large estates. He is a massive and powerfully built dog, slightly arched over the loin, his forelegs straight and hind legs muscular. His head is broad and somewhat rounded between the ears, the muzzle blunt, forehead a trifle wrinkled, dark eyes set far apart, and V-shaped ears falling close to the cheeks. His long, tapering tail hangs straight in repose and forms a slight curve when the Mastiff is in action. The coat is short, coarse, and close-lying. WEIGHT: 135–185 pounds. HEIGHT: males at least 30 inches; females at least 27½ inches. COLOR: apricot, silver fawn, or dark fawn-brindle, with dark muzzle, ears, and nose.
GROUP: Working.

Miniature Pinscher

Like the Doberman but on a much smaller scale, the Miniature Pinscher has existed in his native Germany for several hundred years, although the serious development of the bred began in 1895. He has a terrier's characteristics and instincts for hunting vermin, and is valuable as a watchdog. He is a sturdy and compact little dog with a fearless, lively manner. His head tapers toward the muzzle; the cheeks are lean and the lips tight. The eyes are dark and very bright, and the ears stand erect when cropped. His short, shiny coat covers the body closely.

WEIGHT: 7–10 pounds. HEIGHT: 10–12½ inches. COLOR: solid red; stag red (red with intermingled black hairs); black with rust markings; chocolate with rust markings.
GROUP: Toy.

Newfoundland

Some authorities claim he is descended from Great Pyrenees dogs brought to the coast of Newfoundland by Basque fishermen; others think his ancestors are French Boarhounds. An exceptionally strong swimmer, he has saved many shipwrecked persons from drowning. Strength is his hallmark, together with a peculiar rolling gait. The body is powerfully built and well-boned, the forelegs straight, the hind legs powerful and well-muscled. The head is massive with a broad skull, the muzzle broad and deep, eyes dark and deep-set, and small ears set well back and lying close to the head. The tail hangs straight or with a slight curve, while the coat is very heavy and weather-resistant.
WEIGHT: 100–150 pounds. HEIGHT: 26–28 inches. COLOR: black, or white and black (Landseer).
GROUP: Working.

Norfolk Terrier

Norfolk and Norwich terriers share a common ancestry. Until 1979, the Norfolk was recognized in this country as a drop-eared variety of the Norwich Terrier. Although their appearance seems similar, there are differences between the breeds, resulting in two slightly different breed standards. The Norfolk is one of the smallest of the working terriers, with a body slightly longer than it is high, short and powerful forelegs, and broad, strong hindquarters. His V-shaped ears are small and neatly dropped, slightly rounded at the tip, and carried close to the cheek.

WEIGHT: about 11–12 pounds. HEIGHT: about 9–10 inches. COLOR: red, wheaten, black and tan, grizzle.
GROUP: Terrier.

Norwegian Elkhound

Thousands of years ago, the fearless Elkhound accompanied his Viking masters on their North Atlantic expeditions. The Norwegians have used his outstanding scenting abilities to hunt elk, reindeer, bear, and other large game. He is equally talented at pulling sleds and herding flocks. Built for stamina rather than speed, his body is square and compact, with great staying power. His forelegs are straight, hind legs strong and only moderately angulated, thighs broad and muscular. His head is broad, his muzzle tapers gradually, and his eyes are dark and lively in expression. His thick-haired tail is set high and tightly curled, and his heavy weather-resistant coat is longest on the neck, the chest, and the backs of the forelegs and thighs.
WEIGHT: 48–55 pounds. HEIGHT: 19½–20½ inches. COLOR: variations of gray tipped with black.
GROUP: Hound.

Norwich Terrier

To the students of Cambridge goes the credit for popularizing the Trumpington Terrier, later named the Norwich. The breed was developed in England, and by the 1880's, owning a small ratting terrier became a fad with undergraduates. Known as the Jones Terrier in this country in the 1920's. This is a small but natural type of working terrier with a moderately short body and level back. The legs are short but powerful, the feet round. The head is foxy-looking, that is, fairly broad in skull and tapering toward the muzzle. The ears are small and erect; the eyes are dark and very keen. The coat is very hard and wiry, with slight eyebrows and whiskers.

WEIGHT: about 12 pounds. HEIGHT: under 10 inches. COLOR: red, wheaten, black and tan, or grizzle.

GROUP: Terrier.

Old English Sheepdog

As breeds go, the Old English Sheepdog is not very old at all, his history going back only 150 years. Whatever the length of tail when a puppy is whelped, it is docked so short as to appear tailless, hence the nickname "bobtail." The body is square and compact, the forelegs straight with plenty of bone, and hindquarters round and muscular. In walking or trotting, the Old English has a characteristic ambling or bearlike gait. His head is large, with square and strong jaws, and ears flat to the head. Dark eyes are preferred, but in blue dogs a pearl eye, walleye or china eye is typical. The coat is full, hard, and quite shaggy.

WEIGHT: 70–85 pounds. HEIGHT: males 22-inch minimum; females slightly less. COLOR: gray, grizzle, blue, or blue-merled, with or without white markings, or reverse.

GROUP: Herding.

Otter Hound

Known since the fourteenth century, the Otter Hound is used for otter hunting. During the nineteenth century this sport became a minor vogue in England and Otter Hounds were hunted in packs to control the otters preying upon the fish in rivers and streams. Resembling somewhat the Bloodhound, and with remarkable scenting powers, the Otter Hound is a big, courageous-looking dog, thoroughly at home in the water. Rather ungainly in body, he has a long, gaily carried tail and large webbed feet.

His head is large, with deep-set dark eyes and pendulous ears. His heavy coat is crisp and oily enough to withstand almost any water temperature. WEIGHT: males 75–110 pounds; females 65–100 pounds. HEIGHT: males 24–27 inches; females 22–26 inches. COLOR: any color or combination of colors.
GROUP: Hound.

Papillon

Developed from the sixteenth-century dwarf spaniel, the Papillon was popularized by Madame de Pompadour and other famous ladies of the French court, whose pets were pictured with them in their portraits. The erect ears, flaring like the spread wings of a butterfly, gave this little dog his name. He is a shade long-backed, with a heavily plumed tail carried up and over the body. The head is small, with a moderately lean muzzle. The bone is fine, the feet long and slender, while the coat is long and silky, with a profuse frill on the chest and feathering on the legs. Ears of the drop type, known as Phalene, droop flat to the head and are carried completely down.
WEIGHT: 6–10 pounds. HEIGHT: 8–11 inches. COLOR: always part-color-white with patches of any color.
GROUP: Toy.

Pekingnese

The Pekingese was sacred to Chinese emperors as far back as the Tang dynasty of the eighth century. Theft of a sacred dog was once punishable by death. After the British looted the Imperial Palace at Peking in 1860, one of four dogs smuggled out was presented to Queen Victoria and a vogue began. Here is a dignified toy with courage far beyond his size. His head is broad and massive, muzzle extremely short, broad, and wrinkled. The eyes are dark and prominent. The body is deep, compact, big-boned, and lionlike—heavier in front than in back. The short forelegs are unusual in that the bones of the forearm are bowed. The feathered tail lies over the back to either side, and the coarse, thick coat has a profuse mane which forms a ruff or frill around the neck.

WEIGHT: under 14 pounds. HEIGHT: 6–9 inches. COLOR: red, fawn, black, black and tan, sable, brindle, white, and parti-colored, frequently with black mask and spectacles.

GROUP: Toy.

Pharaoh Hound

One of the oldest domesticated breeds, the Pharaoh Hound's history traces back to Egypt, around 3000 B.C., where he was treasured for his superior hunting ability. He is one of the few sight-hounds that can also track quarry by scent. Here is a medium-size, graceful dog that moves with a free and flowing gait. His lithe body has a nearly straight topline and deep brisket. Slightly longer than he is tall, this elegant hound has a long, lean head with rather small oval amber eyes, flesh-colored nose, and eye rims and lips that blend with his short and glossy coat.

WEIGHT: 40–60 pounds. HEIGHT: males 23–25 inches; females 21–24 inches. COLOR: ranging from tan/rich tan/chestnut, with white markings.

GROUP: Hound.

Pointer

The Pointer has been used in England as a hunting dog since 1650 and in America since 1876. He was one of the first dogs to point game birds, hence his name. He is a clean-limbed, natural dog with a strong, slightly sloping back and long, tapered tail carried straight out. His head is long, moderately wide, with a slight furrow between the eyes. The soft and thin ears hang flat to the cheeks, and the eyes are usually dark. The coat is short, dense, and smooth.

WEIGHT: males 55–75 pounds; females 45–65 pounds. HEIGHT: males 25–28 inches; females 23–26 inches. COLOR: liver, lemon, black, or orange, either combined with white or solid.

GROUP: Sporting.

Pointer, German Shorthaired

The German Shorthaired Pointer is a rather recent development of descendants of the old Spanish Pointer crossed with various scent hounds to add trailing skill to pointing ability. The result was a hunter that points and retrieves. Here is a powerful, aristocratic dog, nicely balanced and clean-cut. His back is short and straight, his hips broad, thighs muscular. His head is moderately broad, the muzzle about as long as the skull, and deep, with full but not heavily hanging lips. Eyes are medium in size, and ears hang flat to the head. The tail is docked; the coat is short, thick, and tough.

WEIGHT: males 55–70 pounds; females 45–60 pounds. HEIGHT: males 23–25 inches; females 21–23 inches. COLOR: solid liver; liver and white—spotted, ticked, or roaned.

GROUP: Sporting.

Pointer, German Wirehaired

Known as the Deutsch-Drahthaar, which, literally translated, means German Wirehair. A distinct breed in Germany since 1870 and one of its most popular hunting dogs, he was used on game birds and waterfowl. First brought to America about 1920, where he achieved considerable popularity. His rough, wiry coat, water-repellent to some extent, protects him in rugged cover and weather.

WEIGHT: about 50–60 pounds. HEIGHT: males 24–26 inches; females smaller. COLOR: liver and white—spotted, ticked, or roaned.

GROUP: Sporting.

Pomeranian

A member of the Spitz family. This perky dog's name traces to Pomerania, where, about a century ago, he was bred down in size. His ancestors were the northern sled dogs of Iceland and Lapland. When first introduced to England during the mid-nineteenth century, some specimens weighed as much as 30 pounds. In spite of his tiny size today, he has kept his make and shape. The Pom's body is short and compact with level topline. A foxy head, small erect ears, dark almond-shaped eyes, thick coat, and plumed tail laid flat over the back complete the picture.

WEIGHT: 3–7 pounds. HEIGHT: 6–7 inches. COLOR: any solid color, with or without lighter or darker shadings of the same color, or with sable or black shadings; particolor; sable; black and tan.

GROUP: Toy.

Poodle

An old-time hunter, herder, and draft dog of Europe, the Poodle closely resembles the Irish Water Spaniel and England's old rough-haired Water Dog. He was originally a fine swimmer, and his hindquarters were trimmed "lion" style to lighten the weight of his coat in the water; thus began the vogue of clipping him in fancy patterns. France, Germany, and Russia all had their Poodles, but he has been regarded as the national dog of France for years. Poodles come in three varieties: Standard or large, Miniature or medium—both in the nonsporting group—and Toy or very small—in the Toy group. Except for size, the dogs are identical. The Poodle is a graceful dog, squarely built, short-backed and strong, with tail docked, high-set, and carried up. The skull is moderately rounded, cheeks flat, muzzle long and fine, eyes oval and dark, and ears thickly feathered and hanging close to the head. The coat is either harsh, dense, and curly or hangs in tight cords of varying length.

WEIGHT: Standard 40–60 pounds; Miniature 12–20 pounds. HEIGHT: Standard, over 15 inches; Miniature, 10–15 inches. COLOR: any solid color— black, brown, blue, gray, silver, apricot, cafe-au-lait, cream, white. GROUP: Non-Sporting.

Poodle (Toy)

The Toy is the smallest variety of Poodle, and is governed by the same breed standard as the Miniature and Standard varieties.
WEIGHT: 6–9 pounds. HEIGHT: under 10 inches. COLOR: solid colors— black, brown, blue, gray, silver, apricot, cafe-au-lait, cream, white.
GROUP: Toy.

Portuguese Water Dog

An ancient breed, also known as the Portuguese Fishing Dog in his native land, where he herded fish into nets, retrieved lost tackle and broken nets, and acted as courier from ship to ship or ship to shore. The breed became almost extinct in the early twentieth century. Among those first interested in the breed in this country were Mr. and Mrs. Herbert Miller of Connecticut, at whose home the Portuguese Water Dog Club of America was founded in 1972. Here is a medium size, robust, and muscular dog with a short back, wide and deep brisket, strong and straight forelegs, and strongly muscled hindquarters. There are two types of coat, wavy and curly; and two acceptable trims, the working-retriever clip and the lion clip.
WEIGHT: males 42–60 pounds; females 35–50 pounds. HEIGHT: males 20– 23 inches; females 17–21 inches. COLOR: black, white, brown, and combinations of black or brown with white.
GROUP: Working.

Pug

The Pug came into existence centuries ago, probably in China. It was brought to Holland by traders, where it became the official dog of the House of Orange in the sixteenth century. The breed's popularity spread to England and France, where it became a favorite of Marie Antionette and Empress Josephine. The Pug is a wrinkle-faced chunk of a toy, short-backed and round-ribbed, and decidedly square. His blunt muzzle is very short indeed. His dark eyes are large and worried-looking, while his soft "button" or "rose" ears are like black velvet. His tail is tightly curled over the hip; a double curled-tail is considered perfection. The coat is short and glossy.

WEIGHT: 14–18 pounds. HEIGHT: 10–12 inches. COLOR: silver or apricot-fawn, with black mask and trace (line extending from the back of the head to tail); black.

GROUP: Toy.

Puli

The Puli has served Hungarian shepherds for more than a thousand years. Although he seems buried beneath a wealth of long hair, his coat is well-suited to extremes of weather. Puppies are born fluffy and, with growth, the soft undercoat naturally tangles with the coarse outercoat and forms long cords. The Puli is a compact, square-looking dog of medium size. His forelegs are straight and the hindquarters well-developed and muscular. The medium-size head is in proportion to the body, with a strong and straight muzzle, dark almond-shaped eyes, and V-shaped ears. The tail is carried over and blends into the backline.

WEIGHT: 25–35 pounds. HEIGHT: 16–17 inches. COLOR: solid colors of rusty black, black, gray, and white.

GROUP: Herding.

Retriever, Chesapeake Bay

Here is one of America's native breeds, developed along the shores of Maryland to retrieve ducks from the rough, icy waters of Chesapeake Bay. His 1½-inch coat is crisp and oily to protect him while swimming. His short body is higher at the hindquarters than at the shoulders, his legs are straight, and his hare feet are webbed. His head is broad with a rather short muzzle. Eyes are medium-large, yellow or amber, and his tail is straight or slightly curved.

WEIGHT: males 65–80 pounds; females 55–70 pounds. HEIGHT: males 23–26 inches; females 21–24 inches. COLOR: any color from dark brown to faded tan or deadgrass.
GROUP: Sporting.

Retriever, Curly-Coated

Descended from the sixteenth-century English Water Spaniel, the Curly-Coated Retriever is believed to be one of the oldest members of the Retriever family. His tight curls shed water and also protect his skin from heavy brush. His body is rather short, his chest deep, feet round and compact, and the tapered tail carried straight out. His head is long with jaws a bit lean, eyes large but not prominent, and curl-covered ears lying close to the head. In fact, as his name suggests, he is a mass of curls right down to the tip of his tail.

WEIGHT: 60–70 pounds. HEIGHT: 23–24 inches. COLOR: black or liver.
GROUP: Sporting.

Retriever, Flat-Coated

Developed in England from dogs brought to British ports by Canadian seafarers, the Flat-Coated Retriever resulted from a combination of the St. John's Newfoundland and Labrador Retriever, together with later crosses possibly involving Setters and Golden Retrievers. Here is a powerful, active dog, short-backed, rather squarely built and muscular, legs straight, well-boned, and thickly feathered. The head is moderately broad, with long and strong jaws, the neck clean, long, and slightly arched, and the chest deep. Eyes are brown or hazel, ears small and falling close to the head. The feathered tail is long, the moderately long coat dense and flat with a high luster.

WEIGHT: 60–70 pounds. HEIGHT: males 23–24½ inches; females 22–23½ inches. COLOR: black or liver.

GROUP: Sporting.

Retriever, Golden

Although it was once believed that Golden Retrievers were descended from a troupe of performing Russian circus dogs, the story has no basis in fact. It is known that the breed was developed in the 1860's when Lord Tweedmouth of Scotland bred a yellow Retriever to a liver Tweed Water Spaniel. Later crosses were made to Irish Setters, other water spaniels, and small Newfoundlands. Flat or wavy, dense and water-resisting, the beautiful coat popularized the Golden, although special prowess as a land and water retriever has also made it many friends. The body is deep and rather short-coupled, the tail long, straight, and feathered. The head

is broad, muzzle powerful, eyes dark and set wide apart, ears medium-size and falling close to the cheeks.
WEIGHT: males 65–75 pounds; females 55–65 pounds. HEIGHT: males 23–24 inches; females 21½–22½ inches. COLOR: Rich golden.
GROUP: Sporting.

Retriever, Labrador

Imported from Newfoundland to England about 1870 by the Earl of Malmesbury, the Labrador was developed there from the St. John's Water Dog into one of the most popular members of the Retriever clan. In the old days he brought hooked fish to the boats, while today he is an especially good water retriever. He's a deep-chested, strong-bodied dog, fairly wide over the loins and muscular in the hindquarters. His long tail, thick at the base and tapering toward the tip, has a rounded appearance which is described as an "otter" tail. His head is wide, clean-cut, his muzzle powerful, ears just moderately large and hanging fairly close to the head. Eyes are preferably brown or black, while the satin-smooth coat is very dense and without wave.
WEIGHT: males 60–75 pounds; females 55–70 pounds. HEIGHT: males 22½–24½ inches; females 21½–23½ inches. COLOR: black, yellow, or chocolate.
GROUP: Sporting.

Rhodesian Ridgeback

Developed in South Africa by the Boer farmers as a big-game hunter and guard. His ancestors probably were brought in from European countries two or three centuries ago, and crossed with native dogs that could withstand the temperature extremes of the South African veld. Unique among purebreeds, the Ridgeback has a distinct ridge down the back where the hair grows in the opposite direction from the rest of the coat. He is a strong, muscular hound-type dog, with a powerful and deep-chested body. The head is fairly long and rather broad, the medium-size ears set rather high, dropped, and carried close to the head. The muzzle is long and deep and the lips clean. The coat is short and glossy.

WEIGHT: males 75 pounds; females 65 pounds. HEIGHT: males 25–27 inches; females 24–26 inches. COLOR: light wheaten to red wheaten. GROUP: Hound.

Rottweiler

When Roman legions crossed the Alps almost 2,000 years ago, they used this breed's Mastiff-type ancestors as guards and cattle herders. Eventually these dogs spread across the Alps into the southern German village of Rottweil, where they were bred with local dogs to produce the Rottweiler. For centuries thereafter, this robust dog drove cattle to market and served as a guard and police dog. He is a stockily built, powerful animal, calm and quiet. His back is short, broad and level, his chest roomy, legs straight, with muscular thighs and rather heavy bone. The head is broad between the ears, with muzzle about as long as the depth of the skull. His almond-shaped eyes have a good-humored expression, while his small ears hang flat. The coat is short but very dense and hard.

WEIGHT: 85–110 pounds. HEIGHT: males 24–27 inches; females 22–25 inches. COLOR: black with rust to mahogany markings. GROUP: Working.

St. Bernard

An ancient breed, the St. Bernard probably descends from the heavy fighting dogs brought into Switzerland by Roman armies in the first century A.D. He gained fame in the Swiss Alps, where, at the Hospice of St. Bernard, dogs were raised and trained to rescue travelers lost in the snow. He is a large, powerful dog with strong back and well-developed hindquarters and muscular and powerful shoulders. The head is imposing with its broad forehead, wrinkles and furrow, and muzzle with loose-skinned lips. His rather high-set ears are medium-sized and lie close to the cheeks, and his lower eyelids fit loosely. The long tail hangs with a slight upward curve at the tip. He comes in two coat types: shorthaired (smooth, dense, and tough) and longhaired (medium length, plain to slightly wavy).

WEIGHT: 150–180 pounds. HEIGHT: males minimum of 27½ inches; females minimum of 25½ inches. COLOR: white with red, or red with white; brindle patches with white markings.
GROUP: Working.

Saluki

Sight-hunter of gazelles in the desert, the Saluki is perhaps the world's oldest domesticated dog. Carvings of his image were found in Sumerian excavations and on Egyptian tombs of several thousand years ago. He was Egypt's royal dog, respected and called the "noble one," even by Muslims, who ordinarily considered dogs as unclean. Here is a dog built for speed; he is tall, long, and slender with deep, narrow chest, arched loin, and long thighs. His head is narrow, too. His closely hanging ears are covered with long, silky hair. The tail, which is set on low, is carried in a graceful curve. The coat is fine, smooth, and silky-textured, moderately feathered on the back of the thighs and the tail.

WEIGHT: 45–55 pounds. HEIGHT: males 23–28 inches; females slightly smaller. COLOR: white, cream, fawn, golden, red, grizzle and tan, tricolor (white, black, and tan), and black and tan.

GROUP: Hound.

Samoyed

The Samoyed takes his name from the ancient Samoyed people of northeastern Siberia, where he served as hunter, draft dog, and herder of reindeer. In more recent times, he has excelled as a sled-dog racer, a pack carrier, and in polar expeditions. Essentially an Arctic type, agile and strong, with deep chest and well-sprung ribs, strong neck, straight front, and especially strong loins, he gives the appearance of being capable of great endurance but without coarseness. His head is broad in skull and wedge-shaped, muzzle tapering, eyes dark and wide apart, lips black and slightly curved up at the corners of the mouth in the appearance of a smile. His well-furred ears stand erect. His heavy coat is a thing of beauty, its underlayer thick and soft, its outer layer longer, harsh, standing off from the body and glistening with a silver sheen.

WEIGHT: 40–70 pounds. HEIGHT: males 21–23 inches; females 19–21 inches. COLOR: white, white and biscuit, cream, or all biscuit.

GROUP: Working.

Schipperke

The Schipperke, or Flemish "little captain," had the job of keeping the Belgian canal boats free of rats. Later he became a fashionable pet when in 1885 Leopold II's queen acquired one. For a small dog he is powerfully made, his body short, thick-set, and cobby. His forelegs are slightly heavier in bone than his hind legs, his rump is nicely rounded, and his tail docked very short. The foxy head tapers from skull to muzzle, the small oval eyes are deep and sharp, while the triangular ears stand erect. The coat, which is full and harsh, is fairly short on the body, and longer around the neck and ears, forming a ruff and a cape, and on the thighs, where it forms a culotte.

WEIGHT: under 18 pounds. HEIGHT: about 12–14 inches. COLOR: black. GROUP: Non-Sporting.

Schnauzer, Giant

The Giant Schnauzer is the largest of the three Schnauzer breeds. He was developed by cattlemen in southern Bavaria by breeding medium-size Schnauzers with smooth-coated sheep and cattle dogs, with later crosses to rough-haired sheepdogs and black Great Danes. Once called the Munchener, he was prized as a superb cattle and driving dog. He resembles, as nearly as possible, a larger and more powerful version of the Standard Schnauzer.

WEIGHT: 65–85 pounds. HEIGHT: Males 25 1/2–27 1/2 inches; females 23 1/2–25 1/2 inches. COLOR: solid black; pepper and salt. GROUP: Working.

Schnauzer, Miniature

The three Schnauzer breeds originated in Germany. The Standard Schnauzer is the oldest of the trio, known since the fifteenth century. The Miniature Schnauzer, exhibited as a distinct breed since 1899, was developed by crossing small Standards with Poodles and Affenpinschers. This is a robust dog, squarely built, with deep brisket, straight topline, and muscular thighs. The head is strong and rectangular, the whiskered muzzle blunt, the oval eyes dark and shadowed by bristling eyebrows. The coat is hard and wiry.

WEIGHT: 13–17 pounds. HEIGHT: 12–14 inches. COLOR: salt and pepper, black and silver, solid black.
GROUP: Terrier.

Schnauzer, Standard

The Standard, or medium-size dog, is the oldest of the three Schnauzer breeds. Probably developed by crossing the black German Poodle and gray wolf spitz with Wirehaired Pinscher stock, the Standard has been a guard and watchdog in Germany since the sixteenth century, his special work that of a rat catcher around stables. He is a robust, heavyset dog, squarely built. His head is long and rectangular, the whiskered muzzle blunt, the oval eyes dark and shadowed by bristling eyebrows. The V-shaped ears are small and carried erect when cropped, and the coat is hard and wiry.

WEIGHT: 30–40 pounds. HEIGHT: males 18½–19½ inches; females 17½–18½ inches. COLOR: pepper and salt or pure black.
GROUP: Working.

Scottish Terrier

Thought to be one of the oldest of British terrier breeds, the Scottie's ancestors were ancient terriers from the Highlands of Scotland. Once known as the Aberdeen Terrier, he hunted all kinds of vermin. He's a compact and powerful dog, with a short back, wide hindquarters, and short, heavy-boned legs, all giving the impression of immense power in a small size. His head is long, the muzzle rather blunt, ears small and erect, and eyes set well under heavy brows. His seven-inch tail is carried up in a slight curve. His coat, about two inches long, is dense underneath and hard and wiry on top.

WEIGHT: 18–22 pounds. HEIGHT: about 10 inches. COLOR: steel or iron gray, brindled or grizzled, black, sandy, or wheaten.
GROUP: Terrier.

Sealyham Terrier

The Sealyham was developed in the last half of the nineteenth century to hunt badger, otter, and fox by Captain John Edwardes. The breed takes its name from Edwardes' estate in Haverford West, Wales. He is a powerful little fellow with good bone, short in back and low on the legs, with large, compact feet. His head is long and broad, with flat cheeks and a powerful square jaw. The oval eyes are fairly wide apart, and the ears are folded level with the top of the head, the forward edge lying close to the cheek. The tail is docked and carried straight up. The coat is hard and wiry.

WEIGHT: about 23–24 pounds. HEIGHT: about 10½ inches. COLOR: all white, or with lemon, tan, or badger markings on head and ears.
GROUP: Terrier.

Setter, English

Probably developed from land spaniels that originated in Spain, crossed with pointing breeds, the English Setter was used in England for bird hunting more than 400 years ago. Credit for developing modern strains goes to Sir Edward Laverack and Sir Purcell Llewellin, two world-famous British dog breeders of the mid-nineteenth century. Here is a handsome, large dog with a flat, long, and beautifully feathered coat. His head is lean, muzzle long and square, with lips fairly pendant. The silky-haired ears droop low, the eyes are dark and bright. The tail is carried straight out, its long fringes tapering to a point at the tip. WEIGHT: 50–70 pounds. HEIGHT: 24–25 inches. COLOR: black, white, and tan; black and white; blue belton, lemon and white, lemon belton; orange and white; orange belton; liver and white; liver belton; and solid white. Note: belton means blended or flecked. GROUP: Sporting.

Setter, Gordon

Scotland's member of the Setter family is the Gordon, the handsome black-and-tan, named for the fourth Duke of Gordon. Once called the "black and fallow setting dog." His lineage dates back to at least the early seventeenth century. The Gordon is a sturdy hunter, well-balanced, with a rather short back, and deep rather than broad head with a fairly long muzzle. His eyes are dark brown, wise in expression, his thin ears hang low, while his feathered tail, thick at the root and finishing in a fine point,

is carried horizontally. The coat is soft and shining, with longer feathering on the ears, underbody, legs, and tail.
WEIGHT: males 55–80 pounds; females 45–70 pounds. HEIGHT: males 24–27 inches; females 23–26 inches. COLOR: black with tan markings.
GROUP: Sporting.

Setter, Irish

Ireland's contribution to the respected family of bird finders first came into prominence in the early eighteenth century. Believed to be the result of English Setter-Spaniel-Pointer crosses with a dash of Gordon Setter. Sportsmen used early Irish Setters for falconry. Originally colored red and white, but solid colors were developed in the nineteenth century. The Irish Setter is a graceful yet substantial dog, deep-bodied and strong. His head is long and lean, muzzle moderately deep and square, ears set low and hanging close to the head. The somewhat almond-shaped eyes are dark to medium brown. The coat is flat, with longer feathering on the ears, chest, underbody, legs, and outstretched tail.
WEIGHT: males about 70 pounds; females about 60 pounds. HEIGHT: males about 27 inches; females about 25 inches. COLOR: mahogany or rich chestnut red.
GROUP: Sporting.

Shetland Sheepdog

Miniature in size, like the ponies for which the rather barren and rocky Shetland Islands are known, the Sheltie is a small edition of the rough Collie. His body is fairly long and rounded with a heavy stand-off coat of straight harsh hair, including an abundant mane and frill and feathered legs and tail. His head is long and wedge-shaped, tapering slightly from ears to nose, cheeks flat, jaws clean and powerful. The eyes are slanting, ears small and semierect, while the long tail is carried low with a slight upward swirl.

WEIGHT: 18–20 pounds. HEIGHT: 13–16 inches. COLOR: black, blue merle, and sable, marked with white and/or tan.

GROUP: Herding.

Shih Tzu

Although its origins are obscure, the Shih Tzu (pronounced sheed-zoo) originated centuries ago, probably in Tibet or China. Its likeness is depicted in paintings and objects d'art of the Tang dynasty, dating about A.D. 624. The breed was called the "chrysanthemum-faced" dog because its facial hair grew in all directions. Its luxurious, long and flowing coat, long mandarin beard, heavily plumed tail, and distinctly arrogant carriage give the Shih Tzu an enchanting appearance.

WEIGHT: 9–18 pounds. HEIGHT: 8–11 inches. COLOR: all colors.

GROUP: Toy.

Siberian Husky

The Siberian Husky was developed centuries ago by the Chukchi people of Siberia as an endurance sled dog and general beast of burden. In fairly recent times, he was used in Alaska as a racer in sweepstakes contests, where his great energy enabled him to track a snowbound course sometimes 400 miles long. He has a powerful body, with deep chest, well-muscled shoulders and hindquarters. His head, of medium size, tapers toward the eyes; his muzzle is of medium length, his lips tight, and the ears erect and well-furred. The keen-lighted eyes are slanting; they can be brown or blue in color, and one of each color is also acceptable. The furry fox-brush tail rides over the back in a graceful sickle curve, and the coat is thick and dense.

WEIGHT: males 45 to 60 pounds; females 35 to 50 pounds. HEIGHT: males 21–23½ inches; females 20–22 inches. COLOR: all colors from black to pure white.

GROUP: Working.

Silky Terrier

Named for his fine silky coat, this tiny dog from Australia was once known as the Sydney Silky, later the Australian Silky. Derived mainly from Australian Terriers crossed with Yorkshire Terriers, he was first shown in his native land in 1907. A charming little fellow of pronounced terrier character and spirit, he is a lightly built, moderately low-set dog, with strong, straight forelegs, well-muscled thighs, and a high-set tail that is carried erect or semierect.

WEIGHT: 8–10 pounds. HEIGHT: 9–10 inches. COLOR: blue and tan.

GROUP: Toy.

Skye Terrier

The Skye Terrier has been bred pure for 400 years or more in his native land, the Isle of Skye, off the northwest coast of Scotland. His long flowing hair protected him against badgers, foxes, and other vicious small animals he hunted. His body is very long and low to the ground—he is twice as long as he is high. His head is long and powerful, tapering to a strong muzzle. The ears may be carried prick or drop. His long body coat hangs straight down each side, parting from head to tail. The hair on the head veils the forehead and eyes and forms a beard and apron. The long feathering on the ears falls straight down from the tips and outer edges.

WEIGHT: 23–30 pounds. HEIGHT: 9½–10 inches. COLOR: black, blue, dark or light gray, silver platinum, fawn, cream.

GROUP: Terrier.

Soft-Coated Wheaten Terrier

Although his origins are obscure, the Soft-Coated Wheaten Terrier has been known in Ireland for more than 200 years, where he was used to hunt small game, to kill vermin, and to guard herds. He is probably an ancestor of the Kerry Blue Terrier. He is a charming medium-size sporting terrier, squarely built, with a deep chest and gaily carried docked tail. His head is rectangular in appearance, with a strong muzzle and dark reddish-brown or brown eyes. He is distinguished by his soft, silky, and gently wavy wheaten-colored coat, which covers his entire body, legs, and head.

WEIGHT: 30–40 pounds. HEIGHT: 17–19 inches. COLOR: any shade of wheaten.
GROUP: Terrier.

Spaniel, American Water

Aptly named, the American Water Spaniel is a true native, developed as a water retriever as well as an all-around shooting dog with a keen nose. Although his origins are obscure, his color, coat, and conformation suggest that he may have been developed from crosses of Irish and English Water Spaniels and Curly-Coated Retrievers. He is sturdily built, of medium size, and his outline displays a symmetrical relationship of parts. His skull is rather broad and full, muzzle deep and square, eyes wide-set (hazel, brown, or dark to harmonize with his coat), long ears falling close and covered with curls. The feathered tail curves in a slight rockerlike shape, while the weather-resistant coat is thick and closely curled.

WEIGHT: 25–45 pounds. HEIGHT: 15–18 inches. COLOR: liver or dark chocolate.
GROUP: Sporting.

Spaniel, Clumber

The Clumber is the heaviest of the English sporting spaniels, named for Clumber Park, the Duke of Newcastle's estate in Nottingham. He is a dignified dog, long-bodied, heavy-boned, and low to the ground. It is thought that his long, low body resulted from crosses to Basset Hounds. His head is massive, its forehead furrowed, the muzzle fairly deep to facilitate retrieving many kinds of game, the jaws long and powerful. Gentle in expression, his large, dark amber eyes are a trifle loose-lidded, while his ears are broad at the top and hang close to his head. His tail is docked and feathered; his weather-resistant coat is straight and flat.
WEIGHT: males 70–85 pounds; females 55–70 pounds. HEIGHT: males 19–20 inches; females 17–19 inches. COLOR: white with lemon or orange markings.
GROUP: Sporting.

Spaniel, Cocker

Smallest of the sporting spaniels, the Cocker is so named because his forebears came from Spain and he was used in early days in England to hunt woodcock. Today he is one of the most popular breeds in North America. In body he is quite square, with short back, deep chest, and nicely rounded and muscular hindquarters. His tail, which is docked, is constantly a-wag. His head is rounded, forehead smooth, muzzle broad, deep, and square. His dark eyes are soft and appealing in expression, his ears long and silky. His slightly wavy coat is soft, with heavy feathering on the ears, chest, underbody, and legs.
WEIGHT: 22–28 pounds. HEIGHT: 14–15 inches. COLOR: black; black with

tan points; any solid color other than black, and any such color with tan points; particolored.
GROUP: Sporting.

Spaniel, English Cocker

During the nineteenth century, England's Cockers appeared in mixed-size litters, the larger specimens developing into Springers to spring game, the smaller dogs into Cockers to hunt woodcock. In 1892 the Kennel Club of England recognized them as separate breeds. Although he shares a common ancestor with his American counterpart and is somewhat the same in many details, the English Cocker is larger, longer in head, and less heavily feathered than his American cousin.
WEIGHT: males 28–34 pounds; females 26–32 pounds. HEIGHT: males 16–17 inches; females 15–16 inches. COLOR: various solid colors (with small amount of white); blue, liver, red, orange, or lemon roan; black and tan.
GROUP: Sporting.

Spaniel, English Springer

Named for the ancient spaniel trait of springing or flushing birds, the English Springer Spaniel became popular as a gun dog in America early in this century. He has a fairly broad head of medium length, a square muzzle with deep but not hanging lips. His long feathered ears hang low; his eyes are dark brown or hazel. His body is fairly short, back straight, and tail docked. His coat may be flat or wavy but it must be thick enough to protect him when hunting in heavy cover. It is medium in length, glossy, and rather fine in texture.
WEIGHT: 45–55 pounds. HEIGHT: 19–20 inches. COLOR: black or liver with white markings; tricolor; black and white or liver and white with tan markings; blue or liver roan.
GROUP: Sporting.

Spaniel, Field

The Field Spaniel, descended from an old branch of the spaniel family, now very rare, was bred long and low for hunting on foot. The type was established by crossing "Welsh Cockers" with Sussex Spaniels. The back is strong and well-ribbed, the chest deep rather than wide, and the bone fairly heavy. The skull is well-developed, the muzzle long and lean with exceptional scenting power. The ears hang in graceful folds, while the dark eyes have a more solemn expression than is typical among dogs of the spaniel group. The tail is docked, feathered, and carried low, while the glossy coat is slightly wavy.

WEIGHT: 35–50 pounds. HEIGHT: about 18 inches. COLOR: black, liver, golden liver, mahogany red, or roan.

GROUP: Sporting.

Spaniel, Irish Water

Tallest of the spaniels. The history of this breed dates back at least one thousand years. In the twelfth century, dogs found in southern Ireland below the River Shannon were called Shannon Spaniels, Irish Water Spaniels, or Rat-tailed Spaniels. Here is a remarkable swimmer and retriever that is adept at hunting wild duck in marshes and lakes. He is short-backed, high on leg, rounded in rump. His forehead is high, his muzzle square and long, eyes keenly alert, and his curl-covered ears hang low. His so-called "rat tail," thick at the root and covered for two or three inches with short curls, is a striking characteristic of the breed. His coat is a mass of tight, crisp curls, and on his head he wears a topknot with a widow's peak between the eyes.

WEIGHT: males 55–65 pounds; females 45–58 pounds. HEIGHT: males 22–24 inches; females 21–23 inches. COLOR: liver.
GROUP: Sporting.

Spaniel, Sussex

Developed in England to be a slow-moving spaniel that hunters could follow on foot, the Sussex was often used for upland shooting. He is not used as a hunter in this country, probably because he lacks sufficient speed for the average sportsman. His back is long and muscular, body low to the ground. The head is big, with heavy brows, square muzzle, and hanging lips. His hazel eyes are soft and appealing, and his thick fringed ears drop low. The tail is docked; his flat coat is heavy with feathering on legs, stern, and tail.
WEIGHT: 35–45 pounds. HEIGHT: 16–17 inches. COLOR: rich golden liver.
GROUP: Sporting.

Spaniel, Welsh Springer

An old breed from Wales, the Welsh Springer was kept as a hunting dog. While very much like the English Springer, he is smaller, somewhat finer, and only red and white in color. His head is moderately long, muzzle straight and square with strong jaw, ears hanging close to the cheeks, and dark eyes. His body is deep and not long, his tail is docked and feathered, and his coat is flat, thick, and silky.
WEIGHT: 35–45 pounds. HEIGHT: about 17–19 inches. COLOR: red and white.
GROUP: Sporting.

Staffordshire Bull Terrier

His ancestors were the bull- and bear-baiting dogs of Elizabethan England. In the early nineteenth century, when dog fighting was popular, Bulldogs were crossed with small terriers, possibly ancestors of today's Manchesters, to get smaller, more agile dogs. This new breed became the Staffordshire Bull Terrier. Here is a robust though agile medium-size dog with level topline, wide front, and deep brisket. His head is short and deep, with a broad skull, very pronounced cheek muscles, and short muzzle, dark round eyes, and rather small rose or half-pricked ears. The coat is short and smooth.

WEIGHT: 24–38 pounds. HEIGHT: 14–16 inches. COLOR: red, fawn, white, black, blue; any of these colors with white.
GROUP: Terrier.

Tibetan Spaniel

An ancient breed that probably has common ancestors with several Oriental breeds including Pekingese and Japanese Chins. Used for centuries by Buddhists of Tibet to keep watch over their monasteries. Accepted for AKC registration in 1984. Here is a lively, silky-coated little dog, a bit longer in body than he is high, with level back, slightly bowed front legs, and richly plumed tail carried over the back. His head, small in proportion to his body, is slightly domed, with a blunt muzzle, expressive dark eyes, and slightly undershot mouth.

WEIGHT: 9–15 pounds. HEIGHT: about 10 inches. COLOR: all colors and mixtures.
GROUP: Non-Sporting.

Tibetan Terrier

Not a member of the terrier family, this exceptionally healthy dog is an ancient Asian breed that originated in the Lost Valley of Tibet. Bred and raised by lamas in their monasteries, Tibetan Terriers were highly prized as companions and good-luck charms by their owners, and treated like children of the family. Here is a powerful-looking, medium-size dog with a square, compact body, well-muscled forequarters and hindquarters, and a well-feathered tail that curls over the back. His head is furnished with long hair which falls forward over the eyes. Thanks to his profuse double coat, he thrives in all kinds of weather.

WEIGHT: 18–30 pounds. HEIGHT: 14–16 inches. COLOR: any color.
GROUP: Non-Sporting.

Vizsla

A pointing breed from Hungary. The Vizsla's origins are obscure but his ancestors probably were the hunters and companions of the Magyars who settled more than a thousand years ago in what is now Hungary. Gentle and tractable, he is a multipurpose dog for work on upland game, on rabbits, and for waterfowl retrieving. Favored by sportsmen as a keen and close working dog. He is a medium-size dog, robust but rather lightly built.

WEIGHT: 45–60 pounds. HEIGHT: males 22–24 inches; females 21–23 inches. COLOR: golden rust.
GROUP: Sporting.

Weimaraner

An all-round sporting dog of German origin, the Weimaraner was selectively bred in the nineteenth century at the court of Weimar for superior hunting and scenting abilities, intelligence, and speed. He has been nicknamed the "gray ghost" because of his unusual gray coloring and light eyes. Clean-limbed and upstanding, he is strongly built, with moderately short back, deep chest, straight forelegs, well-angulated stifles, and straight hocks. His head is moderately long and aristocratic, with a long muzzle and clean-cut neck. His long and lobular ears fall to the side slightly folded, while his eyes are gray, blue-gray, or amber. His tail is docked and his coat is short and sleek.

WEIGHT: 55–85 pounds. HEIGHT: males 25–27 inches; females 23–25 inches. COLOR: shades of mouse to silver gray.
GROUP: Sporting.

Welsh Corgi, Cardigan

The Cardigan Welsh Corgi, one of the oldest breeds in the British Isles, is a low-set, Dachshund-like dog whose ancestors came to Cardiganshire, Wales, with the Celts from Central Europe about 1200 B.C. Rather than just herding, they nip at the cattle's heels and then drop close to the ground when they kick. This is a long, strong little dog, with deep chest and well-sprung ribs, short legs with relatively large and rounded feet, and long tail like a fox's brush. The foxy head tapers toward the eyes and muzzle. The medium-size eyes are dark and widely set, the ears carried erect, rounded at the tip and rather large. The medium-length coat is dense and hard.

WEIGHT: males 30–38 pounds; females 25–34 pounds. HEIGHT: $10^1/_2$–$12^1/_2$ inches. COLOR: Shades of red, sable, and brindle; black or blue merle with or without tan or brindle points.
GROUP: Herding

Welsh Corgi, Pembroke

Not as old a breed as the Cardigan, the Pembroke Welsh Corgi still rates as one of dogdom's ancients, its ancestors having been brought across the Channel to Wales by Flemish weavers in 1107. Later developed in Pembrokeshire from dogs of northern type, the breed has little or no Dachshund traits. The Pembroke Welsh Corgi is a low-set, sturdily built dog, shorter in body than the Cardigan, and with legs that are straighter and lighter in bone. The head is foxy, the muzzle lean, the ears erect with pointed tips. The tail is naturally short or docked.

WEIGHT: 25–30 pounds. HEIGHT: 10–12 inches. COLOR: red, sable, fawn, black and tan, with or without white markings.

GROUP: Herding.

Welsh Terrier

A very old breed, once known as the Black-and-Tan Wire-Haired Terrier, the Welsh has been bred pure as a sporting terrier for more than 100 years in Wales. He is a medium-size, rugged, compact dog with level topline, deep brisket, moderately wide chest, strong legs, and muscular thighs. The head is rectangular, with a strong foreface, deep muzzle, and powerful jaws. The eyes are dark and almond-shaped and the V-shaped ears are carried forward, close to the cheeks. The coat is wiry and hard with a close-fitting thick jacket.

WEIGHT: 18–20 pounds. HEIGHT: 14–15 inches. COLOR: black and tan, or black grizzle and tan.

GROUP: Terrier.

West Highland White Terrier

The West Highland White Terrier's ancestry possibly traces back to the reign of King James I. He was once known as the Roseneath Terrier in honor of the Duke of Argyll's Scottish estate, where the breed originated. He is a spunky little chap with a short, compact body, level back, well-developed hindquarters, and muscular, relatively short legs. His skull, which is fairly broad, is slightly domed and tapers gradually to the eyes. The dark eyes are widely set and sharp; the ears small, pointed, and carried tightly erect. His white coat is one of the breed's most striking features.

WEIGHT: 13–20 pounds. HEIGHT: 10–11 inches. COLOR: white. GROUP: Terrier.

Whippet

Probably developed by crossbreeding small English Greyhounds with various smooth and rough-coated terriers plus a dash of Italian Greyhound, the Whippet evolved in Great Britain about a century or so ago. He was first used for coursing rabbits, but later was raced on the tracks. In fact, he was nicknamed "the poor man's race horse." Here is a true moderate-size sporting hound with considerable speed. His body is slender, deep-chested, and strong, showing a strong natural arch over the loin. The head is lean and the muzzle long and rather fine. The small ears are thrown back and folded, while the dark eyes are large and alert. The coat is short and sleek.

WEIGHT: 18–28 pounds. HEIGHT: males 19–22 inches; females 18–21 inches. COLOR: any color. GROUP: Hound.

Wirehaired Pointing Griffon

First bred about 1870 by a Hollander, Edward Korthals, who popularized the breed throughout France and Germany as a rough, swamp-country sporting dog, skillful at retrieving game on land and in water. He is essentially Pointer in build, although somewhat more heavily cast. Strong and vigorous, he is fairly short-backed and a trifle low on the leg. His head is long and narrow, his muzzle square, eyes large (iris yellow or light brown in color), and nose brown. His moderate-size ears hang flat, while his tail, which is docked, is carried off from the body. His rough, rather shaggy coat is hard and stiff, with downy undercoat, bushy eyebrows, and mustache.

WEIGHT: 48–60 pounds. HEIGHT: males 21½–23½ inches; females 19½–21½ inches. COLOR: steel gray or gray-white with chestnut splashes; chestnut; dirty white mixed with chestnut.

GROUP: Sporting.

Yorkshire Terrier

Named for the English county of Yorkshire, this terrier was developed by workers about 1860 to control rats in mines and mills. He traces back to Waterside Terriers, rough-coated Black-and-Tans, Paisley and Clydesdale terriers. A popular pet in Victorian times, this is a spirited little dog, covered from top to toe with a wealth of glossy, silky hair that is parted down the back and hangs straight to the floor on each side. The body is short and compact with a level topline. The head is small, rather flat on top, with a short muzzle, dark and sparkling eyes, and small V-shaped ears that are carried erect.

WEIGHT: under 7 pounds. HEIGHT: 7–8 inches. COLOR: steel blue and tan.

GROUP: Toy.

Other Popular Breeds

The following breeds—Australian Kelpies, Border Collies, Cavalier King Charles Spaniels, Finnish Spitz, Miniature Bull Terriers, and Spinoni Italiani—may compete in American Kennel Club conformation shows in the Miscellaneous Class, but are not eligible to earn championship points. They may compete in AKC obedience trials and earn obedience titles. Some other breeds included here, such as the American Eskimo, American Toy Fox Terrier, Bluetick Hound, Redbone Hound, and Shar Pei, are not officially recognized by the AKC but are, nevertheless, well-known, distinct in type, and bred pure. Some are registered with the United Kennel Club in Kalamazoo, Michigan.

American Eskimo

The American Eskimo, sometimes called the American Spitz or Eskimo Spitz, is popular in North America. "Spitz" covers an ancient group of northern dogs from which were developed the various sled dogs, Chow Chows, Pomeranians, and Akitas. All these have full coats and richly plumed tails that curl up over the back. The American Eskimo is a typical northern working dog: a wedge-shaped head with a Nordic-type face, dark, expressive eyes, and small erect ears.

WEIGHT: Standard 18–35 pounds; Miniature 10–20 pounds. HEIGHT: Standard 18 inches. COLOR: pure white most desirable.

American Toy Fox Terrier

The American Toy Fox Terrier is descended from old-time English terriers. Despite his small size, he is a game ratter as well as an alert and intelligent pet. The coat is satiny and smooth and slightly heavier at the neck. The nose is black, the eyes round, dark, and prominent, with a soft expression. The ears are large in proportion to the head, and are rounded or "bat" and usually carried erect.

WEIGHT: 5–9 pounds. HEIGHT: 7–11 inches. COLOR: usually white with black, red, or tan markings.

Australian Kelpie

A popular working sheepdog in Australia and New Zealand, he was developed in the 1870's, probably from Collie stock brought to Australia by early settlers. The breed takes the name "Kelpie" from its foundation bitch. Here is a medium-size , lively dog with great stamina. It is said that he can perform the work of many men in a single day. His dark, expressive eyes and pointed ears give him an alert look. He has a short, flat outer coat with a dense undercoat.

WEIGHT: 28–33 pounds. HEIGHT: 17–20 inches. COLOR: black, black and tan, red, red and tan, fawn, chocolate, blue.

Bluetick Hound

A descendant of the English Foxhound and several other fox hounds, the Bluetick is a popular dog with coonhound field-trial enthusiasts. He is fairly large and a fast trailer. The blue ticking with tan markings is a prominent feature.

WEIGHT: 60–70 pounds. HEIGHT: 23–25 inches.

Border Collie

The Border Collie is a very old breed, having been described by Dr. Caius in 1570. His stance is different from that of most dogs. It can be described as an almost perceptible backward stance, as if he were bracing himself to hold back his flock. The Border Collie's back is a trifle longer than he is high, and his tail is carried low with a slight upward swirl. The head is like the old-fashioned shepherd's, shorter and more blunt in muzzle and broader in skull than today's Collie. He has large dark eyes and is known for his specially keen sight. The coat is dense and especially heavy around the neck.

WEIGHT: 30–45 pounds. HEIGHT: 17–18 inches. COLOR: black and white; or black, tan, and white.

Cavalier King Charles Spaniel

A descendant of the English Toy Spaniels of the sixteenth through eighteenth centuries. Dogs resembling modern Cavaliers appear in many Old Master paintings. Here is a graceful, short-coupled dog with a level back, moderately deep chest, and long silky coat. In relation to the English Toy Spaniel, the Cavalier is taller and slightly heavier, with a flatter skull and longer, more finely tapered muzzle. The Cavalier's eyes are not as prominent; it ears are set fairly high and it has a scissors bite.

WEIGHT: 13–18 pounds. HEIGHT: 12–13 inches. COLOR: Blenheim—rich chestnut-red markings on pearly white; Tricolor—black and white with tan markings; Ruby—solid rich red; Black and Tan—black with tan markings.

The Chinese Crested

The small, unique-looking Chinese Crested was first identified in China, although its origins are a mystery. Historians believe that the breed was first brought to America on Chinese sailing ships in the seventeenth century.

The Chinese Crested is slender and finely-boned. Its body is hairless, except for a flowing crest on the head, a plume on the tail, and "socks" on its long, narrow feet. The skin, smooth and warm to the touch, can be any color and often is spotted. Occasionally puppies with a soft veil of hair all over, called "Powder Puffs," appear in hairless litters. The happy-go-lucky Chinese Crested has fastidious habits and is practically odorless.

WEIGHT: 10 pounds in proportion to height. HEIGHT: 9–13 inches. COLOR: any color or combination of colors.

Finnish Spitz

Ancestors of the Finnish Spitz were companions of the ancient Finns, forest people who lived in clans. Their dogs were indispensable allies for hunting all kinds of game from bear to squirrel, and especially birds. The Finnish Spitz, like other members of the spitz family, has the characteristic Nordic look: broad skull, pointed muzzle, small erect ears, dark almond-shaped eyes, squarish symmetrical body, stiff, dense coat, and plumed and curled tail.

WEIGHT: 28–36 pounds. HEIGHT: 15½–20 inches. COLOR: Shades of golden red ranging from pale honey to deep auburn.

Miniature Bull Terrier

Developed in the last century by selected breedings of small Bull Terriers. The first specimens were so small and delicate (show classes were held for dogs under ten pounds) that breeders found it difficult to produce sound animals with typical heads. Renewed interest in the 1920's resulted in a gradual increase in the dog's weight. The Miniature Bull Terrier is a replica of the Bull Terrier in all respects except height and weight.
WEIGHT: under 20 pounds. HEIGHT: under 14 inches. COLOR: white; colored (any color other than white, or any color with white markings, brindle preferred).

Redbone Hound

The Redbone is named after his coloring and is descended from Foxhound stock, with possibly a Bloodhound cross. He is a specialist on coon hunting, but is also used on bear, cougar, and other big game, and instinctively trees his prey.
WEIGHT: 45–60 pounds. HEIGHT: 21–26 pounds. COLOR: red, with permissible small amount of white on chest and feet.

Shar Pei

This unique-looking breed probably originated in Tibet or northern China about 2,000 years ago. He was used as a guard dog and herder, but was unsurpassed as a fighting dog because his bristly hair and loose, wrinkled skin made it nearly impossible for opponents to grip him. He is a medium-size, compact dog, squarely built and close-coupled. He possesses many fighting-dog qualities: curved canine teeth; small, sunken eyes; small ears which lie flat; a large head covered with profuse wrinkles on the forehead and cheeks; a broad and blunt hippopotamuslike muzzle; a tail that forms a circle; and skin that seems excessive for his body. WEIGHT: 35–55 pounds. HEIGHT: 18–20 inches. COLOR: solid colors.

Spinoni Italiani

The Spinoni Italiani, or Italian Pointer, a member of the Griffon family, is descended from ancient hunting breeds of the Piedmont area of Italy. Because of superb sporting skills, he is the most popular gun dog in his native country. He is a hardy, heavy-boned, yet slender-looking dog, squarely built, with strong shoulders, wide chest, heavy boned forelegs, and muscular hindquarters. His dark yellow or ocher eyes give him a gentle and sweet expression. His wiry coat lies rather close to his body, with longer hair covering the eyebrows, cheeks, and lips. WEIGHT: 62–80 pounds. HEIGHT: 23–27½ inches. COLOR: white; white with orange, chestnut, or liver markings; white sprinkled with orange or brown hairs.

Index

By the year 2000, 2 out of 3 Americans could be illiterate.

It's true.

Today, 75 million adults... about one American in three, can't read adequately. And by the year 2000, U.S. News & World Report envisions an America with a literacy rate of only 30%.

Before that America comes to be, you can stop it... by joining the fight against illiteracy today.

Call the Coalition for Literacy at toll-free **1-800-228-8813** and volunteer.

Volunteer Against Illiteracy. The only degree you need is a degree of caring.

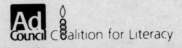

Ad Council Coalition for Literacy

LWA